Race and Religion
among the Chosen Peoples
of Crown Heights

Race and Religion among the Chosen Peoples of Crown Heights

HENRY GOLDSCHMIDT

RUTGERS UNIVERSITY PRESS

NEW BRUNSWICK, NEW JERSEY, AND LONDON

LIBRARY OF CONGRESS CATALOGING-IN-PUBLICATION DATA

Goldschmidt, Henry.
  Race and religion among the chosen peoples of Crown Heights /
Henry Goldschmidt.
      p. cm.
  Includes bibliographical references and index.
  ISBN-13: 978–0–8135–3883–9 (hardcover : alk. paper)
  ISBN-13: 978–0–8135–3897–6 (pbk. : alk. paper)
  1. Crown Heights (New York, N.Y.)—Race relations.   2. New York (N.Y.)—Race
relations.   3. African Americans—New York (State)—New York—Relations with
Jews.   4. African Americans—New York (State)—New York—Public opinion.
5. Jews—New York (State)—New York—Attitudes.   6. Social conflict—New York
(State)—New York.   I. Title.
  F128.68.C76G65   2006
  305.892'4074723—dc22   2005035534

A British Cataloging-in-Publication record for this book is available
from the British Library.

Manufactured in the United States of America

In memory of my mother, Ann Dee Goldschmidt,
who gave me a home in Brooklyn.

In honor of my father, Bernard Goldschmidt,
who raised me there.

With love to my wife, Jillian Shagan,
who made the place new.

CONTENTS

ACKNOWLEDGMENTS

My research and writing have been funded over the years by the International Migration Program of the Social Science Research Council, the Lucius N. Littauer Foundation, Phi Beta Kappa of Northern California, the National Foundation for Jewish Culture, and the Institute for the Advanced Study of Religion at Yale University—as well as the generous support of my family, and my own work at Wesleyan University, Dickinson College, Rutgers University, and elsewhere. I am extremely grateful to every one of the individuals and institutions who supported this project.

Above all, however, my thanks go to the Crown Heights residents—close friends, acquaintances, and total strangers—who agreed to work with me in the course of my research, or at least to tolerate my silly questions. Some made my work in Crown Heights a delight while others made it an ordeal, but all challenged my assumptions and enriched my thinking in ways this text hardly begins to describe. I won't thank any Crown Heights residents by name, as a number of my closest friends in the neighborhood specifically asked me not to. Indeed, with the exception of public figures, and other individuals already known in the media, I will not use my informants' names in the body of the text. In all honesty, I'm afraid some wouldn't want to be closely associated with my work. My understanding of identities like Blackness and Jewishness is substantially different from that of most Crown Heights residents—so much so that my friends in the neighborhood may wonder if I learned anything from them at all. I only hope they will read my work as a heartfelt contribution to the dialogue I have been privileged to hold with them through my research. We may disagree in fundamental ways, but we're in this together—this borough, these identities, their history, our future.

I'm also deeply indebted to my friends and colleagues in academia. To the anthropology faculty at the University of California at Santa Cruz, and above all to the members of my dissertation committee—Don Brenneis, Jackie Brown, Steven Gregory, and Susan Harding—for inspiring and challenging me. To my fellow students at UC Santa Cruz, especially Nina Schnall, who knew before I did that I'd one day write this book. To all the members of my dissertation writing group, and above all to Ben Chesluk and David Valentine (the Writer's Bloc). To the senior colleagues who helped me navigate the intersection of anthropology and Jewish studies, including Hasia Diner, Faye Ginsburg, Barbara Kirshenblatt-Gimblett, and above all Jonathan Boyarin, who has supported my work in more ways than I can count. And to my students and colleagues at Wesleyan University and elsewhere—above all Liza McAlister, for her wit and wisdom.

Of course I would never have finished, or even survived, this book without all the friends and loved ones who keep me in touch with the wonderful world beyond academia. First and foremost Jill, for her careful editing, her Crown Heights savvy, and her (nearly) endless patience with the demands of academic life. Also my whole Brooklyn posse, for food, drink, and general wackiness. Linner anyone? I've got a book to celebrate. And my family, near and far, new and old: Bernie, Toni and Laura, Carl and Anna, Mike and Rena, Ethan and Sarah. My love to you all.

Finally, my editors at Rutgers University Press, Kristi Long and Adi Hovav, were unfailingly supportive and engaged with my work. I couldn't have imagined a better environment in which to bring this project to fruition.

PORTIONS of this book have been published, in different forms, in the following essays. I am grateful to their publishers for permission to reprint them here.

" 'Crown Heights Is the Center of the World': Reterritorializing a
   Jewish Diaspora," *Diaspora: A Journal of Transnational Studies*,
   vol. 9, no. 1 (2000): 83–106.

"Suits and Souls: Trying to Tell a Jew When You See One in Crown
   Heights." In *Jews of Brooklyn*, ed. Ilana Abramovitch and Sean

Galvin (Hanover, NH: Brandeis University Press and the University Press of New England, 2002), 214–223.

"Food Fights: Contesting 'Cultural Diversity' in Crown Heights." In *Local Actions: Cultural Activism, Power, and Public Life in America*, ed. Melissa Checker and Maggie Fishman (New York: Columbia University Press, 2004), 159–183.

"Introduction: Race, Nation, and Religion." In *Race, Nation, and Religion in the Americas*, ed. Henry Goldschmidt and Elizabeth McAlister (New York: Oxford University Press, 2004), 3–31.

"The Voices of Jacob on the Streets of Brooklyn: Black and Jewish Israelites in and around Crown Heights," *American Ethnologist*, vol. 33, no. 3 (2006): 378–396

Race and Religion
among the Chosen Peoples
of Crown Heights

PROLOGUE

"Blacks" and "Jews" at the Laundromat

This book is about Black-Jewish difference in the Brooklyn neighborhood of Crown Heights—a neighborhood known for its history of intermittent conflict between Lubavitch Hasidic Jews and their predominantly Afro-Caribbean neighbors, and above all for the deadly violence of August 1991. The book will focus, for various reasons, on the Jewishness of the Lubavitch Hasidim, but its ultimate goal is to explore the diverse conceptual logics with which both Blacks and Jews in Crown Heights make sense of the differences that divide their neighborhood.

Given this lofty goal, it may seem somewhat strange to begin my analysis in the laundromat at the corner of Empire Boulevard and Brooklyn Avenue. But anthropologists often find far-reaching significance in quotidian detail, by examining what the pioneering ethnographer Bronislaw Malinowski called the "imponderabilia" of everyday life.[1] It is at once our methodological hallmark and occupational hazard. And, in fact, the everyday life of the laundromat may teach us a great deal about Blacks and Jews in Crown Heights, as well as the ways they are often misunderstood.

It's an entirely unremarkable laundromat (or at least it was an entirely unremarkable laundromat, as it has since been replaced by a barbershop). But when I first moved to Crown Heights, in December of 1996, it struck me as somehow remarkable that in a neighborhood known for sensationalized incidents of racial and religious conflict, Blacks and Jews folded their underwear together in this oddly intimate public space. Laundromats are, in fact, contact zones of a sort—one of the relatively few places where Black and Jewish Crown Heights residents are likely to spend more than a few minutes together—and the laundromat on my block was occasionally the scene of interracial and religious dialogue. The bulletin board next to the change machine was often home to a variety of proselytizing tracts, from evangelical Christian pamphlets listing "Signs of Christ's Early Return" to Lubavitch Hasidic flyers promoting Gentile observance of the Noachide Laws (laws the Torah enjoins upon both Jews and Gentiles, which many Lubavitchers consider essential to the dawning of the messianic age). Social interactions were nearly always polite and respectful, but could occasionally get a bit charged. One of the Caribbean women who managed the laundromat once told me of a Hasid who angrily accused her of antisemitism because she wouldn't let him start his laundry five minutes after the "last wash" deadline. And on one Sunday afternoon in August of 1997, the laundromat was home to its own small drama of Black-Jewish conflict.

It was a brutally hot and humid day, and the laundromat was even hotter than the sweltering streets outside. The air-conditioning was broken—if there ever was any—and a dozen dryers ran nonstop, pouring additional heat into the crowded room. The place was packed with customers doing Sunday chores, waiting their turn to wash or dry. A young Black woman was unloading a dryer, accompanied by her four- or five-year-old daughter, while a few young Hasidic women did their laundry nearby. One of the Hasidim began unloading the dryer immediately above the Black woman's dryer, and accidentally brushed up against her daughter. The fog of low-level crankiness was suddenly broken, as the Black woman snapped at the Hasid: "You just see what happens if you hit my daughter!" The other customers—both Black and Jewish—got a bit edgy as the Black woman said, to no one in particular, "Anybody touches my daughter, they're gonna get their ass kicked today." Things settled down for a minute or two, until the Hasid had finished unloading her dryer, and a young Jewish man began putting his clothes in. He was clearly not Hasidic—a small green yarmulke rested precariously on his long curly hair—and was most likely just visiting Crown Heights on one of the Lubavitch community's many outreach programs for non-orthodox Jews. But such fine-grained distinctions were not significant to the increasingly angry young woman. She threw her arms up in disgust and declared, "Y'see how they look out for each other!" A Black man nearby (most likely

Afro-Caribbean to her African American, judging from their accents) pointed out that the Jewish guy had been waiting his turn just like everyone else, but the Black woman continued to fume. She unloaded the rest of her clothes, muttering something about "those people" under her breath.

When she was done it was, unfortunately, my turn. I carried my laundry toward the dryer, but she would have none of it. She took one look at me—like the curly-haired guy, I was White and wearing a yarmulke, but didn't dress like a Hasid—and assured me, "Ain't none of your people gonna get this dryer!" She turned to the Black man who'd defended the other Jewish guy and asked him whether he wanted the dryer, but he— looking embarrassed—said he would wait his turn, then went outside for a cigarette. Undaunted, she told me again, "You people ain't gettin' my dryer!" She then took the Black man's clothes, in his absence, and put them in the dryer, starting it with her own quarter.

I put my clothes in the next open dryer and sat down quietly—hoping to avoid further conflict, and thinking over the field-notes I'd soon go write, just in case I ever wanted to tell this story. When the Black man came back inside, he was startled to find his clothes spinning in the dryer, and awkwardly thanked the young woman for putting them in. He looked mortified, however, so as soon as she left—still muttering under her breath—I walked over and shook his hand to assure him there were no hard feelings. "What do I care whose people are whose?" he said, "I just want to get my wash done."

The struggle over the dryer—a tempest in an overheated teapot— captures a little something of the flavor and texture of Black-Jewish conflict in Crown Heights. But more than that, I'm afraid these events (and, to be honest, my narrative of them) capture the flawed assumptions that all too often define public perceptions of Crown Heights. Indeed, my account of the events in the laundromat was crafted to highlight a number of stereotypic images that shape, and limit, the popular imagination of racial, ethnic, and religious conflict. There is, for example, the taken-for-granted link between heat, humidity, short tempers, and racial tension— an image popularized in explanations of collective violence during the "long hot summers" of the 1960s, and perhaps canonized in Spike Lee's 1989 film *Do the Right Thing.* There's the troubling perception of a Gentile child threatened by Jews—a longstanding trope of European antisemitism that may have shaped some Crown Heights residents' responses to the death of Gavin Cato in August of 1991. There's the endless squabble over limited resources—whether it's government funding, urban space, or just a dryer—that scholars and pundits typically locate at the heart of communal conflict. And finally, above all, there's the widely shared assumption that the social world, in Crown Heights and elsewhere, is populated by homogenous and clearly bounded groups like "Blacks" and "Jews"—"your people" and "my dryer"—the dangerous assumption that African Americans and Caribbean immigrants necessarily form a collective defined by "race," while Lubavitch Hasidim and a secular Jewish anthropologist form a comparable collective defined by "religion."

These assumptions aren't all entirely wrong. Some contain more than a grain of truth, while others take on their own brand of truth as they are shared, and invoked, by Crown Heights residents themselves. But none offer an adequate account of Black-Jewish relations in Crown Heights— not of the conflict surrounding the dryer in August of 1997, or the violence that rocked the neighborhood in August of 1991, or the underlying patterns of racial and religious difference that shape the everyday lives of Crown Heights communities. If we look carefully, for example, we may trace the efforts of the woman in the laundromat to *produce* a binary opposition between "Blacks" and "Jews"—in her willingness to overlook distinctions between Lubavitch Hasidim and other Jews, in her fruitless appeal to a dark-skinned neighbor to join her "people" and share her dryer, and finally in her decision to invest a quarter in the cause of their Blackness. These quotidian details don't somehow disprove the existence of the "Blacks" and "Jews" vying for the dryer, but they do give us a sense of the social, political, and rhetorical processes through which such contested collectives are produced.

That, in short, is my goal in this book: to look carefully at the lives of Crown Heights residents, and the differences that have all too often divided them. This ethnographic analysis of Black-Jewish difference will complicate assumptions about the conflict in Crown Heights, and the nature of collective identity itself. It's long past time to leave the laundromat's "Blacks" and "Jews" behind, and develop a richer understanding of our shared social world.

INTRODUCTION

Race, Religion, and the Contest over Black-Jewish Difference in Crown Heights

The Brooklyn neighborhood of Crown Heights stands out, in significant ways, from its immediate surroundings—and, far more broadly, from the patterns of racial and religious identity formation that have shaped American life since the mid-twentieth century. There is, of course, nothing unusual about the neighborhood's quiet tree-lined streets and bustling commercial strips, or its brownstone row houses and low-rise apartment buildings. The largely working- and middle-class immigrant communities who make their homes there are typical, in many ways, of similar communities throughout New York and other major cities. Crown Heights is certainly not isolated from its surroundings, or from larger social and historical trends. Yet it still stands out in certain ways.

Although it was once a predominantly White and largely Jewish neighborhood, the population of Crown Heights, like the rest of north-central Brooklyn, has been overwhelmingly Black (both African American and Afro-Caribbean) since the early 1970s.[1] In this too, Crown Heights is typical of broader trends. Indeed, it exemplifies the national pattern of "White flight" from city to suburbs that transformed New York and other American cities in the 1950s, 1960s, and 1970s. But today's Crown Heights is different from the adjoining neighborhoods of Brownsville and Bedford-Stuyvesant—and from comparable neighborhoods in Chicago, Detroit, Boston, and elsewhere—in at least one extremely simple, yet infinitely complex, way: the Lubavitch Hasidim, a tight-knit community of orthodox Jews, chose to stay in Crown Heights in the late 1960s when nearly all of their White Jewish neighbors chose to leave.

The Lubavitch community now makes up some 6 to 8 percent of the total population of Crown Heights (as its boundaries are semi-officially defined), and some 20 percent of the population in the limited area of south Crown Heights where most Lubavitchers live. Approximately 65 percent of the population of the neighborhood (again, as semi-officially defined) consists of immigrants from the Caribbean and their families, and approximately 15 percent consists of African Americans whose families have lived in the United States for generations. In addition to the Lubavitch Hasidim and their Black neighbors, there are quite a few Latinos in Crown Heights, a few Asians, and a handful of non-Hasidic Jews— including a small number of Black orthodox Jews and a growing number of non-orthodox immigrants from the former Soviet Union. There is also, I should note, a fair number of Sephardic Lubavitchers, from North Africa and the Middle East, who may not appear "White" by current American racial standards. As I will show throughout this book, none of these communities is monolithic or easily defined. The meanings of their identities cannot be reduced to the seductive clarity of statistics. But the Lubavitch Hasidim nevertheless stand out in today's Crown Heights—in both demographic fact and popular imagination—as a predominantly White community in a predominantly Black neighborhood. And Crown Heights itself thus stands out from other neighborhoods, thanks to the complex relationships between its Blacks and Jews.

Most of the time, Blacks and Jews in Crown Heights live together in peace, if not harmony—intimate strangers, sharing the streets of their neighborhood at a respectful distance. Yet most Crown Heights residents remain acutely aware of what they consider significant differences between Blacks and Jews. The substance of this difference is sometimes hard to pin down. As I will argue, Crown Heights residents rarely agree on its precise nature or political implications. Yet they return, again and again, to what most see as an axiomatic fact: Blacks and Jews are different. "As different," one Hasidic woman told me, "as an animal is from a tree." This is not to say that Crown Heights residents, on the whole, are racists or antisemites, preoccupied with their differences. Most, thank goodness, are not. But they do tend to assume—and assert, and produce—the fact of Black-Jewish difference. It is a structuring principle of everyday life and community politics, of casual conversation and cosmological order.

And on a number of occasions over the past forty years, their sense of difference has been cast in stark relief by violent conflict. Such was the case in August of 1991, when the tragic deaths of Gavin Cato and Yankel Rosenbaum—the former struck by a car in the motorcade of the Lubavitcher Rebbe (the charismatic leader of the Lubavitch community), and the latter stabbed by a Black teenager in the violence that soon followed—touched off three days of conflict between Blacks and Jews that a government report later described as "the most widespread racial unrest to occur in New York City in more than twenty years."[2] In the wake of this violence, Crown Heights was thrust into the media spotlight, the civil and criminal courts, local and national debates on diversity, and popular discussions of Black-Jewish relations.[3] The neighborhood became a symbol of racial and religious conflict, a cautionary tale of difference gone awry.

Since 1991, "Crown Heights" has haunted many other New Yorkers as an image of unbridgeable difference—an image that mirrors Crown Heights residents' own assumptions about the differences that divide their neighborhood's communities. The violence of 1991 followed a number of other local incidents of racial violence (like the 1986 murder of Michael Griffith in the Queens neighborhood of Howard Beach, and the 1989 murder of Yusuf Hawkins in the Brooklyn neighborhood of Bensonhurst) and set the stage, in a sense, for the nationwide crisis of racial violence that followed the 1992 acquittal of the Los Angeles police officers who had beaten Rodney King. New Yorkers in the late 1980s and early 1990s lived under a pall of racial tension. They elected David Dinkins—the city's first, and thus far only, Black mayor—in 1989, hoping he could unite a divided city. And then came "Crown Heights." A seven-year-old Guyanese boy was killed in a tragic, and arguably avoidable, car accident. A twenty-nine-year-old Australian orthodox Jew was stabbed in a brutal revenge murder. Blacks and Jews faced off in angry demonstrations, hurling rocks, bottles, slogans, and slurs. A half-dozen stores were looted, and a few Black youths (and others) assaulted Jews, journalists, and police. For three days the police were unable—some say unwilling—to stop the violence. When they finally did, with overwhelming force and mass arrests, a palpable bitterness lingered in Crown Heights, casting its shadow over an uneasy peace.

As they looked for solutions in the years that followed, New Yorkers found precious little hope for the future. Legal and political processes intended to bring closure to the conflict in Crown Heights instead brought fresh rounds of recrimination until the summer of 2003.[4] Many Crown Heights residents resisted the efforts of community organizations and government agencies to foster interracial dialogue. The Lubavitch Hasidim, above all, remained committed to religious beliefs and practices that encourage them to keep a certain social distance from their non-Jewish neighbors. Crown Heights residents wouldn't mix, and they wouldn't move. The city's vaunted "melting pot" had boiled over. At the very moment when massive waves of transnational migration were changing the face of New York—and the United States as a whole—the conflict in Crown Heights cast doubt on the city's ability to contain its bewildering diversity. How, New Yorkers wondered, can we navigate our increasingly diverse "global city" if we can't even resolve the conflict in Crown Heights?

Yet in a decade and a half of hand-wringing and finger-pointing, few New Yorkers have paused to examine the nature of Black-Jewish difference in Crown Heights. Few have questioned the taken-for-granted assumptions about race and religion that shape the politics—and perceptions—of conflict in Crown Heights. That, in essence, is my goal in this book. I hope to complicate the popular image of "Crown Heights" by posing fundamental questions about the neighborhood's racial and religious differences, and answering these questions through detailed ethnographic research.

I did ethnographic fieldwork in Crown Heights from 1996 to 1998. I lived in the neighborhood for much of that time, and conducted research at what anthropologists will likely recognize as a typical range of field sites. I attended a representative sample of local synagogues and churches, yeshivas and Bible-study courses—some just once or twice, others far more regularly. I attended a number of political (or politicized) events related to the violence of 1991, and I volunteered at a number of community organizations. I did extensive research in relevant archival collections. And perhaps above all, I hung out with lots of Crown Heights residents. I made a few close friends and a great many acquaintances, and conducted scores of tape-recorded interviews with a broad range of people in the neighborhood, including some who had been active in local politics, and others who had not. In all of these settings, I struggled to understand how Crown Heights residents themselves define the identities of, and the differences between, their neighborhood's Blacks and Jews.

Following a great deal of scholarship on collective identity formation, I assumed, from the outset of my field research, that Blackness and Jewishness are complex products of ongoing social processes, rather than stable or unchanging essences.[5] I did not therefore attempt to downplay or debunk the social reality of these identities—as though such "socially constructed" phenomena were not, in fact, real—but I did examine the discourses and practices through which they are produced. By analyzing these discourses and practices, I have worked to develop a more subtle understanding of race and religion. This new understanding will be helpful, I think, to New Yorkers still wrestling with the far-reaching implications of the conflict in Crown Heights—as well as Americans, and others, wrestling with the complex roles of identity and difference in contemporary social life.

Race, Religion, and Other Differences

A simple yet all too often underappreciated fact lies at the heart of my analysis of difference in Crown Heights: the simple fact of complexity itself. "That life is complicated," writes the legal scholar Patricia Williams, "is a fact of great analytical importance."[6] Black-Jewish difference in Crown Heights is, to be blunt, enormously complex. And its complexity, I will argue, is largely a product of its multiplicity.[7]

Although Crown Heights residents, and others, tend to imagine a stark distinction between the neighborhood's Blacks and Jews, they tend to describe this distinction in remarkably different ways. There is, in fact, no single, unambiguous, or agreed upon difference between Blacks and Jews in Crown Heights. Rather, the neighborhood is caught in a tangled web of multiple, competing, and intersecting differences. Crown Heights residents generally agree that Blacks and Jews are profoundly different, but they rarely agree on the nature of this difference. They struggle to explain their differences in terms of race, religion, and other conceptual categories. This unruly multiplicity stands behind, yet undercuts, the popular image of an unbridgeable difference between Black and Jews.

When Afro-Caribbean and African American Crown Heights residents reflect on their tense relationships with their Hasidic neighbors, they tend to describe the difference between Blacks and Jews as a matter of "race"—as a difference, in essence, between "Blacks" and "Whites"—a difference they sometimes express in the pseudoscientific terms of racial biology, but ultimately define in terms of the historical legacies of slavery, segregation, and discrimination in the United States and throughout the Americas.[8] The Lubavitch Hasidim, however, tend to describe the difference between Blacks and Jews as a matter of "religion"—as a difference, in essence, between "Jews" and "Gentiles"—a difference they sometimes express in terms of ritual practice and belief, but ultimately define in terms of Jewish descent from the biblical patriarchs, the Jews' unique covenant with a universal God, and a history of oppression prophesied, according to some, in the biblical text itself.[9]

Of course, the distinction between these racial and religious discourses is not so simple either. At times, we will see, Lubavitchers do speak in terms of race, invoking stereotypical images of Whiteness and Blackness that they share, to some extent, with most other Americans. Contrary to the popular perception of Hasidic Jews as "a people apart"— living in a world of their own, or some previous century—the Lubavitch community has been shaped in profound ways by American society. Though I will argue, throughout this book, that their religious perceptions of collective identity are substantially different from the racial perceptions ingrained in most Americans, this surely does not mean they are somehow ignorant of race. And similarly, though I will argue that Black Crown Heights residents tend to imagine Black-Jewish difference in terms of race, this by no means implies that their diverse religions have no significant impact on their perceptions of self and other.

Indeed, as I will argue at length below, although racial and religious discourses often differ in significant ways, they are inextricably linked— in Crown Heights and elsewhere—and must ultimately be seen as interwoven threads in a fabric of identity and difference that has shaped the lives of Americans and others throughout the modern world. I will explore the intimate ties between race and religion throughout this book, but at the same time I will explore a fundamental fact of life in Crown Heights: Blacks and Jews in the neighborhood tend to understand their differences in substantially different ways—in terms one may often describe as either racial or religious.

"Race" and "religion" are the most significant terms in the categorical contest over difference in Crown Heights, but they are hardly the only ones. On the relatively rare occasions when community leaders or elected officials organize formal dialogues between Blacks and Jews, their differences are typically framed as a matter of "culture." And when Blacks and Jews alike discuss the history of their neighborhood, or envision its future development, they tend to draw distinctions of socioeconomic "class." According to the rabbinic law that shapes nearly every aspect of Hasidic life, Jews are ultimately distinguished from Gentiles by their matrilineal descent from the ancient Israelites—forming a "tribe" or "genealogy" rather than a race or religion. And in the messianic visions of many Crown Heights residents—Lubavitch Hasidim, evangelical Christians, Black Hebrew Israelites, Rastafarians, and others—Jewish difference is defined by the unique status of the Israelites, whoever they may be, as God's "chosen people." The seeming simplicity of Black-Jewish difference is complicated, though never erased, by these multiple, cross-cutting axes of difference—race and religion, class and culture, genealogy and chosenness, to name but a few.

There is far more than abstract conceptual categories at stake in the tension among these different differences. Each of these divergent views of Black-Jewish difference encodes substantially different assumptions about the causes and contexts of conflict in Crown Heights. Each entails different perceptions of local community politics, and different standards of etiquette in everyday neighborly relations. Each implies different hopes and dreams for the future of the neighborhood. Blacks and Jews in Crown Heights thus tend to speak and act at cross purposes, because they don't even agree on the nature of their difference.

Black-Jewish difference in Crown Heights is hardly unique in this contested multiplicity—but, once again, it stands out in certain ways. Collective identities of all kinds are generally defined by a range of overlapping differences, regardless of whether they are ultimately described as "racial," "ethnic," "religious," or what-have-you. Yet in most social contexts, one form of difference takes conceptual and political priority over all others. An enduring consensus holds, for example, that the difference between

Blacks and Whites in the United States is a matter of race. On this, Black and White Americans tend to agree, though they may also stress the significance of other criteria—culture, class, nation, religion, gender, sexuality, and so on—in defining their own sense of self and community. The roles of these other differences in defining Blackness and Whiteness have thus been subsumed—however tenuously or provisionally—within the categorical hegemony of race. Among Blacks and Jews in Crown Heights, however, no single category of identity and difference holds such hegemonic sway. The clarity and hegemony of race and religion have eroded in today's Crown Heights, casting the multiplicity of difference in stark relief, and sparking a heated contest over the nature of Blackness and Jewishness. But how, exactly, did this contest take shape? How did categories like race and religion, and identities like Black and Jew, become so complex in this modest Brooklyn neighborhood?

Above all, I will argue, the answers to these questions lie in the distinctive beliefs and practices of the Lubavitch Hasidim. A careful analysis of the Lubavitch community is therefore central to my broader analysis of Black-Jewish difference. Like other Hasidic Jews, most Lubavitchers are fervently devoted to the observance of religious law, to the charismatic leadership of their Rebbe, and to a Jewish spirituality grounded in mystical, kabbalistic thought that informs most every aspect of their personal and communal lives—including their understandings of individual and collective identity. Indeed, as I will discuss below, many Lubavitchers are particularly devoted to their own distinctive brand of Hasidic thought, and to a distinctive set of claims about the nature of Jewishness itself. Though they are by no means isolated from American racial thought, the Lubavitch Hasidim have organized their community around a religious vision of Jewishness, in a neighborhood—and a nation—where collective identities and social hierarchies are more often defined in terms of race. They've tried to craft a Jewish identity outside of the terms of race, but their effort to do so has been constrained, at every turn, by the inextricable ties between religion and race—by their neighbors' perceptions of their Whiteness, by their complex position in racialized urban politics, and by the inescapably racial dimensions of their own religious discourses and practices. The tensions between the Lubavitch community's religious vision of Jewishness and the widespread American understanding of race have thus led to the contest over difference in Crown Heights.

Let me be quite clear about this crucial point: I am in no way arguing that the Lubavitch community, or its vision of Jewishness, is somehow to blame for the history of Black-Jewish conflict in Crown Heights. I am not suggesting that Lubavitchers have somehow misunderstood or misrepresented their own identities, or that they ought to approach their relationships with their neighbors in a fundamentally different way. Indeed, throughout this book I will defend the ability—dare I say the right?—of Lubavitchers and others to construct their identities and conduct their lives in ways that are meaningful to them. I am arguing, however, that the Lubavitch Hasidim, more than their neighbors, have upset the dominant patterns of American identity formation, revealing unexpected complexities in categories and identities like race and religion, Black and Jew.

I will ultimately argue that this Hasidic resistance to the hegemony of race reveals the conceptual and political limitations of such fashionable concepts as "multiculturalism" and "diversity"—concepts that claim to celebrate difference, yet only accommodate differences of certain kinds. Americans have developed quite a taste for diversity, but we generally prefer it when it's easily digestible—Thai food on Tuesday, Mexican on Wednesday, Caribbean on Thursday, but not too spicy please.[10] Categories like race, and for that matter religion, help us accommodate, and contain, cultural difference by reducing its limitless expressions to familiar and manageable forms—forcing Blacks and Jews, and everyone else, to define their identities and communities in equivalent ways. Blackness and Whiteness are seen as equivalently "racial," while Judaism and Christianity are considered equivalently "religious." Jerk chicken is to gefilte fish as Kwanzaa is to Hanukah, or dreadlocks are to yarmulkes, because all are considered equivalently "cultural." But sectarian religious communities, like the Lubavitch Hasidim, tend to disrupt these reductive equations by insisting upon the categorical uniqueness of their god-given practices and beliefs. There are, by definition, any number of "races" and "religions," but according to Lubavitchers (and others) there can only be one true "chosen people." This singular people is thought to transcend the constraints of the social world. The Lubavitch community's efforts to live by its vision of Jewishness—to live as a divinely chosen people in a diverse Brooklyn neighborhood—thus tests the ability of American society to accommodate radical forms of difference.

I will develop these arguments in the chapters to follow by examining the complex relationships between Blacks and Jews in today's Crown Heights (or rather, the Crown Heights of the 1990s, when I conducted my field research). I will flesh them out here, however, by examining a decisive moment in the history of the neighborhood—the moment, one might say, when the Lubavitch community broke with the prevailing norms of identity formation, and inaugurated the contest over difference in Crown Heights. This was the moment, in the spring of 1969, when the Lubavitcher Rebbe declared that his community would stay in Crown Heights as it became a predominantly Black neighborhood.

Race, Religion, and the Lubavitcher Rebbe

In Crown Heights and many similar communities, the 1960s witnessed the height of White flight—the racially charged out-migration that gave rise to America's "chocolate city" and its "vanilla suburbs."[11] The Black population of Crown Heights had been growing rapidly since the 1940s, but in 1960 the neighborhood was still 70 percent White. By 1970, however, it was 70 percent Black.[12] Just five years after the 1965 Hart-Cellar Immigration Reform Act opened the door to a new wave of Caribbean immigration, the very blocks of south Crown Heights where most Lubavitchers lived had become the demographic center of an Afro-Caribbean community that would soon be numerically and culturally dominant in the entire area.[13]

These were difficult years for many Jews in Crown Heights. An elderly Hasid I met in 1997 recalled that Jews of the time were deeply concerned about "the blight that was coming up from Bed-Stuy." Their fear of their new neighbors was compounded by a number of sensationalized incidents of Black-on-Jewish crime and, in 1964, by the first communal conflicts between local Blacks and Jews.[14] In the mid- to late 1960s, the riots breaking out across America every summer focused national anxiety on the shifting terrain of urban race relations. And in 1968, the bitter conflicts surrounding the teachers' strike in nearby Ocean Hill–Brownsville focused local anxiety, more specifically, on Black-Jewish relations.[15] In Crown Heights, as elsewhere, these anxieties were often provoked by "block-busting" realtors, who profited by underpaying nervous White home sellers while overcharging first-time Black home buyers. In this racially charged context, the Bobov Hasidim—a Hasidic community, like the Lubavitchers, that had settled in Crown Heights in the 1940s as Holocaust refugees—left en masse for Boro Park, a south Brooklyn neighborhood that remains overwhelmingly White and Jewish to this day. Some Lubavitchers undoubtedly talked of leaving Crown Heights in the 1960s. But the vast majority ultimately stayed, and they did so at the impassioned insistence of their Rebbe, Menachem Mendel Schneerson.

It is difficult to overstate the devotion most Hasidic Jews feel toward their Rebbes. Since the early nineteenth century, the various Hasidic communities (of which Lubavitch is one of the largest) have been distinguished from each other by the fervent allegiance of Hasidim to a number of multigenerational dynasties of charismatic leaders, or Rebbes. The Rebbe of each community acts as its spiritual and temporal leader, and serves—according to Hasidic theology—as an intermediary between his Hasidim and their God.[16] He stands, by definition, at the very center of Hasidic life. Yet there are, nevertheless, individual Rebbes who inspire greater or lesser degrees of devotion among their Hasidim. And in the Lubavitch community, in particular, it is nearly impossible to overstate the devotion inspired by Menachem Mendel Schneerson. "The Rebbe," as he is known (unlike his six predecessors, who are known by specific identifying characteristics), led the Lubavitch community from 1951 until his death on June 12, 1994. He rebuilt the community in the wake of the Holocaust, helped initiate a worldwide trend of "return" to Jewish orthodoxy, played a prominent role in local and global Jewish politics, and ultimately inspired a controversial messianic movement among many—though by no means all—of his Hasidim.[17] His authority within the community was virtually unquestioned. And in a public lecture in April of 1969, on the last day of Passover, the Lubavitcher Rebbe took an unequivocal stand against any exodus from the neighborhood where his revered father-in-law, now known as the Previous Rebbe, had put down roots some thirty years before.

FIGURE 1 The Lubavitcher Rebbe speaking at a farbrengen in December 1991.
(Photo by Marc Asnin. Reprinted by permission of Corbis Image Licensing.)

Throughout his decades of leadership, the Rebbe spoke to his Hasidim
nearly every Shabbos and on most Jewish holidays, in ritual performances
known as *farbrengens* (in Yiddish, simply "gatherings"). He typically spoke
before thousands of Hasidim, who packed the community's main synagogue at 770 Eastern Parkway to overflowing. He spoke for hours at a time,
pausing occasionally for his Hasidim to sing in Yiddish or Hebrew, and to
chant the ecstatic wordless melodies of Hasidic *nigunim*.[18] As the afternoon
wore on, these farbrengens often built to a fever pitch of "collective effer-
vescence" (in Emile Durkheim's classic phrase), forging a powerful bond
between the Rebbe and his Hasidim (see figure 1). The significance of the
Rebbe's farbrengens to the Lubavitch community is, once again, difficult
to overstate. In the early 1990s, an elderly Hasid told a friend of mine, simply, "It's like traveling to Mount Sinai each week and getting the Torah
again. Whatever God has to tell us this week is in the farbrengen."[19]

And on the last day of Passover in 1969, God—speaking through the
Rebbe—told the Lubavitch community to stay in Crown Heights. The
Rebbe's farbrengens generally focused on theological questions, allegori-
cal narratives, and fervent exhortations to observe the commandments of

the Torah. He rarely spoke on social or political issues, and when he did
he usually articulated broad principles rather than specific policies. But
this time he was quite clear. He began his lecture:

> In recent times, a plague has spread among our brethren—the
> wholesale migration from Jewish neighborhoods. One result of
> this phenomenon is the sale of houses in these neighborhoods to
> non-Jewish people. Even synagogues and places of Torah study are
> sold. Furthermore, the livelihood of many members of the commu-
> nity becomes undermined or completely destroyed by this precipi-
> tous flight. Since this matter concerns tens of thousands of Jews, I
> feel compelled to express my opinions openly and clearly, and to
> call attention to at least some of the references on the subject in
> Torah law.[20]

The Rebbe went on to cite and discuss over a dozen specific rulings by Talmudic sages and rabbinic authorities that, he argued, forbid Jews from
selling or renting property to non-Jews if there is a chance this non-Jewish
presence will damage the lifestyle or livelihood of a Jewish community.
While his Jewish neighbors were leaving Crown Heights to protect their
middle-class status from "urban blight," and protect their hard-won
Whiteness from Black people, the Rebbe urged his Hasidim to stand firm
against "those who worship idols and stars," and to face down the hostility of "the enemies of Israel." While most American Jews renegotiated
their place in American society by thinking and acting in terms of race
and class, the Rebbe insisted on the primacy of religion in defining Jewish
identity and community.

He warned, above all, that the fabric of religious life and generational
continuity would be torn if Jews moved. "In the old neighborhoods," he
said, "people had found their particular circles, had sunk roots into their
particular Jewish environment. Each person belonged to an organization
devoted in some measure to studying Torah, maintained active synagogue
membership and attendance, and supported charitable organizations. . . .
and their children had in great degree been influenced to follow in the familiar, well-trodden path. All of this is endangered with the move to a
new neighborhood." He specifically discussed the spiritual dangers of
selling synagogues and yeshivas, called attention to the plight of the

"poor, orphans and widows" who cannot move so easily, and encouraged
Jews to work instead to build their local communities. He declared that
leaving a Jewish neighborhood is simply not an individual choice, but a
matter for the entire community to decide. And finally, he quoted from
Deuteronomy to tell his Hasidim: "Do what is right and good in the sight
of the Lord, so that all may go well with you and that you may be able to
possess the good land that the Lord your God promised on oath to your fathers, and that all your enemies may be driven out before you, as the Lord
has spoken" (Deut. 6:18–19).

For most Lubavitchers, the choice was clear. The interwoven authority of the biblical text, rabbinic law, and their beloved Rebbe kept them in
Crown Heights. The essential nature of Jewishness, as they understood it,
stood against the process of White flight that was redefining the identities
of their Jewish neighbors. More broadly, one might say, the religious discourses of the Lubavitch Hasidim stood against the thoroughgoing racialization of American society—insisting on the viability of a Jewish identity
and community defined in other terms.

This religious resistance to the hegemony of race was, at the same
time, a remarkable success and an abject failure. The Lubavitch community remained in Crown Heights, yet remained caught—as thoroughly as
ever—in the grip of race. They "[did] what [was] right and good in the sight
of the Lord," but their "enemies" were hardly "driven out before [them]."
The demographic trends of the 1960s continued unabated, and by the
mid-1970s the Lubavitch Hasidim were the only numerically significant
Jewish community left in Crown Heights. Though the Hasidim increased
their numbers dramatically in the 1970s and 1980s, the neighborhood had
already changed around them, becoming, in Philip Kasinitz's apt description, "the center of West Indian life in the United States."[21] Along
with Flatbush and East Flatbush to the south, the neighborhood is now
home to large communities of immigrants from Haiti, Jamaica, Trinidad,
Guyana, and other Caribbean countries.[22] Each year on Labor Day, the
West Indian–American Day Parade, or Carnival, asserts the demographic
and cultural predominance of these communities by bringing millions of
revelers to Eastern Parkway for the largest annual gathering of Black people in North America—and bringing a boisterous soca party to the doors
of the synagogue where the Rebbe once farbrenged.[23]

Indeed, the Lubavitch community's decision to remain in Crown Heights for religious reasons has ultimately served to highlight the racial dimensions of their collective identity, thanks to their distinctive demographic status as a White Jewish minority surrounded by a Black Gentile majority. In communities throughout the United States where relatively small numbers of Lubavitchers live in predominantly White, and largely Christian, neighborhoods, their Whiteness is generally unremarkable. Their difference—and their Jewishness—thus tends to be defined in religious terms.[24] But the absence of White Christians in Crown Heights, and the resulting binary politics of "Black-Jewish relations," have redefined the links between race and religion—equating Whiteness with Jewishness and Blackness with Christianity in ways that are, perhaps, unprecedented. In simple if somewhat reductive terms, Blacks in Crown Heights are defined by Christianity (or perhaps just non-Jewishness) in ways they are not elsewhere, while Lubavitchers have come to exemplify Whiteness in ways that Jews (and Hasidim, no less) do not elsewhere. The Rebbe's insistence on the primacy of religion has thus led, in turn, to a countervailing insistence on the primacy of race—an ironic twist that highlights the ties between racial and religious discourses and politics.

For example, the Reverend Al Sharpton, who played a controversial role in the events of August 1991, recalled in an interview that as a child growing up in and around Crown Heights, he rarely distinguished Hasidim from other Whites: "They were all one thing to us—I mean, it was a while before I understood the difference between a Hasidic Jew, and another more secular Jew, and a non-Jewish White. It was all one thing to us. . . . Kids growing up in Crown Heights saw them as White, versus Black. That was Whiteness to them, or their first frame of reference to Whiteness." The fact that Lubavitchers may be equated with non-Jews, forming the "first frame of reference to Whiteness" for local Black children, suggests that the politics and demographics of today's Crown Heights have shifted the categories of race and religion in locally specific, and somewhat eccentric, ways. This unusual situation is an unintended result of the Lubavitch community's attempt to define a Jewish identity outside the terms of race.

The distinctive local contours of difference in Crown Heights should not, however, blind us to the broader historical contexts of the neighborhood's racial and religious identities. I will explore four of these contexts in the following sections, expanding the scope of my analysis from section to section, to examine: (1) the history and beliefs of the Lubavitch community; (2) the longstanding ambiguity of American Jewish identities; (3) the co-constitutive ties between "racial" and "religious" discourses of difference; and (4) the continuities between "modernity" and "tradition" that these ties suggest.

The Lubavitch Ideology of Jewishness

The Lubavitch community of Crown Heights is set apart from its neighbors, and most other Americans, not merely by the fact of its Jewishness, but by its distinctive claims concerning the nature of Jewishness and the difference between Gentiles and Jews. This Lubavitch ideology of Jewishness stands in self-conscious, active opposition to the collective identities of most American Jews—and in stark contrast, in certain ways, to the widespread American understanding of race.[25]

Lubavitch understandings of Jewishness often mirror those of other Hasidim and (to a somewhat lesser extent) those of other "ultra-orthodox" Jews.[26] Lubavitchers are united with all ultra-orthodox Jews—Hasidic and non-Hasidic alike—in their meticulous observance of religious law. Although they often differ in their interpretations of specific laws, the ultra-orthodox ultimately agree that Jewish identity may only be defined in terms of the laws of the Torah—laws given to the Jews by God at Mount Sinai, and interpreted over the millennia by divinely inspired sages. Yet despite this consensus, orthodox Jewry has often been divided by controversial social and religious movements. Such was the case in the Jewish communities of Eastern Europe in the eighteenth century, when the popular movement that later came to be known as Hasidism was founded by a mystic and teacher known as the Baal Shem Tov (literally "Master of the Good Name," a term often used to describe folk healers whose therapeutic practices invoked kabbalistic names of God).[27] The early Hasidic movement was bitterly opposed by the leading rabbinic authorities of the time, and though this rift was largely healed in the nineteenth century, Hasidic and non-Hasidic orthodox communities still differ in a number of ways. Hasidim are distinguished, in large part, by their devotion to their Rebbes—a devotion considered idolatrous by some non-Hasidic orthodox

Jews—and by their efforts to infuse the observance of religious law with an enthusiastic spirituality grounded in esoteric mystical thought. The Lubavitch community in Crown Heights shares these core principles and traditions with dozens of small and large Hasidic communities, many of which are now based in the Brooklyn neighborhoods of Williamsburg and Boro Park.[28]

Yet since its origins in White Russia in the late eighteenth century, the Lubavitch community—or Chabad-Lubavitch movement[29]—has been distinguished from other, more inward-looking, Hasidic communities by its efforts to teach Hasidism to a broader Jewish audience. This ethic of outreach dates to the earliest years of the community, but it came to define Lubavitch as an organized social movement in the mid- to late twentieth century.[30] Since the 1950s, under the leadership of the Rebbe, Lubavitchers have become well known—and somewhat controversial—in the broader Jewish world for their aggressive campaigns to encourage orthodox observance and Lubavitch beliefs among secular and non-orthodox Jews. These "mitzvah campaigns" have been marked by full-page advertisements in the *New York Times* and other major papers, and by the presence of young Lubavitchers in the streets of major cities, accosting Jewish passersby—"Excuse me sir, are you Jewish?"—to encourage their observance of religious law. Above all, however, these campaigns have led thousands of Lubavitchers, working as "emissaries" of their Rebbe, to found synagogues, schools, and community centers in hundreds of small and large Jewish communities throughout the world. These "Chabad Houses" are intended to promote and support Jewish orthodoxy, but they have also placed Lubavitchers in a sustained and complex dialogue with the non-Hasidic, non-orthodox, and indeed non-Jewish worlds—a dialogue that has had far-reaching effects on the Lubavitch community itself, setting it apart in many ways from its fellow Hasidic communities.[31]

In the course of these outreach efforts, and as a substantial number of Jews raised in relatively secular families have joined the Lubavitch community, Lubavitchers have come to emphasize a vision of Jewishness as an inherent and inherited property of the soul—an understanding of Jewish identity that tends to level distinctions between secular and orthodox Jews, while accentuating distinctions between Jews and non-Jews.

Lubavitch ideology proclaims, and Lubavitchers generally believe, that Jews are distinguished from non-Jews by a unique "godly soul" (in Hebrew, *nefesh elokis*) inherited from their biblical patriarchs. This distinctive Jewish soul is thought to be fundamentally different from the "animal soul" (in Hebrew, *nefesh bahamis*) shared by Gentiles and Jews. It is thought to link Jews around the world to each other and their God, and to predispose them (whether they know it or not) to follow the commandments of the Torah. The theological foundations of this belief were developed in the eighteenth century by Rabbi Shneur Zalman—the first Lubavitcher Rebbe, and founder of the Lubavitch community—but the doctrine of the godly soul has taken on a new significance, and urgency, as Lubavitchers have worked, over the past fifty years, to convince secular Jews around the world that they already possess the soul of a Hasid.[32]

There is, indeed, a sense of urgency to these efforts. For according to Lubavitchers, and many other orthodox Jews, widespread Jewish observance of the Torah's commandments is the one and only way to usher in the messianic age.[33] Given the unique role of Torah observance in the cosmic drama of redemption—a role that constitutes the essence of the Jewish people's chosenness—the ultimate goal of the Lubavitch community's ongoing outreach campaigns is nothing less than the messianic redemption of creation. And this is, as I've noted, a goal that was very much on the minds of most Lubavitchers in the 1980s and 1990s, as many came to believe that their Rebbe was the messiah. The Lubavitch community's distinctive ideology of Jewishness thus stands at the center of a global social movement, a self-conscious program for identity formation, and an all-embracing narrative of cosmological transformation.

This understanding of Jewishness resonates in certain ways with American views of racial biology—through common tropes of descent and purity, as well as what may be described as a shared bio-spiritual determinism—but it nevertheless stands against a number of basic assumptions about "race" and other American identities. Above all, it aims to supplant the loosely defined identities of most American Jews with the foundational clarity of a god-given Jewish soul. More broadly, though less explicitly, it aims to supplant what Lubavitchers consider a superficial distinction between Blacks and Whites, in Crown Heights and elsewhere, with a divinely sanctioned distinction between Gentiles and Jews. And broadest of all, it aims to supplant the pseudoscience of racial biology with what Lubavitchers consider the eternal truths of the Torah—that is, one might say, to replace a widely accepted body of mythical beliefs with a somewhat less well known one. The Lubavitch Hasidim have thus catalyzed the contest over difference in Crown Heights through their efforts to transform— or resist, or circumvent—American understandings of collective identity.

Of course, Lubavitchers are by no means the only Crown Heights residents whose sense of self and community stands in tension with American patterns of identity formation. Much as their spiritual vision of Jewishness complicates their racial Whiteness, many of their Afro-Caribbean neighbors have built transnational communities that complicate their racial Blackness. The national flags waved—and worn—by the diverse crowd at the Labor Day Carnival mark gaps in the hegemony of Blackness that further destabilize Black-Jewish difference. Yet these transnational identities do not generally form programmatic bases for cultural activism in the Black community, and they rarely define unified perceptions of other communities. Few, if any, Afro-Caribbean Crown Heights residents insist, as a matter of principle, that their neighborhood is populated by Haitians and Russians, for example, rather than Blacks and Whites. Rather, as scholars of Caribbean Brooklyn have shown, most invoke such identities in fluid and situational ways, and continue to view their relationships with White Americans—including their Hasidic neighbors—through the binary lens of race.[34]

The Lubavitch Hasidim, however, have built a community and organized a social movement around an all-embracing religious vision of Jewishness—a vision at odds, in significant ways, with American understandings of race. The contest over Black-Jewish difference in Crown Heights thus unfolds around the inextricable ties, and irreconcilable tensions, between religion and race.

The Ambiguity of American Jewish Difference

This categorical contest is specific to Crown Heights in many important ways, but it is nevertheless shaped by broader patterns of identity formation. It speaks, for example, to the categorical ambiguity that has long surrounded American Jewishness. Much as Crown Heights residents struggle over race and religion, Americans have struggled—and failed—to define Jewish difference in a number of ways.

As I have noted, most Americans view Blackness and Whiteness as matters of "race." By the same token, we tend to describe Christianity and Islam, or Buddhism and Hinduism, as "religions." We see the difference between Haitian and Jamaican immigrants, for example, as a difference of "ethnicity," while the difference between Haitians and Jamaicans in the lands of their birth is thought to be one of "nationality." But American Jewish identity has rarely, if ever, been so clearly defined. It is not—or no longer—generally considered racial, although one is usually born into it. It is often considered religious, yet somehow accommodates nonpracticing nonbelievers. It might be described as ethnic, though it encompasses immigrants from all over the world. It is linked in complex ways to the state of Israel, but few American Jews have rushed to "return" to their national homeland. There is, in brief, no settled consensus in the United States concerning the nature of Jewish difference. Jewishness is often perceived—by Jews and others—as an ambiguous identity that doesn't quite fit the available categories of identity formation.

In the late nineteenth and early twentieth centuries, when a great many American Jews arrived as immigrants from Eastern Europe, Jewish difference was generally defined in terms of race. Jews in the United States were generally—though by no means universally—considered White, but were nevertheless thought to differ from other Whites by virtue of their distinctive "Jewish blood." American Jews of the time often adapted such terms as well, describing themselves as a "race" even as they assimilated with White Gentiles. But as this assimilation proceeded over the course of the twentieth century—and as a binary view of Black-White racial difference supplanted the finer-grained distinctions Americans had once drawn between Anglo-Saxons, Hebrews, Celts, and other White races—Jewishness gradually lost its moorings in race.[35] And without the false certainties of blood, in a society where many Jews don't practice their religion, where few agree on the details of their ethnic heritage, and most are ambivalent about their reborn nation, Jewishness seems to have lost whatever clarity it may once have had. Daniel Itzkovitz's subtle analysis of American Jewish difference in the early twentieth century rings true, in many ways, in the early twenty-first:

As exacting as early twentieth-century American accounts of Jewish difference often become, they are most striking, taken as a
whole, for their inability to arrive at a solid notion of "the Jew."
Jewishness kept slipping within and among the categories of race,
nation, religion, and culture, and the criteria for affiliation and
disaffiliation (notwithstanding the religious law that defines as
Jewish those individuals whose mother is Jewish) were very vulner-
able to contestation. Who belonged? What were the qualifica-
tions?[36]

These questions have still not been answered. Or rather, they have been
answered so often and so variously that American Jewish difference remains, in Itzkovitz's apt phrase, "a difference with no content, or, more
exactly, with a fluid and ever-shifting content that cannot mark Jewishness as distinct."[37]

Of course, there is absolutely nothing about Jewishness itself, independent of its social contexts, that makes it inherently more ambiguous
than other identities. Indeed, to argue as such would merely reinscribe an
essentialist understanding of Jewish difference, comparable in many ways
to that of the Lubavitch Hasidim—a sort of postmodern chosenness, with
the Jews imagined as "a people apart," unique in their ambiguity. This is
clearly not the case.[38] I would argue, however, that for a number of specific historical reasons, Jewishness is somewhat more ambiguous than
most other American identities. This ambiguity may ultimately be rooted
in the complex trajectory of Jewish assimilation in the United States, in
the ambivalent role of European Jews in—but not quite of—colonial Christendom, the ambivalent place of Judaism itself at the historical and theological heart of Christianity, or in some combination of these and other
factors. But whatever its root causes, the ambiguity of American Jewishness clearly helps shape the contest over difference in Crown Heights.

Moreover, this ambiguity is accentuated in today's Crown Heights
by another longstanding trend in American religious life: the role of
Jewishness—as a concept, symbol, or narrative trope—in the racial and religious identities of many Black Americans. As I will discuss in detail in
chapter 5, a substantial minority of Black Crown Heights residents see
themselves as Jews in some literal or figurative sense, and a substantial

majority have at least a passing familiarity—and oftentimes a profound engagement—with the history of the biblical Israelites. The rhetorical figures of "Israel" and "the Jews" occupy central places in the social imaginations of Bible-believing Black communities, whether these figures are inhabited by Blacks themselves or projected onto Jews. The "ever-shifting content" of Jewishness thus shifts back and forth between Blacks and Jews in Crown Heights, further exacerbating the contest over their difference.

Of course, Lubavitchers grant no credence to their Black neighbors' claims on Jewishness—and little credence, for that matter, to what they tend to dismiss as the fuzzy-headed ambiguities of other American Jews. But they nevertheless find themselves in a cultural milieu that challenges the clarity of Jewishness as they understand it.

The Co-constitution of Race and Religion

To make matters worse (at least in the eyes of most Hasidim, and other defenders of Jewish orthodoxy), the Jewish identities of Black Crown Heights residents are only the tip of a far larger iceberg. On a broader historical scale, the cast of "Israelites" in the Americas includes countless communities that have claimed, in one way or another, a privileged tie to the chosen people of the scriptures. Puritan colonists and Mormon pioneers, orthodox Jews and Pentecostal Christians, the White supremacist Christian Identity movement and Black supremacist Nation of Islam, Jamaican Rastafarians and Haitian Rara musicians—these diverse communities, and many others, have used the figure of "Israel" to define both race and religion.[39]

As this unruly crowd of Israelites suggests, the contest over Black-Jewish difference in Crown Heights is but one recent act in a long-running drama. In the United States and throughout the Americas, from the fifteenth century through the twenty-first, racial and religious identities (and others) have been inextricably woven together, to such an extent that "race" and "religion" have each helped define the very nature of the other. Throughout American history, these seemingly distinct discourses of difference have borrowed and contested each other's claims to authority, reinforced and undercut each other's social hierarchies, mixing and mingling in complex dialectics that may rarely be reduced to either term alone. They are, I would argue, co-constituted categories, wholly dependent on each other for their social existence and symbolic meanings.[40]

Yet these co-constitutive relationships between race and religion remain poorly understood for a number of reasons. Perhaps above all, scholars of collective identity formation have paid too little attention to religious
identities, and have often overlooked the role of religion in defining identities based on other—seemingly more empirical—criteria. Although most
scholars readily acknowledge that racial identities may be shaped, for example, by differences of class and gender, they typically assume race has
little to do with mythical narratives of Israelite descent or millennial fantasies of divine redemption.

There are, of course, significant exceptions to this critique. Scholars of
African American and Afro-Caribbean history and culture, for example,
have long been concerned with the religious dimensions of Black identities.[41] And their concerns have been echoed, more recently, in research on
a broad range of topics. Scholars of transnational migration have shown
the role of religion in defining the identities of racialized immigrant communities, as well as shaping their incorporation into American society.[42]
Scholars of American Jewish history have traced the uneven development
of Jewish Whiteness in the twentieth century.[43] Scholars of Latin American
Pentecostalism have examined a range of Christian responses to racial inequality,[44] while scholars of American White supremacist movements have
shown how Christianity may be tied to racial violence and domination.[45] In
a broader global perspective, a number of scholars have explored the links
between Christian missionary work and European colonialism.[46] Others
have highlighted the role of religion in the ethnic, nationalist, and communal conflicts that have divided the Balkans, South Asia, and other parts
of the world,[47] as well as the role of collective identity formation in the recent growth of religious "fundamentalisms."[48] Taken together, these small
but vibrant literatures have offered subtle analyses of the religious lives of
racialized communities in the Americas and elsewhere.

Unfortunately, however, most authors on these subjects haven't ade-
quately conveyed the depth and complexity of the relationships between
race and religion. Their work, I would argue, has too often been limited by
a fundamental misunderstanding of the ways in which diverse categories
of identity (race, nation, religion, gender, sexuality, etc.) coalesce to define
individuals and communities. Much of the scholarship referenced above—
including, let me reiterate, a great deal of important research—has started
from the assumption that race and religion are fundamentally distinct,

clearly bounded categories, and only then traced the ways that these categories intersect. These intersections have typically been accorded a kind
of secondary status—secondary, that is, to the presumed boundedness
and integrity of the categories themselves. However fluidly they may in-
teract in the course of social life, in the eyes of most scholars race and religion manage to retain their analytical clarity and autonomy.[49]

And at times, of course, these categories of identity do seem fairly distinct. I have argued, for example, that Blacks and Jews in Crown Heights
tend to describe their differences in terms of "race" and "religion,"
respectively—thus implying that Crown Heights residents themselves distinguish between these two forms of identity, or at least that such a distinction may usefully be drawn in an analysis of their lives. Indeed, I will
draw such distinctions throughout this book—simultaneously invoking
and interrogating race and religion as categories of analysis. In chapter 1,
for example, I will argue that Black Crown Heights residents offer a racial
narrative of the violence of 1991 when they describe this violence as a
"riot" or "rebellion" against White supremacy, while their Hasidic neighbors offer a religious narrative of the same events when they describe
them as a "pogrom" against a defenseless Jewish community. Here the
distinction between race and religion seems to be more or less clear—and
in a limited sense it is.

But this distinction must not blind us to the underlying ties between
these contested categories. For example, Lubavitch Hasidic narratives of
the pogrom against their community tend to draw upon widespread American stereotypes of Black criminality and violence, while resignifying—or
reinterpreting—these "garden variety" racial fears and fantasies in terms
of a religious understanding of Gentile antisemitism. Religion may therefore be the preeminent category of difference in these narratives, but it is
hardly the only one. To the contrary, it gains its rhetorical force by func-
tioning, in the historian Evelyn Brooks Higginbotham's terms, as a "metalanguage" for race and other differences—a master trope or key symbol,
lending religious meaning to differences that might also be understood in
other terms.[50] In this case, it allows Lubavitch Hasidim to describe the violence Americans all too often associate with young Black men as an expression of the brutality they believe these men share—as Gentiles—with
the Cossacks of the Russian steppes. Religious difference offers Lubavitchers

a compelling account of their relationships with their neighbors not because it operates independently of other differences, but precisely because "it speaks about and lends meaning to a host of terms and expressions, to myriad aspects of life that would otherwise fall outside [its] referential domain."[51] And "religion" is thus inextricably tied to "race," not least through efforts to subsume and redefine it—to define Blacks as Gentiles, criminals as Cossacks, and a riot as a pogrom.

Similarly, for many Black Crown Heights residents, race functions as a metalanguage for religion and other differences, redefining objects, images, and practices that might also be understood in different terms. The black hats and coats worn by many Hasidic men are interpreted, for example, as signs of racial Whiteness. The Lubavitch community's insularity, which Lubavitchers attribute to religious observance, is interpreted as a form of racial segregation—and thus, according to some, as an underlying cause of the Crown Heights riots. "Race" is thus inextricably tied to "religion," not least through efforts to subsume and redefine it—to define Jews as Whites, insularity as insult, and a pogrom as a riot.

The "riot" and "pogrom" of 1991 are thus constructed, in part, through efforts to incorporate each other's terms. Indeed, "race" and "religion" themselves have been co-constituted in just such a dialogic process—a process ongoing for centuries in the Americas and elsewhere. Race and religion each enter into, while emerging from, a composite identity formation that cannot be defined by either term alone. Their articulation in and through this larger formation shapes these categories in fundamental ways. Each is shot through with the other, and may thus be found—indeed, must be accounted for—at the heart of the other's social existence. Analyses of Blackness and Whiteness, in Crown Heights and elsewhere, must account for the traces of Jewishness and Gentileness, while analyses of Jewishness and Gentileness must account for the traces of Blackness and Whiteness. These identities and differences intersect to define the chosen peoples of today's Crown Heights.

An analysis of Black-Jewish difference in Crown Heights therefore cannot take the boundaries of "race" and "religion" for granted. A rather different analytical strategy is required. As the philosopher and social theorist Judith Butler has noted, in a discussion of race and sexuality that parallels my analysis of race and religion:

[T]hough there are clearly good historical reasons for keeping "race" and "sexuality" and "sexual difference" as separate analytic spheres, there are also quite pressing and significant historical reasons for asking how and where we might read not only their convergence, but the sites at which the one cannot be constituted save through the other. This is something other than juxtaposing distinct spheres of power, subordination, agency, historicity, and something other than a list of attributes separated by those proverbial commas (gender, sexuality, race, class), that usually mean that we have not yet figured out how to think the relations we seek to mark.[52]

Today's Crown Heights is a site at which race and religion "cannot be constituted save through [each] other." Like Blacks and Jews themselves, these categories of identity may be distinguished in a number of important ways—but without, for a moment, being inherently distinct.

In sum, we may often describe Crown Heights residents' perceptions of difference as either "racial" or "religious," but we may not therefore assume that these co-constituted categories stem from clearly bounded cultures, set apart from each other in fundamental ways. Though I will argue that race and religion offer divergent accounts of life in Crown Heights, the goal of my analysis is ultimately to show the inextricable ties between these discourses of difference.

Race and Religion, Modernity and Tradition

Above all, I hope, this unified analysis of race and religion will offer a subtle understanding of difference in Crown Heights. As an ethnographer and a Brooklynite, my primary concerns are resolutely local. But looking beyond Brooklyn, such an analysis may also suggest a richer understanding of the role of religion in our ostensibly secular modern society. The distinction between "race" and "religion" is often linked, in turn, to the distinction between "modernity" and "tradition," so by rethinking the first of these co-constituted pairs we may also shed new light on the second.[53]

While religious beliefs have shaped global politics since at least the early middle ages, race is a distinctively "modern" form of identity—the illegitimate child of secular humanism and scientific rationality, dark underbelly of Enlightenment universalism, and ideological grease on the wheels of industrial capital. The concept of race as we know it today did not take shape until the late eighteenth century, and only became a dominant form of hierarchy and identity in the mid- to late nineteenth century. Its development was, and remains, tied to a number of sweeping social trends—including capitalism, colonialism, and the birth of the nation-state—that have reshaped much of the world over the past few centuries.[54] But the question remains: How are we to understand the relationships between race and the diverse forms of identity, religious and otherwise, that preceded it?

Efforts to answer this question have all too often been hindered by the commonsense equation of modernity with secularization. Throughout the twentieth century, scholars and pundits tended to argue—or simply assume—that religion no longer plays a significant role in identity formation, community building, political life, or much of anything else in the "modern" world.[55] Though the self-identity of medieval Christendom was defined in opposition to the "Hebrews" and "Heretics" within its borders, the "Mohammedans" next door, and the "Heathens" everywhere else, many scholars insist that such religious identities have been—or at least ought to have been—swept away by secular modernity, and replaced by identities based on race, class, and nation.

Contemporary religious identities thus tend to be characterized as survivals, or holdovers, from an earlier time. This assumption was all too clear, for example, in American responses to the terrorist attacks of September 11, 2001. Despite our growing fear of religious extremism (not to mention our growing tendency toward extremisms of our own), too many Americans continue to assume a stark opposition between "the West" and "the Rest"—the former imagined as modern, rational, and secular, while the latter is thought to languish in a fantastical world of religious tradition, with identities and politics based on supernatural beliefs we deem unfounded or irrational. Somewhat closer to home, similar assumptions shape American perceptions of sectarian religious communities. For example, in her popular account of Lubavitch family life, the journalist Lis Harris describes a busy Crown Heights grocery store, then observes that: "Except for the thin veneer of modernity represented by the refrigeration, the plastic food wrappings, and the fashionable wrappings of the women, the store seemed to have been freshly transported to Brooklyn from [the author] Sholem Aleichem's [fictional shtetl of] Kaserilevke."[56]

Although this shtetl in Brooklyn is largely a product of her imagination—
or rather, a product of her inability to imagine radical differences *within*
the modern world—its presence is somewhat unsettling to Harris, and to
many others living in what Harris describes as the "ordinary world" of
secular modernity. "On my first daytime visit to [Crown Heights]," she
writes, "I felt as if I had wandered into a dream."[57]

When the inhabitants of this dream world assert themselves in the
public sphere, their perceptions are too often dismissed as products of irrational fantasy or outdated mythology. The Jews and others who left
Crown Heights in the 1960s may be condemned, by some, for their racial
and economic politics, but their decision to leave the neighborhood is
generally seen as a "rational" response to the realities of their time. The
Lubavitchers who stayed, by contrast, are seen as "irrational" and "anti-
modern," because their decision was governed by ancient religious texts
and the charismatic authority of a spiritual leader. Similarly, while narratives of a Crown Heights "riot" are easily understood by most Americans,
narratives of a "pogrom" fall on many secular ears as distant echoes of a
long-dead world. Lubavitchers who describe a pogrom in Brooklyn, or describe themselves as a chosen people, are cast as medieval mystics hiding behind a "veneer of modernity"—out of place, and time, in American
society, where the social realities of race and class are thought to have
supplanted religious myth.

This assumption is rarely challenged by scholarly research on collective identity formation. Indeed, similar assumptions underlie a great deal
of recent scholarship on the history of race. For example, in an otherwise
insightful analysis of this history, the anthropologist Audrey Smedley argues that over the course of the nineteenth century, in the United States
and perhaps elsewhere, race "supersed[ed] all other aspects of identity."
She writes:

> Because of the cultural imperative of race ideology, all Americans
> were compelled to the view that a racial status, symbolized by bio-
> physical attributes, was the premier determinant of their identity.
> "Race" identity took priority over religion, ethnic origin, education
> and training, socioeconomic class, occupation, language, values,
> beliefs, morals, lifestyles, geographic location, and all other human

attributes that hitherto provided all groups and individuals with a sense of who they were.[58]

Smedley is entirely correct to point out the increasing significance of race in the nineteenth century. And yet, I would argue, the hegemony of race was not constructed by "superseding all other aspects of identity." Race did not simply "[take] priority over religion." Discourses of race were constructed in the eighteenth and nineteenth centuries very much as they are in today's Crown Heights—through contested efforts to subsume and incorporate other differences; to resignify other identities in terms of racial biology, lending racialized meanings to religion, ethnicity, class, language, values, and so on. "Race" was clearly *superimposed* on these different differences, but it hardly *superseded* them. Indeed, the enduring presence of these and other differences within the discourse of race was, and remains, essential to its status as "the premier determinant of [human] identity."

The concept of race that emerged in the eighteenth century undoubtedly transformed these preexisting differences in a number of far-reaching ways. Perhaps above all, as the historian George Fredrickson has argued, the imagined biological basis of race tended to foreclose the possibility of conversion that had been open, at least in theory, to the religious others of medieval Christendom—making human differences seem "innate, indelible and unchangeable."[59] Yet when we examine the ties between race and religion, in Crown Heights and elsewhere, we nevertheless find significant continuities between these "modern" and "traditional" discourses of difference. The birth of race thus seems to mark, as the anthropologist Ann Stoler has argued (following the social theorist Michel Foucault), "not the end of one discourse and the emergence of another, but rather the refolded surfaces that join the two"—not a clean break from "premodern" identities like religion, but a rearticulation of their terms.[60]

An analysis framed in terms of this complex play of historical continuity and discontinuity, instead of an artificial divide between modernity and tradition, offers a richer understanding of the relationships between race and religion—and, far more broadly, of the role of religion in contemporary societies. Such an analysis shows that a belief in one's "Whiteness" is no more or less modern than a belief in one's "chosenness," and a racialized flight from "urban blight" no more or less rational than a religious stand against "the enemies of Israel." It suggests, in the words of the anthropologist Talal Asad, that the social world may not be "divided into modern and nonmodern, into West and non-West . . . that the world has *no* significant binary features, that it is, on the contrary, divided into overlapping, fragmented cultures, hybrid selves, continuously dissolving and emerging social states."[61] This reconceptualization of the global social order—an order defined, in part, by reductive oppositions between secular modernity and its religious others—may be the most far-reaching implication of the contest over Black-Jewish difference in Crown Heights.

The Scope and Structure of the Book

Though it is important to note the broad implications of this contest, my analyses of it will be tied, quite closely, to the everyday lives and social imaginations of Crown Heights residents themselves. The chapters of this book explore specific social contexts in which the neighborhood's Blacks and Jews have struggled to define their differences—often, though not always, by trying to define the identities of Lubavitchers and other Jews.

Each chapter examines how Crown Heights residents engage with categories of identity like race and religion, but the various chapters approach these contested categories in somewhat different ways. Chapters 1 through 3 all locate relatively clear distinctions between the "racial" and "religious" discourses of Blacks and Jews, respectively, while chapters 4 and 5 explore perceptions of identity that trouble the boundaries of these reductive categories. The arguments of these chapters may seem somewhat contradictory—drawing a series of distinctions between race and religion that they ultimately undercut—but taken together, they show the ties and tensions between these co-constituted categories, as well as the limits of categorical thought itself.

I begin, like most commentators on Crown Heights, by discussing the violence that rocked the neighborhood in August of 1991. I devote chapter 1 to this violence not because it somehow typifies Black-Jewish relations in Crown Heights—it most certainly does not—but rather because the efforts of neighborhood residents to frame this violence as a "riot" or a "pogrom" cast the distinction between racial and religious difference in particularly clear terms. This distinction reemerges in chapter 2, in my analysis of local settlement patterns and the social geography of Black-Jewish difference. Race and religion define divergent perceptions of the "Jewish neighborhood" in south Crown Heights, yet these perceptions are inextricably intertwined, and the distinction between them is complicated a bit by Black and Jewish concerns with socioeconomic class. Somewhat similarly, in chapter 3 I show how community activists and government agencies attempt to bridge the divide between Blacks and Jews by describing their differences as a matter of culture, rather than race or religion. This chapter revolves around the basic fact that Black and Jewish Crown Heights residents rarely eat together, or socialize in other ways, showing how this social divide is simultaneously interpreted in terms of religious insularity and racial segregation, kosher foods and cultural exchange.

Much as chapters 2 and 3 add "class" and "culture" to the unstable mix of "race" and "religion," chapter 4 explores the intersections of race, religion, and gender. This chapter examines the widely shared assumption that Jews may be distinguished from Blacks at a glance by their bodies, clothing, and/or behavior—an assumption that splinters on lines of race and gender, leaving Crown Heights residents wondering about the identities of strangers. Moreover, the fluid relationships among visual signs of identity—phenotype and fashion, hats and skin, dreadlocks and beards—begin to erode the distinction between race and religion. This distinction is further eroded in chapter 5, when I discuss the biblical and historical narratives on which many Crown Heights residents ultimately ground their identities. I show how Lubavitch Hasidim and Black Hebrew Israelites each use race and religion, in different ways, to support their claims of Israelite descent, yet I argue that these claims to an embodied chosenness cannot be understood in terms of race or religion alone.

Finally, in the conclusion, I discuss the implications of my analysis for a broader understanding of difference in the United States. I argue that the contest over difference in Crown Heights forces us to rethink the categories with which we typically approach America's diversity. An analysis of Black-Jewish difference in Crown Heights may thus help us create a truly multicultural society—a society with room for radical forms of difference, and for chosen peoples who don't quite fit reductive categories like "race" and "religion."

1

Collisions

Race and Religion, a Riot and a Pogrom

Prelude: A Summer Day

August 19, 1991, was one of those perfect summer days. It rained all morning, but the sky cleared by around one o'clock, and Crown Heights residents enjoyed a glorious afternoon. It had been a hot and humid summer, but Monday the nineteenth was cool and dry, with brilliant sun shining through scattered clouds.[1] Neighborhood children like Gavin and Angela Cato—seven-year-old first cousins whose families had come to the United States from Guyana not long before—took advantage of this respite from the dog days of summer and went outside to play. The Lubavitcher Rebbe also took advantage of the pleasant afternoon, and went to visit the grave of his revered father-in-law, the Previous Rebbe, whom he had succeeded as leader of the Lubavitch community some forty years before. As a doctoral candidate conducting research for his dissertation, Yankel Rosenbaum may have been immune to the lure of the weather. I'm told (though I'm not really sure) that he spent much of the day scouring the shelves of a bookstore in Crown Heights.

Just after eight in the evening—at what may be the most beautiful time of a Brooklyn summer day, when the setting sun suffuses the streets, bathing asphalt and brick in a warm golden glow—Angela was teaching Gavin how to ride a bike, and the Rebbe was returning from the cemetery in Queens to his office on Eastern Parkway. Angela held on to the seat of Gavin's bike as he pedaled around the sidewalk in front of their apartment building, on President Street near Utica Avenue, by the intersection of a tree-lined residential block and a bustling, predominantly Afro-Caribbean shopping strip. (Here and throughout this chapter, readers may want to refer to the street map of Crown Heights on page 78.) A witness later described the scene to the playwright Anna Deavere Smith: "What I saw was, the little sister, she was pushin' her brother on the bike, right? She was runnin' and pushin' and runnin' and pushin'. And little brother was dippin' back and forth, dippin' back and forth, right? Little brother didn't know how to ride the bike."[2] The Rebbe, I can only guess, was in the backseat of his car, conferring with his staff, reciting psalms under his breath, or simply gazing out of the window, lost in thought. Perhaps he was meditating on the memory of his father-in-law—his Rebbe—and seeking his guidance in the countless concerns that occupied his days.

Though they shared the same streets and the same summer sun, the Cato children and the Lubavitcher Rebbe lived in substantially different social worlds. They faced a number of common predicaments and everyday experiences—as New Yorkers, immigrants, Crown Heights residents, and members of more or less marginalized minority communities—but they negotiated these predicaments and interpreted these experiences in dramatically different ways. We may locate them, for a moment, in a single space and time—at the corner of Utica Avenue and President Street, just after eight o'clock, on August 19, 1991—but they arrived at this moment, and were destined to leave it, on divergent historical and personal trajectories.

Yet they did meet in this moment. Their paths crossed, for an instant, with far-reaching results. There was a collision. Or rather, there were a number of collisions: of bodies in space, pavement and steel, lives and deaths, histories and identities, perceptions and realities. These collisions reminded Blacks and Jews in Crown Heights that they don't actually live in different worlds—and that they do.

DISCUSSIONS OF Black-Jewish difference in Crown Heights have been defined, since 1991, by the deaths of Gavin Cato and Yankel Rosenbaum, and by the violence that unfolded over the following three days. Yet while these tragic events have established the terms of subsequent debate, participants in these debates have struggled, in turn, to establish the nature of the events themselves. This is, no doubt, the case following most incidents of collective violence. But in Crown Heights, where Blacks and Jews don't even agree on the nature of their difference, the struggle to define the nature of violence has been particularly intense. The collision that killed Gavin Cato precipitated a broader collision of social realities, and this second collision has made it extremely difficult for Crown Heights residents to reach a consensus about the events of August 1991, or resolve the bitterness that has lingered ever since. As Jonathan Rieder notes in his perceptive analysis of the violence of 1991, Crown Heights residents have been unable to bridge "the moral and perceptual chasm created by two groups with quite different readings of the same events."[3]

I will argue in this chapter that the "chasm" has been nearly impossible to bridge because Crown Heights residents' perceptions of the violence of 1991 are inextricably linked to their perceptions of their own collective identities. I argued in the introduction that Black and Jewish Crown Heights residents generally view Black-Jewish difference as a matter of "race" and "religion," respectively, and I will now show how these conflicting views of difference defined conflicting perceptions of violence.

In the first section of the chapter, I will examine Black and Jewish perceptions of the deaths of Gavin Cato and Yankel Rosenbaum. I will show how Black Crown Heights residents viewed Cato's death as a "social accident" reflecting the history of racial inequality in Crown Heights, while their Jewish neighbors viewed it as a tragic but blameless traffic accident. I will then show how Jewish Crown Heights residents viewed Rosenbaum as a victim of the "hands of Esau"—murdered by antisemites whose irrational hatred of Jews ultimately stems from the rivalry between the biblical patriarchs Jacob and Esau—while their Black neighbors viewed him as a victim of a brutal crime with little or no broader significance. In the second section of the chapter, I will examine Black and Jewish perceptions of the conflict that followed Cato and Rosenbaum's deaths. I will show how Black Crown Heights residents viewed this violence as a "riot"—or a "rebellion"—triggered by Black frustration at White privilege, while Jewish Crown Heights residents viewed it as a "pogrom" triggered by baseless Gentile hostility toward Jews.

Crown Heights residents have been unable to resolve the discrepancies between these conflicting perceptions, because conceptual categories and narrative frames like "race" and "religion," "riot" and "pogrom," tend to precede and inform their experiences of events. "Experience," as the historian Joan Scott has forcefully argued, is "always already an interpretation."[4] And in Crown Heights, as elsewhere, this interpretive process often rests on assumptions about identity and difference. If the neighborhood is inhabited by Blacks and Whites—as its Black residents generally believe it to be—then the violence of 1991 appears to be a "riot" or "rebellion," and specific events will be experienced accordingly. But if the neighborhood is inhabited by Jews and Gentiles—as Lubavitchers generally believe it to be—then this violence appears instead as a "pogrom," and specific events will be experienced quite differently. The characters animating these narratives—Blacks and Whites, Jews and Gentiles—are determined in advance, as axiomatic facts, and the actions considered typical of these characters shape divergent perceptions of events.

Yet this interpretive process wasn't as simple or mechanical as these introductory remarks may make it seem. Black and Jewish experiences of the violence of 1991 rested on preexisting narratives of riots and pogroms, but it wasn't always easy to apply these narratives to the chaotic events in the streets of Crown Heights. Categories like race and religion were not waiting patiently, in clear or stable forms, to define paint-by-number perceptions. These categories and narratives are always open to contestation, especially in moments of communal conflict. Their meaning and relevance only emerge in the complex course of events—while the meaning and relevance of events themselves only emerge within such overarching frames. I am not, therefore, arguing that Crown Heights residents' perceptions of violence were entirely determined by stereotypes and assumptions, irrespective of the details of events. I am arguing, however, that their perceptions were never entirely innocent, and were inextricably tied to their collective identities.

This is by no means simply a matter of Blacks and Jews "distorting" events to suit political agendas—though this has happened often enough in debates over the violence of 1991. Rather, we are dealing with the fundamental, and universal, process through which culturally specific narrative forms define the taken-for-granted contours of social reality. We are dealing, in essence, with the world-making power of culture itself. Anthropologists and others have demonstrated, for decades, that mythical and historical narratives shape the everyday lives and political projects of

communities throughout the world—by "constitut[ing]," in Susan Harding's phrase, "the subjects and objects, the meaning and purpose, the motives and goals, of historical action."⁵ My analysis of the violence of 1991
will build on this research by exploring the relationships between narrative and conflict—by showing how the collision between two communities
sharing a Brooklyn neighborhood has been shaped by an underlying collision between divergent narratives of history and identity.⁶

Collision: "A Social Accident" and "the Hands of Esau"

The gap between Black and Jewish perceptions of the violence of August
1991 is not simply a matter of "interpretations" or "analyses," as though
the events themselves stood outside of the fray, resting on their self-
sufficient factuality. To the contrary, Blacks and Jews in Crown Heights
tend to experience, remember, and ultimately *know* the events of 1991 in
profoundly different ways. They disagree on what each side considers
self-evident facts—the color of a traffic light, the speed of a station-
wagon, the presence or absence of an ambulance, the actions and intentions of a mob. These differences are particularly clear in their narratives
of the deaths of Gavin Cato and Yankel Rosenbaum. Beyond the sheer fact
that Cato was struck by a car in the Rebbe's motorcade, and Rosenbaum
was stabbed three hours later, Crown Heights residents dispute nearly
every aspect of these tragic events.

They do offer different interpretations, but above all they disagree on
the relative significance, or interpretability, of specific events. Blacks and
Jews alike tend to emphasize the significance of their own side's victim—
taking his death as the interpretive key to the violence as a whole—while
downplaying the significance of the other's. One death speaks to the patterns of racial or religious difference that structure relationships between
Blacks and Jews in Crown Heights and elsewhere, while the other is merely
a tragic accident or a brutal crime with no deeper meaning or broader
significance. Again, the differences between Black and Jewish perspectives on the violence of 1991 cannot be described—or dismissed—simply
as differences of interpretation. They are fundamental differences of perception, experience, and moral judgment.

In this section, I will narrate the events that sparked the violence of
August 1991, as Black and Jewish Crown Heights residents perceived them.

First, however, I will sketch these events in my own terms. My goal is not to adjudicate between the conflicting accounts that follow, but to provide a heuristic framework in which we might better understand the differences between them. I will therefore stick, as closely as I can, to the events themselves—an impossible task, one could certainly argue, given my own situated perspective. The accounts of Crown Heights residents will then clarify the conflicting perceptions that shaped these events as they unfolded.

I will draw on a range of sources in my account of the violence, and in my accounts of Crown Heights residents' perceptions. None of these sources provides unmediated access to the events of August 1991, or the experiences of the people caught up in them. But they all offer valuable information and insight, as I struggle to reconstruct these events and experiences nearly fifteen years after the fact. I will draw most of my facts, figures, dates, and times from the official account of the violence published in 1993 by the New York State Division of Criminal Justice Services— popularly known as the Girgenti Report, after its lead author, Richard Girgenti. I will draw other details from the news media of the time, and from evidence presented at the 1997 trial of Lemrick Nelson and Charles Price for the stabbing of Yankel Rosenbaum (which I attended in its entirety). I will draw, of course, on my own interviews with Crown Heights residents and others. And finally, I will draw fairly extensively on the interviews conducted by Anna Deavere Smith for her 1992 play *Fires in the Mirror: Crown Heights, Brooklyn, and Other Identities*. These interviews, let me stress again, must not be taken as direct reflections of events and experiences—to the contrary, they are my own edited excerpts from Smith's edited versions of stories told by thoroughly biased observers—but Smith's work nevertheless offers remarkable insight into Crown Heights residents' perceptions of events. Taken together, these sources will provide a subtle and accurate, though partial and fallible, account of the violence of 1991. Let me turn, then, to this violence.

IN AN INSTANT, at about 8:20 P.M., the bucolic summer scene described above was shattered by the sounds of squealing brakes, twisted metal, and breaking glass. The Lubavitcher Rebbe's motorcade was driving down President Street, heading west across Utica Avenue, into the heart of Crown Heights. The Rebbe's car was escorted, as usual, by a patrol car from

FIGURE 2 The wake of the accident that killed Gavin Cato, August 19, 1991. (Photo by John Paraskevas. Reprinted by permission of *New York Newsday*/Tribune Media Services.)

the 71st Precinct, and followed by a station-wagon holding members of his staff. The police car and the Rebbe's car passed through the intersection of Utica and President without incident, and continued on toward the Rebbe's office. But the station-wagon entered the intersection through a red or yellow traffic light—depending who you ask—and was struck by a car heading north on Utica. It careened onto the sidewalk and slammed into the Cato children, crushing them between pavement and steel. Gavin was killed instantly, and Angela was critically injured. Gavin's bike, twisted and torn, came to rest in a pool of blood and motor oil—a macabre reminder of a life snuffed out at play. Gavin's father Carmel was there at the time, and later described the scene to Anna Deavere Smith: "I saw everything, everything, the guy['s] radiator burst all the hoses, the steam, all the garbage buckets goin' along the building. And it was very loud, everything burst. It's like an atomic bomb."[7]

A crowd gathered immediately, and police arrived in seconds. Carmel Cato remembered "all these people comin' around, wanna know what's happening. Oh, it was very outrageous. Numerous numbers." In the chaos of the moment, Cato was restrained by the police as he ran to help his son and niece: "I was [hit], chucked, and pushed, and a lot of sarcastic words were passed toward me from the police while I was trying to explain: It was my kid! These are my children."[8] A group of bystanders tried to lift the station-wagon off the Cato children, while others confronted—or assaulted—its Hasidic driver and passengers. Ambulances arrived within minutes, by about 8:25, but the exact sequence of their arrival and subsequent actions is one of the most controversial aspects of the entire night. A Hatzoloh ambulance (a volunteer paramedic service staffed and funded by orthodox Jews that serves Jewish communities in Brooklyn and elsewhere) was the first to arrive on the scene, followed, a moment or a minute later, by an ambulance from New York's Emergency Medical Service (EMS). The EMS paramedics treated the gravely injured Cato children on the spot, while the Hatzoloh paramedics brought the mildly injured driver and passengers to a nearby hospital. This division of labor fostered a widely shared, but hotly contested, perception that the Cato children and the Hasidim were given unequal medical care—a perception that had a decisive impact on events in Crown Heights in the hours, days, and indeed years to come.

Over the course of the next few hours, from about 8:30 to 11:00 P.M., the crowd gathered at the corner of Utica and President grew larger, angrier, and increasingly violent.[9] Passersby were drawn by the commotion, as well as the floodlights and "Police Line" tape set up around the station-wagon. A predominantly Black audience had packed a nearby park for a B. B. King concert that evening, and some learned of the accident as they walked to a nearby subway station. By 9:07, area residents began calling 911 to report a riot. Blacks and Jews were arguing on the street, shouting epithets at each other. A few Black teenagers threw rocks and bottles at houses and cops. Rumors were flying about the death of Gavin Cato, the treatment his father had received from police, and perceived inequities in the medical care of the children and driver. A Jew who lived on President Street passed by the scene of the accident at 9:15, and reported hearing Blacks yelling "The Jews killed the kids!"

By 10:30, there were between 250 and 500 people gathered at the corner of Utica and President (according to a *New York Times* reporter and a Lubavitch community leader, respectively), and in the words of a City Hall staffer who surveyed the scene, "the shit [was] hitting the fan." Many in the predominantly Black crowd were still just milling around in the street, talking in small groups. But some began chanting "Jews! Jews! Jews!" and screaming "Fuck the Jews!" or "Fuck the cops!" A television news crew arrived at about 10:45 and was greeted with cries of "White motherfucking press!" Rocks and bottles rained down from roof-tops, and police officers were attacked by members of the crowd. At about 10:30, an African American man named Charles Price arrived at the scene. Four years later, while under investigation for inciting the murder of Yankel Rosenbaum, Price told a friend turned FBI informant: "There were so many people up there that motherfuckin' night, man, it was like—God, I thought I was in the 60s."

At thirty-seven years old, Charles Price was twice the age of most in the crowd. He was a longtime heroin addict and a petty thief, and according to testimony at his 1997 trial he was an unlikely leader for a violent mob. But just before 11 o'clock, a tow-truck removed the station-wagon that had struck the Cato children, and a hush fell over the crowd as a police officer carried away Gavin's crushed bicycle. Speaking to his friend turned informant, Price described his reaction:

> Man, it was like a strike of lightning hit me . . . maybe it was because I was high or something, man, I don't know. But I was—it was like, just like a bolt. Because when I walked across that street, and I saw that blood mix with that oil, and I seen them . . . trying to back that [tow-truck] to the station-wagon, and I saw that blood mix with that oil, and they said a little kid was up under there. It was like a bolt of lightning hit me—bam—and the next thing I know I started runnin' my mouth.[10]

Price stepped into the floodlit space at the center of the crowd, where the station-wagon had been. According to witnesses at his trial, he began pacing back and forth, waving his arms, striking his fist in his palm, and speaking to the crowd. On a home video shot from a nearby fire escape, Price can be heard asking the crowd, "Do y'all feel what I feel? Do y'all feel the pain?" He repeated these questions two or three times, until some in the crowd responded by pumping their fists in the air, and chanting rhythmically, "Hoo! Hoo! Hoo! Hoo!" A few voices added "Get the Jews!"

The video didn't record the rest of Price's speech, and witnesses differ on the details. One police officer who testified at Price's trial recalled him saying, "We can't take this anymore. The Jews get everything they want. They're killing our children. We get no justice, we get no respect," while another recalled him asking, "What are we gonna do about this? Are we gonna take this anymore?" then crying out, "No justice, no peace!" A teenager in the crowd described him demanding, "An eye for an eye!"

After five or six minutes, Price's speech turned toward action. Another teenager recalled him declaring, "I'm going up to the Jew neighborhood!" then asking, "Who's with me?" A police officer recalled him saying, "Let's go to Kingston Avenue [the center of Hasidic settlement in Crown Heights] and get the Jews!" At this point, 11:07 P.M., a large portion of the crowd—some witnesses say 50 percent, others 75 or 90 percent, but unquestionably a crowd of hundreds—ran west on President Street, toward Kingston Avenue. Some were heard chanting the slogan of Black protest politics: "No justice, no peace!", while others quoted the hip-hop theme song of the summer: "You down with O.P.P.? Yeah, you know me."[11] As the crowd headed west it splintered into small groups, and some in these groups threw rocks and bottles at property and police. They broke the windows of a few homes, and burned a number of cars. And for the first time all evening, they began assaulting Jews.[12]

The worst of these attacks occurred at about 11:20, at the corner of President Street and Brooklyn Avenue, five long blocks from the scene of the accident that had killed Gavin Cato. Yankel Rosenbaum—a twenty-nine-year-old non-Hasidic orthodox Jew from Australia, who was living in Crown Heights while conducting research for a doctorate in Jewish studies—was walking on President Street, entirely ignorant of the violence unfolding throughout the neighborhood, when he was attacked by a group of fifteen to twenty rioters. One Black teenager in this group later described Charles Price crying out, "There's one! Get him!" A Hasidic woman who had stopped her car at a nearby traffic light recalled hearing somebody yell, "There's a Jew! Get the Jew! Kill the Jew!" The crowd surrounded Rosenbaum, punching and kicking him. The police arrived moments later, but just as they did Lemrick Nelson—a sixteen-year-old native Brooklynite, whose parents had come to New York from Trinidad—stabbed Rosenbaum four times in the back and torso with a folding pocketknife.

The knife had the word "KilleR" scratched in its handle, the letters painted in red on black.[13]

Lemrick Nelson was arrested, and Yankel Rosenbaum was brought to Kings County Hospital, a few blocks away. His condition was serious, but did not seem life threatening. He was conscious and alert, and spoke with a number of visitors, including Lubavitch community leaders and Mayor David Dinkins. The mayor was assured that Rosenbaum would recover, but doctors in the Kings County emergency room had not noticed, or treated, one of his four stab wounds. Three hours after he was stabbed, at 2:30 A.M. on August 20, 1991, Yankel Rosenbaum died of internal bleeding and a punctured lung.

THESE, IN BRIEF, are the tragic events that inaugurated the violence of 1991. But the underlying logic—or rather, competing logics—of these events remains obscure. As a number of scholars have shown, events that lead to outbreaks of collective violence are rarely, if ever, unambiguously "racial," "ethnic," or "religious" in character.[14] Indeed, in the chaotic hours after the accident that killed Gavin Cato, no single understanding of events, or unwavering intent, governed the actions of those in the crowd. The violence and anger of many at the scene were directed toward police as much as—if not more than—at Jews. Some in the crowd, giddy with adrenaline, clearly shifted their focus from moment to moment. One Black teenager was caught on tape by a television news crew jumping up and down, waving his arms wildly, and yelling, "Hey, hey, put me on tv man!" He then paused for a moment, as though recalling why he was there, and threw his fist in the air—only now yelling, "Fuck the fucking Jews!"[15]

Yet the violence of August 19 culminated in the stabbing of Yankel Rosenbaum and attacks on other Jews, rather than a march on the 71st Precinct house, or some other expression of collective anger. The conflict in Crown Heights was ultimately defined in terms of "Blacks" and "Jews," "race" and "religion." How, then, did this framing take shape? How did the collective identities of Crown Heights residents come to structure the violence in their neighborhood?

Charles Price's words, along with those of other unnamed orators, were important elements in this process of framing and interpretation.

Price helped galvanize the crowd at the scene of the accident, giving shape and direction to the violence that followed—directing it toward Jews in general and Yankel Rosenbaum in specific. But Price was hardly alone in his understanding of events. He undoubtedly inflamed the sentiments of the crowd, but these sentiments preceded any such "incitement." In order to understand how the death of Gavin Cato led to the stabbing of Yankel Rosenbaum—and how these deaths, taken together, led to a conflict between Blacks and Jews—we must examine these events in greater detail, from both Black and Jewish perspectives. From the moment of the accident, Black and Jewish Crown Heights residents experienced the events of August 19, 1991, in terms of dramatically different narratives of Black-Jewish difference. These racial and religious histories, as Crown Heights residents brought them to bear on the present, turned a collision between a station-wagon and two young children into a collision between Blacks and Jews.

IN THE EYES of many Black Crown Heights residents, the circumstances of Gavin Cato's death fit—and confirmed—longstanding patterns of White racism and privilege in Crown Heights and elsewhere. Although the accident surely came as a shock, it was nevertheless experienced, through the lens of "race," as a variation on an all too familiar theme.

Indeed, a Black witness at the scene described his initially blasé reaction to the events leading up to Cato's death. He told Anna Deavere Smith that when he and his friends first saw the station-wagon enter the intersection of President and Utica, "We was watchin' the car weavin' and we was goin' 'Oh, yo, it's a Jew man. He broke the stop light. They never get arrested.' At first we was laughin', man, and we was like, 'You see! They do anything and get away with it.' And then we saw he was out of control, and we started regrettin' laughin', because then we saw where he was goin'. . . . And then we was like, 'Oh my god, man, look at the kids!' "[16]

A number of witnesses claimed the car that struck the Cato children was hurtling down President Street at speeds up to 65 miles per hour, and drove through a red light in an effort to catch up with the Rebbe's car.[17] A few also claimed that the station-wagon's driver, an Israeli Lubavitcher named Yosef Lifsch, was drunk—a charge echoed in subsequent weeks by some Black activists and neighborhood residents. Many Black Crown

Heights residents viewed such reckless driving as typical of the Lubavitch Hasidim, who "do anything and get away with it." Moreover, many saw the Rebbe's police escort—the patrol car leading the motorcade—as a clear sign of the "preferential treatment" Lubavitchers have long been thought to receive from local police and other state agencies (a charge I will discuss in detail in chapter 2). For Black Crown Heights residents, Gavin Cato's death thus raised troubling questions of personal negligence and social inequality.

Few, if any, dispute the fact that Cato's death was, in essence, an accident. But many nevertheless feel, in the words of the Reverend Clarence Norman, Sr.—pastor of the predominantly African American First Baptist Church of Crown Heights, and a longtime activist in local and citywide politics—that: "That accident did not *happen*. That accident was *caused*. What would have happened if [the driver] had waited just two seconds, and let the motorcade go? He knew where the motorcade was going. . . . But he took the chance, and went through that light, and an automobile struck him, knocked him, and he killed a child—and [correcting himself] a child was killed. . . . It's wrong to say 'he killed a child,' but a child died as a result of his indiscretion." For many Black Crown Heights residents, this "indiscretion" resonated with a history of injuries Black communities in the Americas have suffered at the hands of callous and negligent Whites. As the liberal Jewish commentator Arthur Hertzberg later observed in the *New York Times*, when Blacks saw the Rebbe's motorcade hurtling—in their view—down President Street, some may have seen "the ghosts of slavemasters riding into their quarters and not caring whom their horses might trample."[18]

This perception was confirmed, for many, by perceived disparities in the medical treatment of the Cato children and the driver and passengers of the car that hit them. As I have noted, the first ambulance to arrive on the scene was staffed by orthodox Jewish volunteers. This Hatzoloh ambulance treated the Hasidim—who had been injured in the accident and/or at the hands of angry witnesses—and took them from the scene, while a number of EMS ambulances treated the Cato children. According to some Black witnesses, the Hatzoloh ambulance arrived as much as a minute or two before the EMS ambulances, and its crew ignored the gravely injured Cato children while attending to the passengers of the car that hit them. The same witness quoted above described his anger at this turn of events:

> Here comes the ambulance, and I was like "That's not a city ambulance!" . . . Everybody started comin' around, right, 'cause I was talkin' about "These kids is dyin' man!" I'm talkin' about "The skull of the baby is on the ground man! And he [the driver] is walkin'!" I was like "Don't let him get into that ambulance!" And the Jews, the Jews was like "Private. Private ambulance." I was like "Grab him." But my buddies was like "We can't touch them." . . . I was going mad. I couldn't believe it.[19]

Rumors about the actions—and inaction—of the "Jewish ambulance" spread through the crowd at the scene of the accident, and through the community in the days that followed. The Hatzoloh ambulance's seeming disregard for the Cato children resonated with a widely shared view of the Lubavitch Hasidim as an insular community concerned only with its own affairs, to the exclusion of the surrounding neighborhood. As the Reverend Heron Sam—pastor, at the time, of the predominantly Afro-Caribbean Saint Mark's Episcopal Church, and another longtime activist in local politics— summarized the events following the accident: "When the [Hatzoloh] ambulance came, they were more concerned to take care of their own than to worry about some boy—some Black boy—who lay dying on the street."[20]

Many Black Crown Heights residents were angrier about this seeming disregard for the Catos' lives than they were about the accident itself. For example, an African American man who lived in Crown Heights in the early 1990s, and participated in the violence of 1991, told me in 1998: "When the accident first took place, we wasn't so much angry about the accident. It was the disrespect of the Jewish ambulance coming along and totally disregarding two children lying under a car bleeding to death, and attending to the Jewish folks inside the car that had minimal damage. That's what created the whole scenario. That's what sparked the whole thing off." The split-second decisions of a few police officers and paramedics thus had far-reaching effects on the subsequent history of Crown Heights.

In sum, according to many Black Crown Heights residents, Gavin Cato was killed because the Lubavitcher Rebbe's motorcade was barreling down

President Street with no concern for its Black residents, an irresponsible driver ran a red light and slammed into two Black children, and a callous private ambulance left these children to die while whisking the driver from the scene. These events "sparked the whole thing off" because they resonated with Black perceptions of a history of racial violence in Crown Heights and elsewhere—casting the Lubavitch Hasidim as the latest in a long line of White communities wielding unjust, state-sponsored power over the lives and deaths of their Black neighbors.

The Reverend Al Sharpton articulated these widely shared sentiments in his eulogy for Gavin Cato, delivered on August 26 at a local Baptist church. Speaking before an overflow crowd of mourners, activists, dignitaries, and press, Sharpton argued:

> The world will tell us [Gavin] was killed by accident. Yes, it was a social accident. It's an accident for one group of people to be treated better than another group of people. It's an accident to allow a minority to impose their will on a majority. It's an accident to allow an apartheid ambulance service in the middle of Crown Heights. It's an accident to think that we will keep crying, and never stand up and call for justice. That's the accident.

Sharpton then went on to criticize the Hasidic community in terms many observers considered antisemitic—for example by linking "diamond merchants" in Crown Heights and Tel Aviv to the apartheid regime in South Africa. When he returned to the specifics of Gavin Cato's death, he placed Cato, a recent Caribbean immigrant, in an honored lineage of African American martyrs. He told the Cato family:

> Don't worry, Carmel. Don't worry, Grandma. I prayed and called heaven this morning. This boy is all right. He's in the hands of an eternal God. In fact, they told me he was in the playroom. They introduced him to four little girls who got killed in Birmingham one morning. Yusuf Hawkins and Michael Griffith—they'll babysit him. Don't worry. They'll bring him over and introduce him to his uncle, Brother Malcolm. Don't worry about Gavin. But let us, in Gavin's name, build a new nation for our people.

Finally, Sharpton linked the demonstrations following Cato's death to a vision of Black history and destiny that stretched from ancient Africa to the present day. He told the "young people" in the audience:

> Don't apologize. Don't be ashamed and don't back up. You come from a great people. In your blood runs the blood of Shaka Zulu. In you blood runs the blood of Imhotep, Moses, Jesus, Frederick Douglass and Marcus Garvey. In your blood runs the blood of Malcolm X and Fannie Lou Hamer. Stand by, don't ever sit down! Forward ever, backward never! We will win because we're right. We will win because we're strong. God is on our side.[21]

By attributing Cato's death to the structural inequality of an "apartheid ambulance service," linking the accident to previous incidents of racial violence—from the infamous 1963 Birmingham church bombing to the murders of Yusuf Hawkins and Michael Griffith in the New York neighborhoods of Bensonhurst and Howard Beach—and linking the protests that followed to a collective defined by African "blood," Reverend Sharpton clearly framed the violence of 1991 as a matter of race. His references to Moses, Jesus, and "an eternal God" highlight the ties between religion and race, as does the fact that his narrative of Cato's death was offered from the pulpit of a Baptist church. But Sharpton nevertheless argues, implicitly at least, that Black-Jewish difference is a matter of race, because Gavin Cato was a victim of the "social accident" of American apartheid.

NEEDLESS TO SAY, most Lubavitch Hasidim saw the circumstances of Cato's death quite differently. Lubavitchers generally dispute what their neighbors see as evidence of Jewish negligence and privilege in the accident that killed Cato. Indeed, most view such charges as baseless grounds for an antisemitic attack on their community. Just as Blacks saw Cato's death in terms of a longstanding pattern of racial inequality, Jews saw Black responses to it—including the murder of Yankel Rosenbaum—in terms of a longstanding pattern of religious antipathy. Rosenbaum's death was thus seen, through the lens of "religion," as a variation on an all too familiar theme.

According to the occupants of the car that struck the Catos, and most other Jews in Crown Heights, the stoplight was still yellow when the station-wagon entered the intersection of Utica and President.[22] The station-wagon's driver denied speeding to catch up with the Rebbe, and an accident reconstruction expert hired by his attorneys estimated his speed at 30 to 35 miles per hour.[23] The driver, and police, vehemently denied the charge that he had been drinking. And perhaps above all, according to Hasidim, it was the threat of violence against the Hasidic driver that led to the controversial, and misunderstood, division of labor between the Hatzoloh and EMS ambulances. Most Hasidim argue that the Hatzoloh paramedics arrived at the scene of the accident just moments—not minutes—before the EMS ambulances, and were explicitly instructed by the police to remove the injured Hasidim from the scene, out of a justified fear for their safety, and in an attempt to calm the angry crowd.

In sum, according to Lubavitchers, the death of Gavin Cato was a tragic accident, and nothing more. Most are honestly horrified—and quickly angered—by any suggestion to the contrary, because they tend to interpret claims that negligence or privilege led to the accident as accusations of depraved or intentional murder. As a Lubavitcher named Roslyn Malamud explained to Anna Deavere Smith, speaking in a heated tone:

> What happened on Utica Avenue was an accident. Jewish people do not drive vans into seven year old boys! Do you want to know something? Black people do not drive vans into seven year old boys! Hispanic people do not drive vans into seven year old boys! It's just not done! People like Jeffrey Dahmer [a serial killer in the news at the time], maybe they do it. But average citizens do not go out and try to kill seven year old boys. It was an accident![24]

An accident and nothing more—with no deeper meaning or political implications, racial or religious. In the eyes of most Hasidim, their community does not wield the power to cause what Reverend Sharpton described as a "social accident." The concept simply does not apply to the actions of Jews in a Gentile society.

But unfortunately, according to Hasidim, the crowd at the scene of the accident was all too willing to blame the Jews. As Rabbi Joseph Spielman, a Lubavitch community leader whose sons were passengers in the station-wagon, described to Anna Deavere Smith: "The driver, seeing that he had hit a child, leapt out of the car, and tried to physically lift the car. Well as he was doing this the Afro-Americans were beating him already. He was beaten so badly he needed stitches in the scalp and the face, fifteen or sixteen stitches. And also, there were three other passengers in the car that were being beaten too."[25] At a number of press conferences and public events in the following weeks, Lubavitch leaders recalled a traffic accident on Kingston Avenue, two years before, in which a Black motorist killed a Hasidic child, and Hasidim on the scene reportedly brought the man a cup of coffee to calm his nerves. But in this case, they repeatedly pointed out, a blameless accident was taken as pretext for antisemitic violence.

While their neighbors tend to see them as a privileged White minority operating an "apartheid ambulance service," Hasidim tend to see themselves as an embattled Jewish minority living amid a hostile Gentile majority. Hasidic understandings of the violence that followed the Cato accident are shaped by a sense of the capricious power Gentiles have all too often wielded against Jews. According to most Lubavitchers, their neighbors' perceptions of the accident rested on antisemitic stereotypes reinforced by demagogic Black leaders, in a calculated effort to foment violence against Jews. Rabbi Spielman argued, for example, that rumors about the actions of the driver and paramedics were "fed amongst the Black community. And it was false, it was totally false, and it was done maliciously, only with the intent to get the riots, to start up the resulting riots."[26]

To many Lubavitchers, suggestions of Jewish responsibility in the death of Gavin Cato resonated with the painful legacy of medieval and early modern blood libels, in which European Jews were accused of murdering Christian children to use their blood for ritual purposes—and were often attacked by their neighbors as a result.[27] Hasidim were horrified to hear some Blacks at the scene of the accident accuse "the Jews" of "killing our children." They remained nervous a week later, when Reverend Sharpton took "the innocence and humility of a child" as a central theme of his eulogy for Cato, and a flyer posted around the neighborhood by a coalition of Black nationalist organizations warned of a "Hasidic/Police conspiracy to murder and brutalize our children."[28] In 1997, a Lubavitch community activist told me:

Listen. People talk about the pogrom of '91, y'know. But there were two—it wasn't just a pogrom. Before the pogrom there was a blood libel. How do I mean that? Because an Italian's car went out of control, went through a light and hit a Jew's car, and pushed that car up onto a sidewalk, and a Black kid was killed, and a Black kid went to the hospital. Now that's called an automobile accident. But they turned it into—they equate it with a cold-blooded murder [by comparing the accident with the stabbing of Yankel Rosenbaum]. *Time* magazine comes out with "An Eye For An Eye" [thus equating the two deaths]. . . . It's ridiculous! It was a blood libel!

According to most Hasidim, this blood libel led directly to the murder of Yankel Rosenbaum by an antisemitic mob.

Although the vast majority of Black Crown Heights residents condemn the stabbing of Yankel Rosenbaum in no uncertain terms, their narratives of the violence of 1991 tend to minimize the antisemitic (or anti-White, for that matter) intent of his killers. They generally describe the murder as a brutal crime, and nothing more—with no deeper meaning or implications, racial or religious. They describe Lemrick Nelson as a mixed-up kid, drunk on beer and adrenaline, who attacked Yankel Rosenbaum in the heat of the moment. And when they describe Charles Price at all (Price's role in the violence is often overlooked by both Black and Jewish Crown Heights residents), they describe him as a washed-up drug addict, whose objectionable words had little to do with the violence that followed. Most Lubavitchers, however, view Price and Nelson—and the rest of the mob that assaulted Rosenbaum—as murderous bigots driven to violence by their deep-seated hatred of Jews. Nelson, it was rumored, had once painted a swastika on his Jewish landlord's door. And to Lubavitchers at least, Price's call to "Get the Jew!" speaks for itself. Yankel's brother Norman Rosenbaum undoubtedly spoke for most Lubavitchers when he told a rally at City Hall, "my brother was killed on the streets of Crown Heights for no other reason than that he was a Jew!"[29]

For most Lubavitch Hasidim, the murder of an innocent Jewish bystander, who had nothing to do with the death of Gavin Cato, revealed the antisemitism at the heart of the violence of 1991—and indeed, at the heart of Black-Jewish relations, in Crown Heights and elsewhere. According to

Hasidim, the violence of 1991 reflected a history of Gentile antisemitism stretching from today's Crown Heights back to biblical times. Many Lubavitchers ultimately attribute this violence to an underlying antisemitism that they consider an essential component of the character and identity of all non-Jews—an endemic and eternal hatred, rooted in Gentile jealousy over Jewish chosenness, and the bitter rivalry between the patriarch Jacob and his twin brother Esau, whom orthodox Jews consider the "fathers" of all Jews and Gentiles, respectively. For example, a Lubavitch yeshiva student once explained Black-Jewish relations in Crown Heights by telling me simply: "Esau hates Jacob and Jacob hates Esau." Sensing I wasn't convinced, he picked up a Bible and asked me, pointedly: "Do you think this is just a storybook? Do you think the Torah is a thing of the past?"

I will explore Lubavitch narratives of Jacob and Esau in far more detail in chapter 5, when I examine how both Black and Jewish Crown Heights residents claim descent from the biblical Israelites. For the moment, however, it is important to note the role of these narratives in shaping Jewish perceptions of the death of Yankel Rosenbaum. The role of biblical narrative in Crown Heights politics was clear in August of 1996, at a memorial service and political rally marking the fifth anniversary of Rosenbaum's death. Speaking before a few hundred Hasidim, a handful of Blacks, a stage full of prominent politicians, and eight or ten television news cameras, Rabbi Shmuel Butman—a prominent but controversial Lubavitch community leader—linked Rosenbaum's murder to a number of symbolically potent Bible stories. He began by comparing the stabbing to Cain's murder of Abel, then turned his attention to the eternal conflict between Jacob and Esau. Butman told the crowd:

> We further see in the Bible [where it says]: "Hakol kol Yaakov, v'hayadayim y'dai Esav." "The voice is the voice of Jacob, and the hands are the hands of Esau." After the hands of Esau have committed this atrocious murder . . . the voice of Jacob—and in our case the voice of Jacob Rosenbaum—is calling out and says to us: "I have waited, day after day, week after week, month after month, year after year, for everyone who attacked me to be apprehended, and it is the responsibility of everyone, of all public officials, of all honest

and decent citizens, to work that every one of those attackers should be apprehended and that justice should finally be done!"

By citing—and then speaking—the "voice" of the patriarch Jacob, Rabbi Butman tied the murder of Yankel Rosenbaum (whose first name is a diminutive form of Jacob) to what he views as an inherent difference between Jews and Gentiles. The passage he quoted, Genesis 27:22, draws a distinction between "the voice of Jacob" and "the hands of Esau," which many Lubavitchers, and other orthodox Jews, interpret as a prophetic description of the intellect and spirituality of the children of Jacob, in contrast to the violence and materialism of the children of Esau—character traits most Lubavitchers thought were clearly evident in their Black neighbors' behavior during the violence of 1991.

Much as Reverend Sharpton's reference to an "apartheid ambulance service" and "the blood of Shaka Zulu" linked the death of Gavin Cato to a history of White supremacy and Black resistance, Rabbi Butman's reference to Jacob and Esau equated Yankel Rosenbaum's killers with the entire Gentile world, and Rosenbaum himself with the entire Jewish people. Rabbi Butman thus framed the events of August 1991 within a history of religious violence. Though his rhetoric also demonstrates the ties between religion and race—for example by implicitly invoking the violent criminality all too often attributed to young Black men—he ultimately argued that Black-Jewish difference is a matter of religion, because Yankel Rosenbaum was a victim of "the hands of Esau."

Both Sharpton and Butman thus defined Cato and Rosenbaum's deaths in terms of their broader understandings of Black-Jewish difference. Yet while they may have shared this rhetorical project, they articulated dramatically different views of that difference—views that may be described, in general terms, as "racial" and "religious." It is therefore hardly surprising that Crown Heights residents tend to talk at cross-purposes when they discuss the violence of 1991. Their conflicting perceptions of this violence are tied to a contest over the nature of their difference.

IN THE WAKE of these contested events, Black and Jewish activists alike turned to the media and the courts in an attempt to prove—or at least to popularize—their own perceptions. In the weeks following the accident, Black Crown Heights residents, activists, and elected officials repeatedly called for the prosecution of Yosef Lifsch, the driver of the station-wagon that had hit the Catos. Some demanded he be prosecuted for murder, while others called for a grand jury investigation into the circumstances of the accident. Calls for Lifsch's arrest rang out in numerous demonstrations on the streets of Crown Heights. The *New York Amsterdam News*, the city's best known Black newspaper, noted on August 24 that arrests were made quickly in the stabbing of Yankel Rosenbaum, while "no one has been arrested for the murder of the child"—further proof, according to some, of racial inequality in Crown Heights.[30] Needless to say, Lubavitchers considered such calls for Lifsch's arrest baseless. Hasidic leaders held a series of press conferences to argue against convening a grand jury investigation. A Hasid captured on television news coverage of one such event carried a homemade sign observing, simply, that "Traffic Accidents Are Not Racial."

A grand jury was ultimately convened to weigh charges of criminally negligent homicide against Yosef Lifsch. On September 5, following two weeks of hearings and one hour of deliberations, the grand jury declined to issue an indictment. Lifsch was on a plane hours later, returning home to Israel. Lubavitchers felt vindicated, but Black activists led demonstrations against the prosecutor who had failed to win an indictment, accusing him of racism and political bias. Many Black New Yorkers, and others, were suspicious of Lifsch's hasty return to Israel. Within days of the grand jury's decision, Reverend Sharpton announced the Cato family's plans to bring a multimillion-dollar civil lawsuit against Yosef Lifsch, the Lubavitcher Rebbe, the police department, the Emergency Medical Service, and the City of New York. As far as I know no such suit was ever filed, but the Cato family did eventually win a $400,000 settlement from the city, in December of 2001, based on their claim that Gavin Cato had received inadequate medical care from the city's EMS ambulance.[31]

On August 27, by contrast, Lemrick Nelson was charged with murder. Nelson was ultimately convicted of stabbing Yankel Rosenbaum, and Charles Price ultimately pled guilty to inciting the crowd that attacked him. But their fates were not decided until the spring of 2003, almost twelve years after the violence of 1991, and the torturous progress of their

cases undercut the finality of these verdicts. Nelson was first tried, and acquitted, in New York State criminal court in 1992.[32] He was then retried, in
1997, on federal civil rights charges—accused of denying Yankel Rosenbaum his constitutionally guaranteed rights by stabbing him to death
because he was Jewish.[33] Price was first arrested in the summer of 1996,
following a lengthy investigation, and was tried along with Nelson in 1997.
Both were convicted, in February of 1997, of violating Yankel Rosenbaum's
civil rights, and sentenced to long prison terms for the statutory equivalent of second degree murder. The court did not distinguish between
"racial" and "religious" violence, but their civil rights convictions reflected the jury's finding that their actions were motivated by some sort of
bias.

Their convictions were overturned, however, in January of 2002, when
an appellate court found that their federal judge had manipulated the jury
selection process, in a well-intentioned but unconstitutional effort to en-
sure a racially balanced jury. Price pled guilty to federal charges of incitement in April of 2003, rather than face a second trial. Nelson was tried, for
the third time, in May of 2003—and was convicted, for the second time, of
stabbing Yankel Rosenbaum. This time he admitted that he had, in fact,
stabbed Rosenbaum, but his lawyers argued—to no avail—that the stabbing had nothing to do with Rosenbaum's Jewishness. However, in a
bizarre final twist, the jury found that the stabbing did not actually cause
Yankel Rosenbaum's death. As a result of this counterintuitive verdict
(which the jury reportedly based on evidence of malpractice by Rosenbaum's doctors that had not even been presented in court), Nelson was ultimately sentenced to just ten years in prison—less than one year more
than the time he had already served while awaiting his various trials.[34]

These inconclusive verdicts included something for everyone in
Crown Heights—and something for everyone to be angry about. Many
Black neighborhood residents see the contrast between Price and Nelson's convictions and the grand jury's refusal to indict Yosef Lifsch as evidence of the race-based "preferential treatment" Lubavitch Hasidim
receive from the state. Yet many Jewish neighborhood residents see Lemrick Nelson's relatively light sentence as a slap on the wrist for an antisemitic murder. These controversies ultimately cannot be resolved, because
Crown Heights residents do not agree on the nature of the violence that

took the lives of Gavin Cato and Yankel Rosenbaum—victims of racial inequality or religious bigotry, "a social accident" or "the hands of Esau."

Collision: A "Riot" and a "Pogrom"

The deaths of Gavin Cato and Yankel Rosenbaum were followed by three days of violence the Girgenti Report later described as "the most widespread racial unrest to occur in New York City in more than twenty years."[35] But the nature of this violence is not so clear. Was it, in fact, "racial" unrest? Blacks and Jews in Crown Heights disagree, and their disagreement is reflected in the terms with which they refer to these events. The state's official account views these events as "disturbances." But Black Crown Heights residents generally recall a "riot" in their neighborhood (as do most other New Yorkers, and most of the media). Some, with more radical politics, even speak of a Crown Heights "rebellion." Yet Lubavitchers nearly all remember the violence of 1991 as a "pogrom." To the Lubavitch Hasidim it was, as one community leader later put it, "the first pogrom here on American soil."

Fundamental questions are at stake in these seemingly superficial differences of terminology. Was the violence in Crown Heights motivated by race or religion? Were the Jews acting as Whites, or the Blacks acting as Gentiles? And who was ultimately at fault—Blacks, Whites, Gentiles, or Jews? Narrative frames like "riot" and "pogrom" answer these questions in terms of what many Crown Heights residents see as the essential characters of Blacks and Jews.

MOST BLACK CROWN HEIGHTS residents view the violence of 1991 as a reaction, misguided or not, to a history of racial inequality in the neighborhood—a history crystallized, as we've seen, in the death of Gavin Cato. For example, the Reverend Heron Sam told Anna Deavere Smith, in what Smith portrays as a matter-of-fact tone, that after Cato's death, "The people showed their anger. They set fires, upturned police cars, looted, and I believe, in retaliation, murdered one of the Hasidics. But you see, this was just the match that lit the powder keg. It's going to happen again. And again, and again."[36] For as long, Sam implies, as the "powder keg" of inequality in Crown Heights is not defused.

Nearly all Black leaders dismiss Reverend Sam's provocative suggestion that Black youths in Crown Heights may be excused for murdering
"in retaliation," and some question the assumption that Jews in Crown
Heights are privileged above their neighbors. Yet most still describe the
violence of 1991 as a reaction to oppression and deprivation. For example,
Richard Green—an activist and educator, and director of the influential
Crown Heights Youth Collective—described the riots as symptomatic of
the bitter futility pervading the lives of Black youth in Crown Heights and
elsewhere. Green told Smith:

> Those young people [who rioted] had rage like an oil-well fire that
> has to burn out. . . . I can show you that rage every day right up and
> down this avenue. We see, sometimes in one month, we see three
> bodies in one month. That's rage, and that's something that nobody
> has control of. . . . Those youths were running on cops without
> nothing in their hands. Seven- and eight- and nine- and ten-year-
> old boys were running at those cops with nothing. Just running at
> 'em. That's rage. Those young people out there are angry and that
> anger has to be vented, it has to be negotiated. And they're not
> angry at the Lubavitchers. They're just as angry at you—and me, if it
> comes to that.[37]

While Reverend Sam casts the Jews of Crown Heights as a privileged White
elite, Richard Green views the Hasidim, much like their neighbors, as victims of a broader social malaise. But both envision the violence in Crown
Heights as an expression of enduring anger and frustration, of hostility
accrued through a history of deprivation—at the hands of Lubavitchers,
other Whites, or broader social forces. In each case, this "rage" lies waiting to explode, like a "powder keg" or an "oil-well fire."

This social and psychological link between deprivation, hostility,
and violence has constituted the hegemonic narrative of an American
"race riot" since at least the late 1960s, when it was canonized in the
1968 *Report of the National Advisory Commission on Civil Disorders*. Sur-
veying the racialized collective violence that rocked America's cities
nearly every summer in the mid-1960s, the Kerner Commission (headed
by Otto Kerner, then governor of Illinois) famously warned that: "Our
nation is moving toward two societies, one black, one white—separate

and unequal."[38] The commission traced the chain of events leading up to a "typical" race riot as follows: "discrimination, prejudice, disadvantaged conditions, intense and pervasive grievances, a series of tension-heightening incidents, all culminating in the eruption of disorder at the hands of youthful, politically-aware activists," and ultimately concluded that: "White racism is essentially responsible for the explosive mixture which has been accumulating in our cities since the end of World War II."[39]

This explanation of racial violence is, no doubt, contested from a broad range of perspectives—not least by conservative counterdiscourses describing such "riots" as products of racialized moral pathology. In an effort to counter such critiques, some more militant Black Crown Heights residents and community leaders describe the violence of 1991 as a "rebellion" or "uprising." For example, a flyer posted by "Brooklyn Comrades" in 1997 (following the federal civil rights convictions of Charles Price and Lemrick Nelson) argued that, "It was right to rebel in '91 and it's right to rebel against racism and oppression anytime!" Such calls to rebellion imagine the violence of 1991 as an organized political movement, rather than an explosion of politicized rage, but narratives of a "riot" and "rebellion" share the basic assumption that this violence was a response to racial inequality. For most Black Americans, and many Whites as well, this link between racism, deprivation, and anger has become an axiomatic, commonsense explanation of collective violence. It was, we will see, how most Blacks in Crown Heights experienced and narrated the violence of August 1991.

The violence of Tuesday and Wednesday, the twentieth and twenty-first, took three distinct but overlapping forms: peaceful protest marches turned into pitched street battles, as large groups of Blacks and Jews exchanged volleys of rocks and bottles; a half-dozen stores—owned by Blacks, Jews, and others—were looted on Utica Avenue; and small groups of predominantly Black men assaulted Jews, journalists, police, and property. Most Black Crown Heights residents, including many who condemn this violence in no uncertain terms, describe these actions as forms of political protest—moral or immoral, misguided or not—against racial inequality.

The Reverends Al Sharpton and Herbert Daughtry, along with Sonny Carson and other Black leaders, led protest marches on Tuesday and

FIGURE 3 Black youths throwing bottles at Jews in Crown Heights, August 21, 1991. (Photo by John Paraskevas. Reprinted by permission of *New York Newsday*/Tribune Media Services.)

Wednesday—drawing 200 to 400 people each day—to demand the arrest and prosecution of Yosef Lifsch.[40] Groups of Lubavitchers also gathered each day, in front of the synagogue at 770 Eastern Parkway, to demand increased police protection. Although Reverend Sharpton later told me that he organized marches in Crown Heights to "[give] people there a way to peacefully vent their feelings," violence soon broke out between Black and Jewish demonstrators. When their competing demonstrations met, Blacks and Jews threw rocks and bottles at each other, and at the police trying to keep them apart. Even among Black activists and journalists, accounts differ as to who cast the not-just-proverbial first stone. The *New York Amsterdam News* described Hasidim hurling rocks at peaceful Black demonstrators, while the Afro-Caribbean journalist Peter Noel described Black youths throwing first, and Lubavitchers responding in kind.[41] Either way, many Black Crown Heights residents saw these stone-throwing marchers as "Gavin Cato's avengers."[42]

FIGURE 4 Jewish youths throwing stones at Blacks in Crown Heights, August 21, 1991. (Photo by John Paraskevas. Reprinted by permission of *New York Newsday/Tribune Media Services*.)

This physical violence was accompanied by the rhetorical violence of slogans and slurs. Most Black marchers chanted call-and-response rallying cries like "No justice, no peace!" and "Whose streets? Our streets!"—slogans familiar from previous protests following other incidents of racial violence. But some in the crowd added chilling and vindictive slurs, targeted specifically at the Jews of Crown Heights, including "Heil Hitler!", "Hitler didn't finish the job!", "Death to the Jews!", and "Back in the ovens!" Lubavitchers—and many other New Yorkers—took these slogans as evidence of the demonstrators' pervasive antisemitism, but some Black Crown Heights residents dispute this assessment. One who participated in the violent demonstrations later claimed that such slogans were calculated to offend the Jews of Crown Heights, with whom the demonstrators were angry for reasons that had nothing to do with their Jewishness. He told me: "We know what pisses Jews off! . . . We know, in the orthodox community, that the moment we walk in talkin' about 'Heil Hitler! Hitler didn't kill you off!' there's a problem. It's called provocatory! Being provocative. And that's all it was."

Most Black Crown Heights residents and community leaders reject such glib explanations, and many have condemned what they—like their Jewish neighbors—view as a disturbing trend of antisemitism in their community. But some nevertheless see these slurs as further evidence of the marginalization of today's Black youth, rather than evidence of malicious or bigoted intent. Richard Green, for example, views the bitter irony of Black teenagers chanting "Heil Hitler!" as a sign of their inadequate understanding of the past—their own past as well as that of their neighbors. Green told Smith: "[Black youths in Crown Heights] have no role models, no guidance. They're growin' up on their own out there. . . . So when they see a Lubavitcher, they don't know the difference between 'Heil Hitler' and whatever else. They don't know the difference. You ask 'em to say who Hitler was, and half of 'em wouldn't even know—three quarters of them wouldn't even know. . . . Just like they don't know who Frederick Douglass was, or Booker T., or Mary McCleod Bethune."[43] Here again, the violence of 1991 is read as a product of the conditions of racism and poverty faced by Blacks in Crown Heights and throughout America's cities.

On Tuesday evening, August 20, after the day's marches had come to an end, violence continued on the blocks surrounding the intersection where Gavin Cato had been killed, as several stores on Utica Avenue were looted and burned. The looters targeted stores selling coveted commodities like sneakers and jewelry, but many nevertheless viewed their actions as a form of protest—not simply theft. The one person I spoke to in the course of my research who admitted taking part in this violence told me enthusiastically: "Yes! I participated in the riots, and I was looting." Taken aback by his honesty, I asked whether he saw himself as a "rioter" or a "demonstrator." He explained: "It came to a point where it wasn't about demonstrating. A demonstration is organized, and we had some [demonstrations]. But then at night we had rioting and we had looting. And what we did was, all the stores that disrespected us—y'know, where we had reasonable cause, where they had more support for the Jews than they had for the Black community—those were the stores that got vamped on." But, I pointed out, some of the stores looted were Black owned. He agreed, and took this as further evidence that the violence of 1991 was targeted against anyone—Black or White, Jew or Gentile—who had perpetuated racial inequality in Crown Heights.

Finally, on Tuesday and Wednesday evenings, small groups of predominantly Black youths roamed the streets of Crown Heights engaging in further violence—attacking Jews, journalists, police, and a couple of cabbies; hurling rocks through the windows of homes, synagogues, and a firehouse; and overturning and burning a number of police cars. The worst of these attacks occurred on Tuesday evening, when a Lubavitcher named Isaac Bitton was brutally beaten by a dozen or more people, as his young son cowered nearby.[44] The attack on Bitton was headline news in most New York newspapers, as was his rescue by the Black journalist Peter Noel. Once again, my only informant who took part in the violence (though not, to my knowledge, in the attack on Bitton) took pains to insist that none of these attacks were directed against Jews, per se. He told me repeatedly, "We didn't attack no Jewish homes!" and he ridiculed the Hasidic claim that rioters targeted Jews by looking for the mezuzahs on their doorposts: "These 'mezuzahs' you're talkin' about," he scoffed, "We don't even know what that shit is!"

I pushed him on this point, and he reiterated his claim that Jews in Crown Heights were only attacked because the rioters saw them as representatives—and beneficiaries—of broader social inequalities:

Listen. No Jewish home, to my knowledge, was just singled out and vamped on. If there was a Jew who happened to be going to his house . . . and we just seen him going in somewhere, we vamped on his ass. That was the bottom line. It was no holding back. See, what pissed the [Black] community off—Jews have been getting special, preferential treatment in Crown Heights, a neighborhood they don't make the majority of. . . . They control the neighborhood! They control the school board. They control the economic flow. So there's a problem here. There's no equilibrium in that community.

Although many Black activists and neighborhood residents agree with this assessment of Crown Heights, the vast majority rejected such justifications for violence, and resolved to work toward racial "equilibrium" by nonviolent means. But a flyer posted soon after the violence by a coalition of Black nationalist organizations nevertheless captured the views of some in Crown Heights. Beneath a photograph of a young Black man thrusting an uprooted street sign through the windshield of a police van, the text declared: "The Black Liberation Movement is proud of our youth, who took to the streets to defend Black children, and fight the Racist police and Hasidic conspiracy to destroy our community. White America, Black Uncle Toms, and Police Agents call you Hoodlums—we call you the children of Malcolm X." To some Black Crown Heights residents, the violence of 1991 was thus an attack "by any means necessary" on the White power structure—a structure in which, some feel, their Hasidic neighbors play a small but crucial part.

THE LUBAVITCH HASIDIM, however, saw this violence entirely differently. As we have seen, most Lubavitchers dispute Black claims that the circumstances of Gavin Cato's death reflected racial inequalities in Crown Heights. Some may agree with the Kerner Commission's assessment that "White racism is essentially responsible for the explosive mixture which has been accumulating in our cities since the end of World War II," but most do not see themselves—as Jews—playing a significant part in this troubled history. They saw no legitimate reason for their Black neighbors to "retaliate" against them, in Reverend Sam's phrase, and they surely do not accept Black nationalist visions of a "Racist police and Hasidic conspiracy to destroy [the Black] community."

Rather than beneficiaries of racial inequality, Jews in Crown Heights see themselves as victims of religious bigotry. Just as their neighbors linked the violence of 1991 to the history of American racism by describing it as a "riot," Lubavitch Hasidim linked this violence to the history of European antisemitism by describing it as a "pogrom"—a term that calls to mind Kishinev and Odessa rather than Detroit and Watts. According to most Lubavitchers, and many other Jews, the term conveys three essential facts about anti-Jewish violence through the ages: a pogrom is an outbreak of violence based solely on antisemitism, in which Jews are targeted for no other reason than the fact of their Jewishness; a pogrom is a one-sided attack on a more or less passive Jewish community; and a pogrom is conducted with the encouragement, or at least tacit approval, of the state and police.[45] These familiar plot lines shaped Lubavitch perceptions of the violence of 1991.

Lubavitchers generally feel little need to offer evidence of the antisemitic intent of the people who attacked them in August of 1991. To most, there is nothing more preposterous than suggesting motives *other* than antisemitism for collective violence against Jews. But many nevertheless point to what they see as the horrifying antisemitic rhetoric of their assailants, from the "blood libel" that sparked the violence to the cries of "Heil Hitler" that rang through the following days. Michael Miller—a non-Hasidic orthodox Jew who is the director of New York City's Jewish Community Relations Council—undoubtedly spoke for most Lubavitchers when he expressed his outrage at the words of the protesters. He told Anna Deavere Smith:

> Not only were there cries of "Kill the Jews," there were cries of "Heil Hitler." "Heil Hitler!"—from *Blacks*? "Hitler didn't finish the job!"—in *Crown Heights*? "You better turn on the ovens again!"—from *Blacks in Crown Heights*? And Hitler was no lover of Blacks! The hatred is so deep seated. The anti-Judaism! The anti-Judaism—if people don't want to hear me use the word anti-semitism—knows no boundaries. And I'll be damned if [the common Black accusation of] "preferential treatment" is gonna be the excuse for a single rock, bottle or pellet thrown at a Jewish person, or the window of a Jewish home.[46]

According to Miller, and most Lubavitchers, Black charges of racial inequality in Crown Heights were merely "excuse[s]" for violence—attempts to mask the antisemitism of the pogrom in a more socially acceptable form—but the bigoted rhetoric of some Black Crown Heights residents revealed the underlying truth of the violence of 1991.

In Lubavitch eyes, and memories, these Black antisemites were the sole source of violence in August of 1991. Although most journalists reported exchanges of rocks and bottles between Blacks and Jews, most Hasidim recall a nonviolent Jewish community subjected to unprovoked assault by a rampaging mob. Rabbi Shmuel Butman—the community leader who later attributed Yankel Rosenbaum's murder to "the hands of Esau"—made this point forcefully on August 21, 1991, at a funeral procession for Rosenbaum that turned into an emotionally charged protest march. Standing over the hearse bearing Rosenbaum's casket, and speaking to a crowd of a few hundred Hasidim, Butman assessed the violence of the previous two days:

> It is important to note, friends, what we have said before: That what happened here, in this community, is not an incident of two sides. Everyone knows that this was not a confrontation between the Jewish community and the Black community. This was a one side confrontation! When we were children we knew that the word "pogrom" was only a word that belongs in the history books. We knew that the words "Heil Hitler" were only words that were said fifty years ago. Unfortunately, we in this neighborhood have now seen a pogrom with our own eyes! . . . This was a pogrom that we thought was only going to exist in books. Unfortunately we saw it right here, on the streets of Crown Heights.[47]

Nearly all Lubavitchers in Crown Heights echo Rabbi Butman's assessment of a "one side confrontation." One Hasid I spoke to was furiously angry at the media's portrayal of Blacks and Jews in the neighborhood as "two warring camps." She described her memories of the violence of 1991, then told me: "This was not 'two warring camps.' This was Jews being attacked and hiding. That's what it was about! . . . I mean you had these evil people [Reverend Sharpton and other activists] coming into the neighborhood, taking crowds down streets, cursing Jews, yelling antisemitic things, throwing stones. We were being attacked!" Another complained about the widespread "myth" that the violence of 1991 was "violence between the races or religions." The word "between," she explained, implies reciprocal violence, and in fact: "That's not at all what happened. It was a pogrom. A pogrom is an uprising against Jewish people just because they're Jews, and that's all it was. There's no other way to call it."

This "uprising" continued unabated on Tuesday and Wednesday, the twentieth and twenty-first. Despite deploying over 800 officers in Crown Heights each day, the police seemed unable to stop the violence.[48] Indeed most Lubavitch Hasidim, and quite a few other New Yorkers, feel that

FIGURE 5 The police presence in Crown Heights, August 22, 1991. (Photo by David Cantor. Reprinted by permission of AP/Wide World Photos.)

then Mayor David Dinkins and Police Commissioner Lee Brown—both of whom are Black—were not really trying to stop the violence. Rather, many claim that Dinkins and Brown instructed the police to let Blacks in Crown Heights "vent their anger" against the Hasidic community. A number of Jewish victims of violence have described what they consider troubling indifference—if not outright misconduct—on the part of police. Isaac Bitton, for example, said the police simply stood at their posts, a few feet away, as a mob assaulted him and threatened his young son. He kept telling himself, he later told me, that they would intervene to save him: "In my mind—even half conscious, because of the brick I got in my head— I knew [that the police were nearby]. I said [to myself], they're right behind, they're gonna come any second. And they didn't come." Roslyn Malamud summed up the perspective of many Lubavitch Hasidim when she told Anna Deavere Smith: "The fault lies with the police department. The police did nothing to stop it."[49]

On Thursday the twenty-second, the police more than doubled their deployment in Crown Heights and changed their crowd control tactics.[50] Over 1,800 officers in riot gear kept Thursday's marches relatively peaceful, finally ending the violence in the neighborhood—more or less. But many Jews in Crown Heights were profoundly disillusioned by the police department's handling of the violence. The mayor's decision—as they saw it—to deny them police protection reflected the same antisemitism that motivated the violence itself, but the inaction of the police was far more disturbing than the actions of a mob, as it demonstrated the antisemitism of the state. One Hasid described her sense of shock after the violence of 1991: "You think you're a citizen," she said, "with certain rights and protections. And then it all drops out from under you." Another shook her head gravely as she told me: "It's hard to believe in America, to believe in those values, after an experience like that."

Just as the violence cast doubt on the promise of America—a country the Rebbe had always called a "land of loving kindness" for its just treatment of Jews—for many Lubavitchers it brought to mind troubling memories of European history. Hasidim often drew parallels, for example, between the violence in Crown Heights and the experiences of Jews in Nazi Germany. One told me: "I feel a new closeness to my brothers in Europe from the last generation. I know now what a pogrom was." A full-page advertisement placed by a Lubavitch community organization in the *New York Times* on September 20, 1991, claimed simply: "This year Kristallnacht took place on August 19th right here in Crown Heights." Some Lubavitchers, and many other Jews, felt this invocation of Kristallnacht—the infamous "night of broken glass" of November 1938—cheapened the horror of the Nazi Holocaust. Yet as the violence of 1991 unfolded, many Jews in Crown Heights experienced such disturbing parallels on a visceral level. One Lubavitch community leader, who told me he shies away from using the term "pogrom" out of respect for the victims of European antisemitism, nevertheless felt what he later described as "moments of Germany" in August of 1991. One night, at two in the morning, he got a phone call informing him—in error, it turned out—that a synagogue in Crown Heights was on fire. His voice shook as he told me: "I, for that moment, had the image of Germany."

For some Jews in Crown Heights, these images of the past were too much to bear. On Monday morning, August 26—as sporadic demonstrations continued in a peaceful but tense Crown Heights—an elderly Jewish woman named Brokha Estrin leapt to her death from the window of her apartment on President Street, just a block from the scene of the accident that killed Gavin Cato and the epicenter of the violence that unfolded after his death. The police denied any connection between her suicide and the events of the previous week, but most Lubavitchers believe Estrin—a Holocaust survivor and relatively recent immigrant—was driven to take her own life by the pogrom that wracked her new home. One Lubavitch leader told a journalist that her death was "a direct result of the protests and antisemitic remarks over the past week."[51] Anna Deavere Smith spoke with a young Hasidic chaplain at Kings County Hospital, who recounted a conversation with Estrin's son on the day of her death:

> [He] told me that his mother committed suicide because she was, um, she was terrified. She jumped out of the third floor of her apartment building and committed suicide. . . . [She] had come from Russia eleven years ago, because of the hardships there, and when this thing started to happen in Crown Heights it was just too painful. It was like—like there was no place to go. It's like you're trapped. Everywhere you go there's Jew haters.[52]

And so, according to most Lubavitchers, the "first pogrom here on American soil" claimed another innocent Jewish life.

NOT SURPRISINGLY, when I interviewed him in 1998 Reverend Al Sharpton dismissed the charge that he and other activists had led an antisemitic pogrom against the Lubavitch community with the tacit approval of the mayor and police. When I asked what he felt lay behind such accusations, he replied: "I think that there are two communities [in Crown Heights] that, to some degree justifiably, hold feelings of victimization. And I think the real challenge is for responsible people, on both or either side, to say: 'Wait a minute. Let's deal with facts.' " These facts are hard to come by, however, when the basic contours of social reality are hotly contested— when Reverend Sharpton, for example, describes himself as a "responsible" leader giving Blacks in Crown Heights "a way to peacefully vent their feelings," and Lubavitchers describe him as an "evil [person]" leading a mob of Gentile "Jew haters."

As in the controversies surrounding the deaths of Gavin Cato and Yankel Rosenbaum, Crown Heights residents turned to the courts in an effort to establish the facts of the violence of August 1991. A number of individual Lubavitchers and Lubavitch community organizations filed a multimillion-dollar civil suit against Mayor Dinkins, Police Commissioner Brown, and the City of New York, claiming that the city and its leadership had acted with antisemitic intent by withholding police protection from the Hasidic community during the violence in Crown Heights. Although the suit focused specifically on the actions of the mayor's office and the police, according to many of the plaintiffs it was an effort to prove, in far broader terms, that the violence of 1991 had been a pogrom.

After years of pretrial proceedings, the case against Dinkins and Brown was dismissed in August of 1997. The judge ruled that they had not acted with "improper discriminatory intent" during the violence in Crown Heights, and were thus entitled to the qualified immunity from prosecution that the law grants elected officials for actions taken in public service. The case against New York City itself was allowed to proceed, but the dismissal of the case against Dinkins and Brown cast doubt on its legal viability. In April of 1998, however, the city's attorneys chose to settle out of court. The plaintiffs received $1.1 million from the city, as well as a formal apology from then Mayor Rudolph Giuliani, who lamented his predecessor's "clearly inadequate response" to the violence in Crown Heights.

But this settlement didn't settle a thing. Speaking from the pulpit of a Black Baptist church in Bedford-Stuyvesant, Reverend Sharpton lambasted Mayor Giuliani's "one-sided, lopsided apology"—to thunderous applause from the well-heeled congregation. On April 6, 1998, *New York Newsday* ran a front-page photograph of Carmel Cato next to a banner headline reading: "Don't Forget My Son." The mayor's apology was excoriated on a number of editorial pages, and a public war of words broke out between Giuliani and his predecessor, after Dinkins charged that, "Rather than risking a small but influential community's anger at a future ballot box, the mayor is throwing a tremendous amount of money at the plaintiffs on a baseless claim." As with the grand jury investigation of Yosef Lifsch, and the repeated trials of Lemrick Nelson and Charles Price, a process that was supposed to bring closure to the conflict in Crown Heights instead ignited another round of controversy and accusation.

Indeed, Lubavitchers themselves were far from content with Mayor Giuliani's apology. The Hasidim with whom I discussed it were well aware of the political considerations that may have motivated his contrition. And besides, some said, it was David Dinkins, not Rudolph Giuliani, who put their lives at risk in 1991. Dinkins is the antisemite, they insisted, not Giuliani. Dinkins should have apologized, but he remained unrepentant. I spoke with one of the plaintiffs just after the settlement was announced, and asked if she was happy with the resolution of her case. She laughed, and drawled "Naaah." She claimed that she, at least, was never interested in the money. All she wanted was an opportunity to set the record straight—to sit on the witness stand, if need be, and tell the world what really happened in Crown Heights. In her eyes, Giuliani's apology had not set the record straight, for one simple reason. "Y'see," she explained, "we [the plaintiffs] were all promised—once or twice, and even more than that—we were told that the apology would include the word 'pogrom,' and an official recognition and acknowledgement that it was a pogrom." But instead the mayor had referred to "four days of rioting," which he described as a terrible "human tragedy," and as long as he continued to deny reality, my acquaintance said, his apology would mean nothing to her. It was crucial, she told me, for him to use the word "pogrom," simply because, "What it is, it is—and that's what you call it. It either is or it isn't."

Conclusion: Narrative and Experience, History and Identity

But the violence of 1991 both is *and* isn't. It was and wasn't a riot and a pogrom, between Blacks and Whites and Jews and Gentiles, acting on the basis of race and religion. Crown Heights residents' discussions of this violence—much like Crown Heights residents themselves—are caught, to this day, in the tensions between these different differences.

My own account of this violence has been shaped, in fundamental ways, by this irreducible multiplicity. In place of the singular and certain truths Crown Heights residents tend to assert about the events of August 1991, I have offered multiple, competing, and sometimes ambiguous "narratives," "experiences," and "interpretations." While I have tried to determine, as precisely as possible, how Crown Heights residents viewed the violence in their neighborhood, I have made little effort to confirm or deny their conflicting perceptions—to wade through the swamp of rumor and innuendo, imagination and fantasy, sorting fact from fiction according to my own views of events. Of course I do have my own understandings of the violence of 1991 (based simultaneously on extensive research and idiosyncratic judgments) and these have, no doubt, shaped my analysis in significant ways. But my goal in this chapter, like the chapters to follow, has been to elucidate the lives and experiences of Crown Heights residents—not to claim privileged access, as a scholar, to ostensibly objective truths.

This principled agnosticism may be somewhat troubling to those Crown Heights residents, and others, who claim—or at least seek—unambiguous or absolute truths about historical events like the violence of 1991. Indeed, it has been fashionable in recent years among some scholars and pundits to condemn accounts like mine for their supposed sins of moral and epistemological relativism. How, readers may well ask, can we possibly hope to understand history and society if we don't work to separate fact from fiction, reasonable accounts from unreasonable ones, accurate perceptions from inaccurate ones? It is, some may feel, a scholar's responsibility to determine, for example, whether the station-wagon that struck the Cato children ran through a red or yellow traffic light, whether Mayor Dinkins actually withheld police protection from the Lubavitch community, and ultimately whether Black-Jewish difference is best described as "racial" or "religious." A failure to do so, some may argue, betrays an amoral acquiescence to the vagaries of cultural difference, and a lack of respect for the cold hard facts of the social world.

These are, of course, legitimate concerns. They speak to fundamental issues of social scientific method, as well as critical questions about the role of scholarship in public life. We—academics, New Yorkers, and others—undoubtedly need a subtle and accurate understanding of the violence of 1991 if we wish to avoid such violence in the future. I would argue, however, that any attempt to distill ostensibly singular and objective truths from the contested perceptions of diverse communities betrays a lack of respect for the social reality of narrative and experience—and thus precludes any real understanding of historical events like the violence in Crown Heights.

The multiple and competing narratives I have examined in this chapter—stories of race and religion, a riot and a pogrom, a "social accident" and a "blood libel," "four little girls who got killed in Birmingham" and "the hands of Esau [that] committed this atrocious murder"—are themselves cold hard facts of the social world. They gave meaning and structure to the experiences of Crown Heights residents in August of 1991, shaping their reactions to the violence in their neighborhood, as well as their roles in unfolding events. Any attempt to downplay or deny the significance of such narratives—looking through them, as it were, to the truths thought to lie beneath—marks a failure to engage with the complex, vibrant social worlds where Crown Heights residents actually live. An analysis of narrative and experience, in their irreducible multiplicity, must therefore lie at the heart of our understanding of the violence of 1991—and at the heart of a truly moral response to the painful legacy of collective violence.

More broadly, I would argue, such an analysis of narrative must be central to our understanding of collective identity. This chapter has shown how Crown Heights residents' identities take shape within historical narratives, while shaping the contours of these narratives in turn. In Crown Heights and elsewhere, "Blacks" and "Jews" are defined as actors in the drama of history, while "race" and "religion" help set the stage on which these actors play their parts—providing detailed scripts for social life, as well as the themes that constitute their historical being. Narratives of a "riot" and "pogrom," for example, establish powerful continuities between past and present—continuities that are defined by, while simultaneously defining, the fundamental nature of Blackness and Jewishness.

Gavin Cato and Yankel Rosenbaum's deaths became meaningful events in the eyes of Crown Heights residents thanks to these dialectical relationships between narrative and experience, history and identity. In less contested social contexts these dialectics establish the orderly succession of events we recognize as "history." In Crown Heights, however, they led to a historiographic tug-of-war, as Blacks and Jews competed to tie their shared present to divergent pasts. Crown Heights residents inhabit intersecting but irreconcilable histories, and the tragic collisions of 1991 have echoed ever since in the space of this multiplicity.

2

Geographies of Difference

Producing a Jewish Neighborhood

New York City is often described, by New Yorkers and others, as a city of neighborhoods—a patchwork metropolis made up of distinctive places, with flavors and characters all their own. "The Village" could never be mistaken for "Midtown," "Kew Gardens" for "Astoria," or "Williamsburg" for "Brooklyn Heights." The boundaries of such places are often tied to the identities of the city's racial, ethnic, and religious communities. Blackness and Whiteness are conveniently localized at symbolically charged sites like "Harlem" and "Bensonhurst," while immigrants are imagined to live in enclaves like "Chinatown" and "The Lower East Side." The concept of the neighborhood—and it is a *concept*, not just a place on a map—thus shapes the contours of urban politics and social relations.[1]

Most Crown Heights residents, both Black and Jewish, describe "Crown Heights" as a distinctive place with a flavor and character all its own. And many imagine part of south Crown Heights as a "Jewish neighborhood" intimately tied to the collective identity of the Lubavitch Hasidim. This shared sense of communal boundaries has shaped the contours of Black-Jewish relations in a number of complex ways. For example, as I described in chapter 1, Charles Price's incitement to violence on August 19, 1991 invoked a spatial sense of Black-Jewish difference. Price reportedly told the crowd at the scene of the accident that killed Gavin Cato, "I'm going up to the Jew neighborhood! Who's with me?" then cried out, "Let's go to Kingston Avenue and get the Jews!" He thus envisioned the Jews of Crown Heights as a geographically bounded community, defined by its ties to a distinctive place—a "Jew[ish] neighborhood" built around "Kingston Avenue." But what, exactly, are the boundaries of this place? And how, exactly, does it differ from surrounding places? How, in other words, have Crown Heights residents imagined and produced a spatial difference between Blacks and Jews? These are the central questions I will address in this chapter.

There is, in fact, an area of relatively concentrated Jewish settlement in south Crown Heights—an area that differs to some extent from nearby areas, with regard to racial and religious demography, socioeconomic class, and certain other social indicators. This chapter will describe and historicize these differences in detail, but let me sketch them briefly here. There are about 12,000 Jews, all but a few of whom are Lubavitch Hasidim, living in a fifty-odd square-block area of south Crown Heights—an area some Lubavitchers describe as the whole of "Crown Heights"—which is more or less bounded by Eastern Parkway to the north, Lefferts Avenue to the south, Nostrand Avenue to the west, and Rochester Avenue to the east (see figure 6). Jews only make up about 20 percent of the population of this area, but in north-central Brooklyn, which is overwhelmingly Black for miles in every direction, this substantial minority is enough to mark the area as "Jewish."

Jewish life in Crown Heights is centered, to a large extent, on Kingston Avenue. The world headquarters of the Lubavitch community (including a large synagogue, a yeshiva, and a small office building) is located at the corner of Eastern Parkway and Kingston Avenue, and the six blocks of Kingston between Eastern Parkway and Empire Boulevard are home to many Jewish communal institutions and Hasidic-owned stores, some of which cater to local Jewish needs for kosher food, religious texts, and ritual items (see figure 7). The residential blocks straddling this stretch of Kingston, between New York Avenue to the west and Troy Avenue to the east, form the densest area of Jewish settlement in Crown Heights, where Hasidim make up almost 40 percent of the population (again, see figure 6). This limited area is also home to some of the most beautiful and well-kept housing in central Brooklyn—blocks of spacious and elegant brownstone and limestone row houses, smaller brick row houses with tiny front lawns, low-rise apartment buildings with airy inner courts, and a block or two of honest-to-goodness mansions. Not surprisingly, the median income in this area is higher than in nearby areas with poorer housing.

FIGURE 6 The approximate boundaries of "Crown Heights" according to various neighborhood residents. The largest outlined area is the whole of Crown Heights, as its boundaries are semi-officially defined—an area in which Hasidim make up 6 to 8 percent of the total population. The medium-sized outlined area is the "Jewish neighborhood" of Crown Heights, as most Lubavitchers see it, in which Hasidim make up approximately 20 percent of the population. The smallest outlined area marks the densest concentration of Jewish settlement in Crown Heights, where Hasidim make up approximately 40 percent of the population. (Copyright Hagstrom Map. Used by permission.)

FIGURE 7 Signs of Jewishness on Kingston Avenue. A drugstore welcomes the messianic age, proclaiming the Lubavitcher Rebbe to be the messiah. (Photo by the author.)

Perhaps surprisingly, however, the median income of Jews in this area—who make up, we must remember, less than half of the population—is lower than that of their immediate Black neighbors.

These, in brief, are the facts on the ground that make part of Crown Heights appear, to many, as a distinctive "Jewish neighborhood." But this perception of communal space is hardly self-evident or uncontested. Although Blacks and Jews alike may assume—and produce—the Jewishness of this area, we cannot take this equation of space and identity at face value. A growing number of scholars have shown in recent years that such ties between "peoples" and "places" are difficult to produce and sustain—demonstrating, in the words of Akhil Gupta and James Ferguson, that "all associations of place, people, and culture are social and historical creations to be explained, not given natural facts."[2] These critical analyses of place-making and identity formation have generally focused on nations and cultures thought to be "rooted" in the very soil, but they also force us to reevaluate our assumptions about urban spaces like a "Jewish neighborhood." Many anthropologists, myself included, still stress the importance of "local" social contexts, but as Jacqueline Brown reminds us, we must avoid "the reductionism that would simply equate the local with . . . the kinds of places that actors use to symbolize it—like neighborhoods." Rather, as Brown makes clear, "Locality is best studied . . . as the outcome of power-laden processes through which the social is marked and defined spatially."[3]

Although the area of Jewish settlement in south Crown Heights does differ in certain ways from surrounding areas, we cannot simply assume that this space forms a clearly bounded "neighborhood." We cannot assume that the social forces defining Black-Jewish difference in Crown Heights start or stop—or ought to stop—at Eastern Parkway or any other boundary. As we will see, the boundaries of "Crown Heights" and its "Jewish neighborhood" are hotly contested, and the substance of their spatial distinction is not always clear. We must therefore examine the diverse ways Crown Heights residents define the boundaries of their social lives—in terms of race, class, religion, and other criteria of spatial difference. We may begin to do so by examining the efforts of Crown Heights residents, and others, to distinguish "neighbors" from "outsiders" during the violence of 1991.

"Neighbors" and "Outsiders"

Charles Price's rhetoric of Jewish spatial difference resonates with—and
in a limited sense corroborates—the common Hasidic charge that many
of the rioters of August 1991 came to Crown Heights from elsewhere in
order to attack its Jewish community. Teenage boys, many Lubavitchers
claim, flocked to Crown Heights from poorer and Blacker neighborhoods
like Brownsville and Bedford-Stuyvesant—"going up to the Jew neighborhood," as Price put it, to "get the Jews." And worst of all, Lubavitchers
often complain, the Reverend Al Sharpton brought in busloads of demonstrators, who soon grew violent. "Yellow school-buses," I was repeatedly
told, "He brought them in on yellow school-buses with Jersey plates!" This
experience of violation by "outsiders" indexes an enduring sense of
neighborhood and community boundaries.

This view of the violence of 1991, and the underlying spatial dynamics
of "Crown Heights," was articulated passionately by Roslyn Malamud, a
Hasidic woman interviewed by Anna Deavere Smith for *Fires in the Mirror*.
Malamud told Smith:

> Do you know that the Blacks who came here to riot were not my
> neighbors? I don't love my neighbors. I don't know my Black neigh-
> bors. . . . I told you we don't mingle socially because of the differ-
> ence of food and religion and what have you here. But the people in
> this community want exactly what I want out of life. They want to
> live in nice homes. They all go to work. They couldn't possibly have
> houses here if they didn't. . . . They want to send their kids to col-
> lege. They wanna live a nice quiet life. They wanna shop for their
> groceries and cook their meals and go to their Sunday picnics! They
> just want to have decent homes and decent lives! The people who
> came here to riot were brought here by this famous Reverend Al
> Sharpton—which I'd like to know who ordained him? He brought a
> bunch of kids who didn't have jobs in the summertime. I wish you
> could see the *New York Times*—unfortunately it was on page
> twenty—I mean, they interviewed one of the Black girls on Utica Av-
> enue, and she said: "The guys will make you pregnant at night and
> in the morning not know who you are." And if you're sitting on a
> front stoop and it's very, very hot and you have no money and you

have nothing to do with your time and someone says, "Come on,
you wanna riot?" You know how kids are. . . . My Black neighbors? I
mean, I spoke with them. They were hiding in their houses just like
I was.[4]

In Malamud's eyes, the racially charged "Jew neighborhood" envisioned by
Charles Price appears instead as a race-neutral neighborhood of "decent
homes and decent lives." Yet Malamud nevertheless defines this space
in contrast to stereotypical images of Black poverty, indolence, and
promiscuity—a world of morally charged and racialized difference she locates at the border of her imagined community, "on Utica Avenue." Malamud's solidarity with her middle-class Black neighbors is thus constructed
at an intersection of racial, religious, and socioeconomic differences.
These overlapping differences allow Malamud to describe Crown Heights
as a clearly bounded "neighborhood" that may then be violated by outsiders like "this famous Reverend Al Sharpton."

I raised this criticism in an interview with Reverend Sharpton, and he
responded by invoking an equally complex mix of spatial identities and
differences. He did not deny bringing demonstrators to Crown Heights in
August of 1991, but he interpreted his actions through a spatial logic, and
a definition of "Crown Heights," that do not mark him as an outsider to
the neighborhood.[5] Above all, he argued that he came to Crown Heights
at the request of Gavin Cato's grieving father, Carmel: "The first response
that I have to that—to the 'outsider' claim—is that it is almost, uh, hu-
morous. Because the first thing that the critics will not deal with is I came
in at the request of the Catos. So you can't, at one level, say that people in
Crown Heights should deal with this, when people in Crown Heights did
decide to deal with it by calling on Reverend Sharpton." Here Sharpton accepts the political significance of locality, yet grounds his activism in the
agency of Carmel Cato—undeniably an "insider" to the violence of 1991,
despite the fact that the Cato family lived just steps from Utica Avenue, at
the border of Roslyn Malamud's "decent" neighborhood. Sharpton makes
a similar argument in his autobiography, when he discusses his controversial role in Crown Heights and the many other incidents of racial conflict he has been involved in over the years. He writes:

I've regularly been called an outside agitator, but I have never
taken a case, from Howard Beach to Brawley to Bensonhurst . . .

where the victims . . . didn't call and ask me to help them. I only become involved if I am invited. . . . I am a minister, and I respond to requests. Suppose Mrs. Robinson called me and said she needed my help and I said no. To me, that would be more of an indictment against my credentials as an activist than going into a strange place where I'm not a local.[6]

He casts doubt on the significance of locality, however, when he sums up this pastoral conception of social activism: "I see my activities as part of my ministry," he writes, "what I call my Christian walk, helping the needy, protecting the weak."[7] This "Christian walk" subsumes Crown Heights—along with Howard Beach, Bensonhurst, and all such "local" communities—in the global space of a universal ministry, cutting across the boundaries of these neighborhoods much as evangelical missionaries cross the borders of Third World nation-states.

In our interview, however, Sharpton shied away from such critiques of locality, and focused instead on tracing his roots to Crown Heights. Yet his portrait of "Crown Heights" was rather different from Roslyn Malamud's. He pointed out:

The other thing people must remember is that I was born in Crown Heights. I was born in Kings County Hospital. I lived on Lincoln Place and Albany [Avenue], and I lived in the Albany Projects—all of which is in Crown Heights. And the church I grew up with, as junior pastor—Washington Temple—is in Crown Heights. . . . So, I mean, it's not like I was considered by the Blacks in Crown Heights as an outsider. I come out of Crown Heights.

But what "Crown Heights?" Or rather, whose "Crown Heights?" The landmarks Sharpton mentions all lie outside of the "Jewish neighborhood" in south Crown Heights—an area, as I've noted, that Lubavitchers often describe as the whole of "Crown Heights." Kings County Hospital lies a few blocks to the south, in an area sometimes called Wingate and often considered part of East Flatbush. The other three locations—Lincoln and Albany, the Albany Projects, and Washington Temple—lie to the north of Eastern Parkway, in an area many Hasidim see as the south side of Bedford-Stuyvesant, or Bed-Stuy, although it is semi-officially defined as north Crown Heights. Sharpton recalls his childhood in this area by pointing to a Pentecostal church and a low-income housing project, implicitly contesting the image of Crown Heights as a "Jewish neighborhood" filled with "decent," middle-class homes—depending, that is, on how one defines "Crown Heights."

I pointed out to Reverend Sharpton, however, that many people have "come out of Crown Heights," and moved to distant suburbs. He wouldn't consider the Jews and others who left in the 1960s "locals," would he? By way of an answer, he told me a story that underlined his enduring connections to the neighborhood. He described a conversation he had with a Lubavitch community activist in August of 1997, when they both attended a rally organized by a Black activist in Crown Heights:

> Funniest thing happened . . . the guy that was with Rabbi Hecht, I forget his name, he said to me "You used to live where?" I said "On Lincoln Place." He says "And then you moved to 1107 Lenox Road." I said "That's right." I said "How'd you know that?" . . . He said "I was the landlord your mother used to pay rent to." That's how much they know I'm not an outsider. . . . He was my mother's landlord when she raised me on welfare, when we moved from Crown Heights into Brownsville.

Here Sharpton gestures at the complex web of relationships linking Blacks, Jews, landlords, tenants, and others in such interconnected spaces as Crown Heights and Brownsville. He implicitly notes the class differences between Crown Heights and its surrounding neighborhoods, but nevertheless marks himself as a Crown Heights "insider" by virtue of his position in the socioeconomic network that tied his family to the neighborhood, even from their home in nearby Brownsville.

Like Roslyn Malamud, Charles Price, and others, Reverend Sharpton imagines the geography of Crown Heights in terms of race, class, and religion—through symbolically charged places and tropes like a "Jew neighborhood" and a "Christian walk," "decent homes" and the "Albany Projects," promiscuous teenagers on "Utica Avenue," and a welfare mother raising her family in "Brownsville." But Sharpton complicates Malamud's attempt to distinguish clearly between neighbors and outsiders by appealing to contested community boundaries, interconnected socioeconomic processes, and divergent conceptions of space and social action. In addition to marking himself as an "insider," he raises important questions about the definition of "Crown Heights." Is the neighborhood bounded or divided by Eastern Parkway? Is it linked to Brownsville in spite of—or because of—the disparate lives of a Jewish landlord and his Black tenants? Is there room on Kingston Avenue for a "Christian walk?"

Such questions cannot be answered simply by locating a "neighborhood" on a map. Rather, we must locate "Crown Heights" in the history of politically charged efforts to produce such a place and distinguish it from other places. That is my goal in the rest of this chapter. By examining the social history of the area, I will show how the "Jewish neighborhood" in south Crown Heights has been distinguished from surrounding areas in terms of race, class, and religion. In the following three sections, I will first explore the racialized history of Black and Jewish settlement in Crown Heights, then examine the complex socioeconomic patterns that have emerged from a century of real-estate development and community activism, then trace the simultaneously local and global religious geography of the Lubavitch community. Finally, in conclusion, I will show how the identity of the Lubavitch Hasidim has been forged at the intersection of these geographies of difference.

Racial Boundaries: "The Crown of a Good Name"

In a 1987 farbrengen, the Lubavitcher Rebbe offered his own interpretation of "Crown Heights." The Rebbe explained that the neighborhood was alluded to—prophesied, in a sense—in the ancient Mishnaic text *Pirkei Avos*, the *Ethics of the Fathers*. In section 4:13 Rabbi Shimon says: "There are three crowns: the crown of Torah, the crown of priesthood, and the crown of royalty. But the crown of a good name rises above them all." According to the Rebbe, Rabbi Shimon's use of the Hebrew verb *oleh* ("rises above") implies that "the crown of a good name" exceeds the other three crowns in its physical elevation, as well as its ethical significance. Rabbi Shimon's "crown of a good name" is thus, quite literally, the highest crown—or "Crown Heights."

Given the Rebbe's central role in the Lubavitch community, it is hardly surprising that ten years later, in the course of my fieldwork, a number of Hasidim repeated his interpretation of "Crown Heights" as the definitive meaning of the place where they lived. I asked a prominent Lubavitch author and translator what the Rebbe meant by this. What can we learn about today's Crown Heights by way of this ancient allusion? "The meaning behind that," he explained, "was the idea that this community should be a source of a good name—a role model of what an ethical and unified community is about." And, he assured me, the Rebbe's interpretation of Rabbi Shimon's crowns was not intended for the Jews of Crown Heights alone. The moral obligation to build a community that merits "the crown of a good name" is incumbent on Blacks and Jews alike.

I was oddly inspired by this ecumenical gloss on the ethical connotations of "Crown Heights." Perhaps, I thought, by investing the English name of his interracial neighborhood with the authority and symbolism of the Mishnaic sages, the Rebbe truly was trying to show "what an ethical and unified community is about." But there's far more in a name than any one speaker can capture—even the Lubavitcher Rebbe. The Rebbe's interpretation of "Crown Heights" as a "good name" for a model community resonates with a history of usage that goes back to the 1910s and 1920s, when the neighborhood as we now know it took shape. But more often than not, the name "Crown Heights" has signified the opposite of a "unified community." Strange as it may seem in a neighborhood whose population is now over 80 percent Afro-Caribbean and African American, "Crown Heights" has generally signified a model community for Whites, founded on the exclusion of local Blacks. This racialized pattern forms a central strand in the history of Crown Heights and its "Jewish neighborhood."

IN THE EARLY NINETEENTH CENTURY, the area of today's Crown Heights was something of a no-man's-land, a sparsely populated tract of farms and forests in between the villages of Bedford and Flatbush, to the north and south.[8] The first substantial settlements in the area were Carrville and Weeksville, neighboring Black villages founded in the 1830s in the northeast corner of today's Crown Heights, on land purchased and developed by African American entrepreneurs. By the 1870s, the area roughly bounded by today's Atlantic Avenue, Eastern Parkway, Albany Avenue, and Ralph Avenue was home to about 650 African Americans, including a significant portion of Brooklyn's Black elite, as well as a number of prominent Black institutions, including two churches—Methodist and Baptist—a public school, orphanage, old age home, and cemetery. The southern and western area of today's Crown Heights, including the area of present-day Jewish settlement, remained largely undeveloped as Carrville and Weeksville flourished. The dominant social institution in this area was the Kings County Penitentiary, built in 1846 on what is now Carroll Street between Nostrand and Rogers Avenues.

By the 1840s, if not earlier, much of the area of today's Crown Heights was popularly known as "Crow Hill." Most historians agree that the name Crow Hill was coined in derogatory reference to the Black community of Carrville and Weeksville, whose residents were sometimes known as "crows." Others say the "crows" in question were the penitentiary's inmates, or perhaps even actual crows. Either way, the name referred primarily to the slopes and crest of a hill that ran just south of today's Eastern Parkway, from Carrville in the east toward the Litchfield estate (today's Prospect Park) in the west—an area bounded, perhaps, by today's Park Place, Empire Boulevard, Washington Avenue, and Ralph Avenue.[9] The area just south of Crow Hill (today's Wingate) held an impoverished shantytown known as Pig Town, and the area north of Crow Hill (today's north Crown Heights or south Bed-Stuy, depending who you ask) was a wealthy section of Bedford known as Saint Marks.

These independent towns were not to last, however. The population of Brooklyn grew almost tenfold in the late nineteenth and early twentieth centuries, from about 260,000 in 1860 to over 2.5 million in 1930, and with the help of a growing mass-transit system many of these new Brooklynites moved into outlying areas like Crow Hill. City planners drafted a street grid in 1855 to guide the future development of the area, and construction began in earnest in the 1870s. But this new development came at the expense of the area's African American population. Much of Carrville, including the Citizen's Union Cemetery (located near today's Lincoln Terrace Park), was demolished in 1870 to make way for the broad boulevard of Eastern Parkway. And in the years that followed, the village of Weeksville, which lay askew of the new street grid, was largely destroyed by new development to the north of the Parkway. By the turn of the century, Carrville and Weeksville were no more.[10]

The development of Crow Hill to the south of Eastern Parkway accelerated in the early twentieth century. The penitentiary was torn down in 1906, and replaced by a Jesuit college. New subway lines linked the area to downtown Brooklyn and Manhattan. And over the course of the 1910s and 1920s, the empty lots defined by the 1855 street grid were filled in with new housing. This was the birth of "Crown Heights." It's hard to say just when the name was first used, but the area's real-estate developers and middle-class residents seem to have felt that the name "Crow Hill"—with its connotations of African Americans, prisoners, and undeveloped woodlands—would not do to describe their new neighborhood. For a while, the area was known as the "Parkway District." But by 1916 (when Crown Street was developed) it was commonly termed "Crown Heights" in real-estate advertisements, newspaper coverage, and (we can only suppose) the everyday lives of neighborhood residents. Much as these upwardly mobile European immigrants occasionally dropped a few letters from their names to mark their entry into the middle class, the underdeveloped "Crow Hill" added a few letters to become the upscale "Crown Heights."

A 1922 article in the *Brooklyn Daily Eagle* captured the area's transformation in a few striking images. The headline read: "Cop Warns Epicurean Goats To Lay Off Crown Heights," and the text described one of the minor headaches of the new neighborhood's middle class. It seems that goats from nearby Pig Town—which remained largely poor and undeveloped—were coming up the hill for a taste of upscale garbage. The *Eagle* explained:

> Only a few years ago the Crown Heights section was a stretch of vacant lots overgrown with brush and old gin bottles, and from Pigtown the goats came over on picnics. . . . For a while after Crown Heights was built up the Pigtown herd ambled over mainly through habit, and a sentimental streak that brought a tear at the thought of all these fine rubbish lots being given over to solid brick buildings and flowered lawns. But when the residents began showing their garbage the situation took on a brighter aspect. The garbage in Pigtown is notoriously low grade. . . . It in no way compares to the excellent cabbage, the delicatessen bismark herring, the sour anchovy paste, the mellow tomatoes and the clobbered milk in the Crown Heights pails. Since ascertaining this fact, the Pigtown goats have rushed over every morning for breakfast.[11]

Some thirty years earlier, the *Eagle* had run a sarcastic profile of "Crow Hill Goats," gently mocking a Brooklyn bumpkin living "a stone's throw from the penitentiary" who raised his own goats for their milk, and claiming

FIGURE 8 **"Brush and old gin bottles." Near the corner of today's Empire Boulevard and New York Avenue in the early 1920s. (Photographer unknown. Reprinted by permission of the Brooklyn Historical Society.)**

that, "Crow Hill has also been dubbed Goat Town, because of the number of these interesting animals found at large."[12] By 1922, however, goats were no longer welcome. The problem was, as the *Eagle* put it, "The [Pig Town] goats have none of the finer instincts that a Crown Heights goat would have, if there were any goats in Crown Heights." So a police officer herded the goats back to Pig Town, where he gave summonses to two Lefferts Avenue residents for allowing them to wander.

Despite the occasional goat, by the 1920s "Crown Heights" was already—as the Rebbe would note some sixty years later—a "good name" for a model community. But Crown Heights was hardly the "ethical and unified community" that the Rebbe (or his translator) envisioned. Like so many of the city's new middle-class neighborhoods, Crown Heights was founded on the exclusion of the local Black population, the semi-rural poor, and anybody else lacking the "finer instincts" of the new community. Urban planners tore down Carrville, Weeksville, and an African American cemetery to make way for the new street grid. Real-estate

developers replaced "brush and old gin bottles" with "solid brick buildings and flowered lawns." And these buildings' residents called the cops
to chase the goats back to Pig Town. Thus was "Crown Heights" born on
the rubble of "Crow Hill."

FROM THE EARLY 1920S through the early 1960s, Crown Heights was an
overwhelmingly White neighborhood, home to a rapidly assimilating elite
of recent European immigrants. It was also predominantly, and as time
went on increasingly, Jewish. The heart of Crown Heights lay on the crest
and slopes of what had once been Crow Hill, and by the early 1930s this
area was home to a broad range of "White ethnics"—immigrant families
from Germany, Scandinavia, Ireland, Italy, and Eastern Europe. Jews were
attracted to the neighborhood by the marketing savvy of Jewish real-estate
developers, and soon made up about 35 percent of the local population.[13]

Crown Heights was a solid middle-class neighborhood, with a median family income of about $4,000 a year in 1930 (compared to the
$2,500 of the working poor in nearby Brownsville, and the $8,700 of the
wealthy on Manhattan's Upper West Side).[14] There were, of course, pock-
ets of wealth and poverty in the area. The imposing homes of President
Street's "Doctor's Row" were matched by the sumptuous apartment
buildings on Eastern Parkway near Grand Army Plaza, while many of the
side streets north of the Parkway were filled with crowded and crumbling
tenements. But on the whole, as Alfred Kazin notes in his memoir of
childhood in Brownsville, the Jews of Crown Heights were "middle-class
Jews, *alrightniks*, making out 'all right' in the New World." Indeed, Kazin
quips, as a working-class child "they were . . . Gentiles to me as they went
out into the wide and tree-lined Eastern Parkway."[15]

Although it is impossible to trace the process with any precision, it
seems that over the course of the 1930s and 1940s, the perceived boundaries of "Crown Heights" expanded to fit the shifting terrain of White ethnic, middle-class settlement. In the early 1930s, the Saint Marks area,
north of old Crow Hill, was generally considered part of Bedford, not
Crown Heights. It was home to an elite community of native-born White
Protestants, along with a few very wealthy Jews and other immigrants.
Over the course of the 1930s, however, Saint Marks was divided from the
rest of White Bedford by a fast-growing Black neighborhood along the industrial and commercial corridors of Fulton Street and Atlantic Avenue.

This narrow strip of undesirable housing had long been a center of Black settlement, but in the 1920s and 1930s a large influx of African Americans from the South, along with a small number of Afro-Caribbean immigrants, began to build the community that would later become Black Bed-Stuy.[16] In a process of White flight that would become all too familiar to Brooklynites in the coming years, wealthy native-born Whites left Saint Marks, opening it up for White ethnic settlement to the south, and further Black settlement to the north. It was in this context, it seems, that the White residents (and realtors) of Saint Marks broke their longstanding ties with Bedford and cast their lot with Crown Heights.

By the 1940s, the commonly recognized boundaries of "Crown Heights" had thus expanded to include a vast area of north-central Brooklyn, more or less bounded by Atlantic Avenue or Fulton Street to the north, Empire Boulevard or Lefferts Avenue to the south, Washington Avenue or even Flatbush to the west, and Rochester or Ralph Avenue to the east. This expansive definition of Crown Heights was enshrined, in the 1950s, in a number of city government reports, although one such document called it "a somewhat artificial community."[17] It was institutionalized, in the 1960s, in the original boundaries of Brooklyn's Community District Eight, and it remains the semi-official definition of "Crown Heights" to this day (again, see figure 6).

By the 1950s, the population of Crown Heights was far more Jewish than it had been in the 1930s. Many of the neighborhood's Irish, Italians, and other White ethnics moved out after World War II, and were replaced by relatively secular Jews, along with a few thousand Hasidim— Lubavitchers and others—who arrived in Crown Heights as Holocaust refugees. In 1950 the neighborhood was 89 percent White, with a small but growing Black population clustered around Atlantic Avenue in the north. Some 50 to 60 percent of this White population was Jewish (as was an unknown but probably minuscule portion of the Black population). These 75,000 or so Jews supported some thirty-four synagogues, from Reform to Hasidic. In 1950, the median family income in most areas of Crown Heights was still comfortably above the Brooklyn-wide average, although the inclusion of predominantly Black communities around Atlantic Avenue brought a number of significantly poorer families into the neighborhood.[18]

This was the Crown Heights—the "Jewish neighborhood"—where the Lubavitch Hasidim began to build their distinctive community. There were a handful of Lubavitchers in Crown Heights as early as 1925, but the community truly took root when the Lubavitcher Rebbe of the time, Yosef Yitzchak Schneersohn, arrived in the United States and settled in Crown Heights in March of 1940.[19] The Previous Rebbe (as he is now known) purchased an imposing brick mansion at 770 Eastern Parkway, between Kingston and Brooklyn Avenues, while his son-in-law Menachem Mendel Schneerson, who would succeed him as Rebbe a decade hence, moved into a modest apartment on President Street between Brooklyn and New York Avenues. Since 1940, the Previous Rebbe's home and office—known simply as "770" by all Lubavitch Hasidim—has been the spiritual and political center of the Lubavitch community.

The assimilated "alrightniks" of Crown Heights did not always welcome their new Hasidic neighbors. Although many American Jews were concerned with the fate of Holocaust refugees, the Hasidim seemed to test the limits of this ethnic and religious solidarity. The art historian Linda Nochlin, for example, grew up in Crown Heights in the 1930s and 1940s, and later recalled viewing Hasidim as "little men wearing odd, identifiable garments" that made them look like "black beetles."[20] Many Hasidim, it seems, were well aware of such perceptions. In an interview conducted in 1993 by the Crown Heights History Project, an elderly Lubavitcher who had lived in Crown Heights since the 1940s claimed that the secular Jews who left the neighborhood in the 1960s did so because, "They didn't want to live in an area where there were Hasidic Jews, who wear the black hats and black suits and so forth."[21]

Despite this chilly reception, the Hasidic communities of Crown Heights grew quite rapidly in the 1950s, as additional Holocaust refugees settled in the neighborhood. It is impossible to say just how many Hasidim lived in Crown Heights at the time, but there seem to have been about 3,000 to 4,000—mostly Lubavitchers and Bobovers—in the neighborhood by 1960.[22] This unscientific estimate puts the Hasidic communities of the 1950s at about 5 percent of the local Jewish population and 2 percent of the local population as a whole. Most Hasidim lived near the traditional heart of Crown Heights—Lubavitchers just south of Eastern Parkway, where they remain today, and Bobovers to their north—but day-to-day Hasidic life encompassed the whole of the neighborhood. One of the largest Lubavitch yeshivas was located in the northwest corner of Crown Heights, on Dean Street between Bedford and Rogers Avenues—just around the corner from Washington Temple, where young Alfred Sharpton was junior pastor in the early 1960s.

AS THE CLOSE PROXIMITY of a Hasidic yeshiva and a Pentecostal church should remind us, the Hasidim were hardly the only new arrivals to Crown Heights in the 1940s and 1950s. The neighborhood's African American and Afro-Caribbean population grew fourfold between 1940 and 1957, by which point some 37,000 Blacks made up about 25 percent of the local population.[23] The area of concentrated Black settlement around Atlantic Avenue began expanding to the south, toward Eastern Parkway, and a few Blacks even moved south of the Parkway.[24] Needless to say, these newcomers were not the first Blacks to live in old Crow Hill. But they were the first to move, in significant numbers, into a neighborhood that had been overwhelmingly White for decades.

Immigrants from the Anglophone Caribbean were among the first Blacks to purchase brownstones south of Eastern Parkway, on the same blocks that were home to many Lubavitch Hasidim. In *Brown Girl, Brownstones*, a novel of Barbadian immigrant life in Brooklyn in the 1940s, Paule Marshall chronicles the struggles of upwardly mobile Caribbean immigrants to buy their own homes, and the central place of "Crown Heights" in the landscape of their American dreams. The mother of Marshall's young protagonist spends her days "scrub[bing] the Jew floor to make a penny" (and eventually does much worse) out of her burning desire to own a home in the middle-class neighborhood of Crown Heights—"up with the white people, if you please." As she explains to her ne'er-do-well husband:

> Every West Indian out here taking a lesson from the Jew landlord and converting these old [Bed-Stuy] houses into rooming houses— making the closets-self into rooms some them!—and pulling down plenty-plenty money by the week. And now that the place is near overrun with roomers the Bajans [Barbadians] are getting out. They going! Every jack-man buying a swell house in ditchy Crown Heights. Percy Challenor and them so gone! Iris Hurley in a house with more wall-to-wall carpeting than the law allow.[25]

But as Barbadian immigrants moved "up with the white people" in the 1940s, and growing numbers of Blacks joined them in the 1950s and 1960s, the "white people" nearly all moved out. As I described in the introduction, these decades of White flight marked the transformation of Crown Heights from an overwhelmingly White and predominantly Jewish neighborhood to an overwhelmingly Black and predominantly Afro-Caribbean one. The neighborhood remained 70 percent White in 1960, but was 70 percent Black by 1970. It quickly became, in Philip Kasinitz's description, "the center of West Indian life in the United States."[26]

The one demographic constant in these turbulent years was the rapid growth of the Lubavitch community, which stayed in Crown Heights at the behest of its Rebbe. The community grew by leaps and bounds in the late 1960s and early 1970s, as its substantial natural growth (derived from relatively large families) was supplemented by a large influx of newly orthodox Jews, drawn to Crown Heights by the community's increasingly successful outreach campaigns. Yet while the Lubavitch community grew—perhaps doubling in size between 1965 and 1975—Crown Heights changed around it.

By 1990, as I noted in the introduction, the neighborhood as a whole (as its boundaries are semi-officially defined) was roughly 65 percent Afro-Caribbean, 15 percent African American, 10 percent Hispanic, 8 percent White—a minority that was, in turn, almost entirely Hasidic—and tiny fractions both Asian and Native American. North Crown Heights (north of the Parkway) was almost 85 percent Black, with equal parts African Americans and Afro-Caribbean immigrants, a small Hispanic minority, and an enclave of largely White "yuppies" in the area around Grand Army Plaza. South Crown Heights was about 80 percent Black, with an overwhelming Afro-Caribbean majority, small African American and Hispanic minorities, and about 12,000 Hasidim living in the blocks around Kingston Avenue. In the 1980s, the Lubavitch Hasidim were the fastest growing segment of the local population, and this growth has likely continued in the years since (although it may have slowed following the Lubavitcher Rebbe's death in 1994). And in the late 1990s, as New York's housing market boomed, a small number of non-Hasidic Whites filtered into Crown Heights from nearby gentrified neighborhoods, looking for more affordable housing. But despite these recent developments—and the inherent fluidity of urban space—there is no chance, in the foreseeable future, that Crown Heights will again become the White, Jewish neighborhood that it was in the 1950s.[27]

YET IN THE EYES of many Hasidim, Crown Heights remains a "Jewish neigh-borhood" to this day. In 1998, for example, a Hasidic woman in her late thirties told me, bluntly, "It's not really a Black neighborhood here at all. They just have nothing to do with it." Speaking in terms of the "politically correct" education she had received before becoming Hasidic, she ex-plained that she was concerned for the feelings of her Black neighbors, liv-ing in a Jewish neighborhood where they can never feel at home. She wondered "how it feels to the Blacks here to be so invisible." But a few min-utes earlier, the same woman had promised me she was "an expert" on Black-Jewish relations, because she lives "just surrounded by Blacks." She referred to a predominantly Haitian church around the corner from her house, and complained to a friend that, "Coming from the subway I have to walk right by that big Voodoo place." Yet somehow, a Hasidic Jew living "surrounded by Blacks," next to a "big Voodoo place," could still claim that "It's not really a Black neighborhood here at all." When I pressed her on this seeming contradiction, pointing out that Crown Heights is about 80 percent Black, she limited her claim to the densest area of Jewish settle-ment in the neighborhood—where she herself doesn't actually live. "Yeah," she said, "but not these six blocks. Here it's really just Jewish."

The shifting geography of her claim points toward one of the ways Lubavitchers maintain their sense of living in a "Jewish neighborhood." There is, as I have noted, a relatively small area of Crown Heights—the blocks around Kingston Avenue between Eastern Parkway and Empire Boulevard—where Hasidim make up almost 40 percent of the population. This is the "six blocks" described here as "just Jewish." And there is a larger area of south Crown Heights where Hasidim make up about 20 percent of the population (again, see figure 6). This, according to many Lubavitchers, constitutes the whole of "Crown Heights." Just as the boundaries of the neighborhood expanded in the 1930s to include the predominantly White area of Saint Marks, they contracted in the 1960s—in the eyes of many Hasidim—to include only those areas with some remaining Jewish popula-tion. Lubavitchers thus cling to the time-honored, but increasingly threat-ened, definition of "Crown Heights" as a White, Jewish neighborhood.

The northern border of the neighborhood is particularly significant in this regard, as it marks the boundary between Crown Heights and Bed-Stuy—a Black neighborhood in both demographic fact and popular imagination. While most city agencies and Black neighborhood residents see Atlantic Avenue or Fulton Street as the northern border of Crown Heights, many Lubavitch Hasidim feel the neighborhood stops at Eastern Parkway. By grafting the almost entirely Black area between Eastern Parkway and Fulton Street on to "Bed-Stuy," Lubavitchers strive to maintain the Jewishness of "Crown Heights." In 1976, the Lubavitch community gained a measure of official recognition for its perceived northern border when Hasidic activists successfully lobbied to have Brooklyn's Community District Eight—a district defined in 1968 according to the expansive definition of Crown Heights that developed in the 1940s—split into today's Districts Eight and Nine, with Eastern Parkway as the line between them. The creation of the new Community District Nine, for south Crown Heights, was fiercely contested by local Black leaders, as it gave Lubavitch community leaders a greater role in managing city services and economic development in their immediate area.[28] Though Community District Eight is officially defined as "north Crown Heights," the division between Districts Eight and Nine lends credence to the Hasidic sense of Eastern Parkway as the border of their neighborhood, rather than its axis.

This Hasidic perception of the neighborhood's northern border is hardly limited to the arena of urban politics. Indeed, most Lubavitchers treat Eastern Parkway as the northern border of their everyday lives, and are reluctant to cross its tree-lined expanse. This reluctance has faded somewhat since the late 1990s, when the high cost of housing in south Crown Heights led a small but growing number of Hasidim to venture north, but the Parkway remains a symbolically charged divide. At a Shabbos dinner in 1997, I spoke with a group of young women living in the dormitory of a school for newly orthodox women and girls on the north side of Eastern Parkway, between Kingston and Albany Avenues. Although their school lay less than fifty yards from the heart of the Lubavitch community, at the corner of Eastern and Kingston, they viewed the trip to their dorm at night as a terrifying ordeal, because they had to walk the last quarter-block on the north side of the Parkway. I agreed that the neighborhood can be rough for women walking alone at night, but expressed my doubts that the north side of the Parkway is any more dangerous than the south side. Oh no, they told me, it's much worse. "It's a different world over there" said one. Another called Eastern Parkway "the Green Line"—comparing it to the

FIGURE 9 Eastern Parkway. Six lanes of traffic, two pedestrian promenades, the boundary between Community Districts Eight and Nine, and in some eyes "the Green Line." (Photo by the author.)

militarized border dividing the state of Israel from the occupied West Bank—a metaphor that came to mind just moments after a heated conversation about a suicide bombing that had killed four Israelis in Tel Aviv that day (see figure 9).

By the same token, Hasidim sometimes refer to the east side of their neighborhood—the blocks between Troy and Rochester Avenues—as "the West Bank." One Hasid living on Union Street between Schenectady and Utica Avenues joked that he lives "on Union between East and West Beirut." Unlike the area north of the Parkway, most Hasidim do consider this area part of "Crown Heights." But these blocks have Jewish populations of just 10 or 12 percent, and Hasidim often claim to face greater hostility from their Black neighbors there than in other parts of the neighborhood. This contested space is where Yosef Lifsch struck and killed Gavin Cato—on the corner of President Street and Utica Avenue—and where Charles Price told an angry crowd, "I'm going up to the Jew neighborhood!" Price stood fifty yards from a synagogue and surrounded by Jewish homes, yet somehow he wasn't in "the Jew neighborhood." Even in Hasidic eyes, he was on "the West Bank."

Lubavitchers thus draw on the rhetoric of the nation-state—and specifically, the Jewish state—to define the boundaries of their "Jewish neighborhood."[29] In place of the subtle variations in racial demography and social
class that cross-cut Crown Heights and its surrounding neighborhoods,
they see unambiguous borders: "It's a different world over there."

THESE BORDERS TAKE SHAPE within the history of racialized spatial
difference—and spatialized racial difference—I have charted in this section. Ever since the neighborhood was built on old Crow Hill, out of the
rubble of two Black villages and a penitentiary, "Crown Heights" has been
a "good name" for a White community. Contemporary struggles over the
boundaries of the neighborhood unfold around the contradiction between this longstanding rhetorical figure and present-day demographic
realities. Local Blacks tend to cite the semi-official boundaries of Crown
Heights—boundaries produced in the 1940s, according to the segregation-
ist logic of a growing White community. Lubavitchers, however, tend to
assert a more limited definition of Crown Heights—a definition that con-
tradicts its semi-official boundaries, but attempts to preserve its threatened Whiteness and Jewishness. The Reverend Al Sharpton can thus
claim, in good faith, to "come out of Crown Heights" because he spent
much of his childhood north of Eastern Parkway, while Roslyn Malamud
can complain, in equally good faith, that Reverend Sharpton is an "outsider" with no business in the neighborhood. Each of these views is true,
in its own way, to the fraught history of "Crown Heights."

But the racial boundaries I have charted here are not the only way to
define the neighborhood. As I will show in the next section, these racial
geographies intersect, in complex ways, with geographies based on socioeconomic class.

Class Distinctions: "Eight Blocks Away
Is the End of the World"

In the United States and elsewhere, experiences of race are often insepa-
rable from experiences of class.[30] I have, therefore, already traced the class
geography of Crown Heights in general terms. Crown Heights, we have
seen, has long been imagined as a middle-class neighborhood—home

to "solid brick buildings and flowered lawns" in the 1920s, to "swell house[s] . . . with more wall-to-wall carpeting than the law allow" in the 1940s, and to "decent homes and decent lives" in the 1990s. This middle-class status has often been linked to the neighborhood's Whiteness, but geographies of race cannot simply be conflated with geographies of class. Spaces defined by racial difference and class distinction may overlap at crucial points, but they are not coextensive. In this section I will examine how real and imagined socioeconomic differences shape distinctions between Crown Heights and other areas, distinctions between the "Jewish neighborhood" and other parts of Crown Heights, and distinctions between Blacks and Jews living in Crown Heights.

A number of the issues I will address came together in a crisis that rocked one small corner of Crown Heights in April of 1977. Eight years after the Lubavitcher Rebbe decreed that his Hasidim should stay in the neighborhood, the stress of life in the "inner city" was just too much, and a piece of the community collapsed. A wall fell down—a cement retaining wall that kept the garages behind a block of homes on Montgomery Street from tumbling into the alley behind a building on Empire Boulevard. Kept them from tumbling, that is, until a stretch of the wall gave way with a "thundering roar," reducing nine garages to a pile of cinder-block. The Jewish home- and garage-owners called for help from Rabbi Samuel Fogelman, a Lubavitch community leader who was the newly elected chairman of the newly created Community Board Nine. Rabbi Fogelman called for help, in turn, from local politicians and federal agencies, but to no avail. He then called up a journalist from the New York Times, and explained that the situation was a crisis because, "The people in those houses are too old and too poor to pay for fixing the wall. . . . These people are going to be wiped out, God forbid." He explained that although it may seem a minor problem, the collapsed wall had far broader—even apocalyptic—significance: "We [the Jews of Crown Heights] are making history. Eight blocks away is the end of the world."[31]

Many things portend "the end of the world" in the profoundly messianic Lubavitch community, but Rabbi Fogelman was referring to the poverty and social dislocation that border Crown Heights to the north and east. The journalist assumed he meant "pocked and impoverished Brownsville," but he could just as well have meant parts of Bed-Stuy, or

Crown Heights itself. Fogelman envisioned these communities' poverty at a distance from his own—"eight blocks away"—yet his community too was home to people who could be "wiped out, God forbid" because they were "too old and too poor to pay for fixing the wall." Their practical predicament, and Rabbi Fogelman's efforts to assist them, illustrate the conceptual predicament of working- and middle-class Crown Heights residents struggling to sustain "decent homes and decent lives" just blocks away from "the end of the world." In this section, I will examine how Lubavitchers and other Crown Heights residents have maintained this fragile sense of class-based spatial distinction—and how this distinction has been mapped, in turn, on to distinctions between Blacks and Jews.

THERE ARE SUBSTANTIAL differences in socioeconomic class between Crown Heights and some of its surrounding neighborhoods. No one statistical index can capture the lived experience of class, but we may sketch these differences by comparing the incomes of neighborhood families. In 1990, Crown Heights families—including those in both north and south Crown Heights—had a median income of about $25,000, which placed them well below the median of $30,033 for all Brooklyn families, but still within the bounds of the borough's middle class.[32] The incomes of Crown Heights families were 20 percent lower than those of families in Flatbush and East Flatbush to the south, and far lower than those of families in gentrified Park Slope, across Prospect Park to the west. But they were 25 percent higher than those of families in Bed-Stuy to the north, and 45 percent higher than those of families in Brownsville to the east.[33]

These geographic differences in socioeconomic class reflect the history of housing development in central Brooklyn. Crown Heights residents live in everything from squalid tenements and housing projects to luxurious single-family homes and apartment buildings—a mix of housing that allows for a mixed-class neighborhood, averaging out at working- or middle class. By contrast, when Brownsville was developed in the late nineteenth and early twentieth centuries, it was almost entirely filled with tenements for the poor and working class, many of which were replaced, in the 1960s and 1970s, by huge swaths of public housing—a change that did little to improve Brownsville's economic fortunes.[34] Bed-Stuy, like Crown Heights, was built as a mixed class neighborhood. It is, however, an older neighborhood than Crown Heights, so its low-income housing once consisted largely of "old-law" tenements (built before 1901, when New York's Tenement House Commission set strict standards for low-cost housing), many of which have been replaced by troubled public housing projects.[35] Flatbush and East Flatbush, again by contrast, were developed around the same time as Crown Heights, but with more single-family homes and less class diversity.

Crown Heights was built at the literal and figurative intersection of these trends. The area to the north of Eastern Parkway was largely developed by the 1910s, as late-nineteenth-century urbanization expanded south from the former town of Bedford.[36] It included mansions and brownstones for the wealthy and middle class, right around the corner from tenements for the poor. But many of the grander homes in north Crown Heights deteriorated for lack of maintenance during the decades of White flight—and capital flight—that began in the 1950s, while many of the old-law tenements in the area were replaced by public housing. The area to the south of Eastern Parkway, by contrast, was developed in the late 1910s and 1920s. This timing proved decisive for the subsequent history of the neighborhood, as the 1920s witnessed an unprecedented boom in upper-income housing development throughout New York City. It was, in the words of a Jewish real-estate magnate of the time, "a period of the grossest exploitation, a period of wild excitement in real estate."[37] Thanks to a tax exemption tilted toward upper-income housing, as well as the general prosperity of the time, the benefits of this "wild excitement" went largely to the middle and upper classes. In south Crown Heights and elsewhere, most of the housing built in the 1920s consisted of spacious row houses and apartment buildings—middle-class homes that still stand today (see figure 10).

Housing—like biology—is not exactly destiny, but these differences in the built environment have contributed to an enduring pattern of class difference between north and south Crown Heights. In an extensive 1972 study of neighborhood housing and socioeconomic conditions, New York's Department of City Planning concluded that "No one section [of Crown Heights] can be identified exclusively as a poverty area or an upper-middle-class enclave," but acknowledged that "If any generalization can be made, it is that many families south of Eastern Parkway have higher

FIGURE 10 A typical block in south Crown Heights. Limestone row houses, with low-rise apartment buildings in the background. (Photo by the author.)

incomes than those north of the roadway."[38] Indeed, in 1970 the median income of families in south Crown Heights was 28 percent higher than that of families in north Crown Heights. Two decades later the difference had shrunk to 16 percent, but 25 percent of families in north Crown Heights still lived below the poverty line in 1990, as opposed to 17 percent in south Crown Heights (and a Brooklyn-wide average of 20 percent).[39]

We may thus begin to see the outlines of Roslyn Malamud's neighborhood of "decent homes and decent lives," as well as a loose correlation between this class-based space and the "Jewish neighborhood" charted above. Crown Heights is, in fact, better built and better off than some of its surrounding neighborhoods, and south Crown Heights is better built and better off than the area to its north. Moreover, the heart of today's Hasidic community—the area of 40 percent Jewish settlement straddling Kingston Avenue between Eastern Parkway and Empire Boulevard—is better built and better off than any other section of Crown Heights. As I have noted, these residential blocks are lined with spacious and elegant row houses and apartment buildings. Mansions break this middle-class pattern (on President Street and Eastern Parkway) more often than tenements. Families living in this limited area have incomes 20 to 40 percent higher (depending on the specific census tract) than those of families in Crown Heights as a whole.[40] This is where Roslyn Malamud lives, in what Anna Deavere Smith described as a "huge beautiful house on Eastern Parkway."[41] This is where Hasidim come—from all over the neighborhood— to shop on Kingston Avenue, where they often come to pray, and where their Rebbe used to farbreng at 770 Eastern Parkway. There is, therefore, a spatial correlation between Jewish settlement, better housing, and higher incomes. In other words, the Lubavitch Hasidim tend to live in the nicest and wealthiest section of Crown Heights.

Yet we must take care not to conflate their "Jewish neighborhood" with this neighborhood of "decent homes and decent lives." In the 1940s and 1950s, when large numbers of Hasidim first moved into Crown Heights, the same blocks of brownstones at the center of today's Hasidic community were among the most desirable blocks to the upwardly mobile Afro-Caribbean immigrants who formed the core of today's Caribbean majority.[42] This is, perhaps, where Paule Marshall imagined "Iris Hurley [living] in a house with more wall-to-wall carpeting than the law allow." Although the demographic center of the Caribbean community has since moved south to Flatbush and East Flatbush, one can hardly say that these well-to-do blocks near the Parkway—which are, we must remember, 60 percent Black—are no longer a "Caribbean neighborhood." Moreover, since the 1970s Lubavitchers have increasingly settled to the south, east, and west of their community's geographic core. In 1990, about 65 percent of Jews in Crown Heights still lived in the core area of 40 percent Jewish settlement,[43] but as their population has grown Hasidim have moved into existing housing and new developments in less well-off sections of Crown Heights. The area of 20 percent Jewish settlement that Hasidim see as their "Jewish neighborhood" thus includes both Black and Jewish wealth and poverty.

Finally, although Jewish homes may be clustered in the best-off part of the neighborhood, we may not therefore assume that Jews in Crown Heights are better off, as a whole, than their Black neighbors. Indeed, the opposite seems to be true. In 1990, the per capita income of Jews in Crown Heights was about 15 percent lower than that of Blacks in the neighborhood as a whole, and almost 20 percent lower than that of Blacks in south Crown Heights. The per capita income of Jews living on the nicest blocks at the heart of the Hasidic community—where both Blacks and Jews had comparatively high incomes—was about 30 percent lower than that of their immediate Black neighbors.[44] Due to the large size of many Hasidic families, these per capita figures may exaggerate the disparity between Black and Jewish family incomes.[45] But the trend is still clear: despite their spatial association with wealth, Jews in Crown Heights seem to be a bit worse off—and are certainly no better off—than their Black neighbors.

And despite these subtle socioeconomic differences, a fundamental fact is also clear: Blacks and Jews in Crown Heights are in more or less the same socioeconomic boat. Neither community enjoys a clear position of material privilege relative to the other. Indeed, their income parity is striking in comparison to the dramatic disparity between Black and White incomes in Brooklyn as a whole.[46] Although the social geography of Crown Heights has been shaped by differences in socioeconomic class, these differences do not map, in any simple way, onto the racial and religious differences between the neighborhood's Blacks and Jews.

YET NEIGHBORHOOD RESIDENTS and others, both Black and Jewish, nevertheless tend to assume that Jews in Crown Heights are better off than their Black neighbors. Blacks often point to imagined Jewish wealth as a sign of the Hasidic community's supposed privilege, while Jews point, in turn, to imagined Black poverty as proof that they are "saving the neighborhood" by remaining in Crown Heights. These perceptions often draw on racist and antisemitic stereotypes, but they may also be shaped by day-to-day experiences of the spatial correlation between Jewish settlement and upper-middle-class status. In other words, Jews in Crown Heights may seem wealthier than they are by virtue of living in proximity to wealth. And finally, these perceptions also point to another important element of the spatial politics of difference in Crown Heights: the active role of Hasidic community leaders in securing "decent homes and decent lives" for Jews in Crown Heights.

In an interview conducted in 1993 by the Crown Heights History Project, an Afro-Caribbean woman in her twenties articulated all three of these perspectives on the class position of her Jewish neighbors. She described Crown Heights as divided into "the haves and the have nots," and when asked if she herself had seen evidence of Jewish privilege in the neighborhood, she replied:

Oh yeah. Millionaire's Row, on President Street. They got a twenty-four hour watch from Kingston on down. They got cops on the block—the cops over there on Eastern Parkway and Kingston, patrolling that church they got over there [770 Eastern Parkway]. They get everything. There's a bank over on Kingston Avenue where they can trade in their food stamps. . . . They on the welfare, they got how many kids, and they living better than me. I gotta live in a slum building. Some of them live in all them newly renovated places. They don't gotta think twice about nothing. They just got it made in the shade. The poorest Jew is not the same as the poorest Black person. The poorest Jew is probably living like a middle-class Black person in Crown Heights.[47]

This interviewee takes the spatial association of Jews and wealth as her starting point by (incorrectly) assuming the Jewishness of "Millionaire's Row" (i.e., Doctor's Row) on President Street. She then veers off into a litany of antisemitic stereotypes, in which Jews appear as both devious bankers and welfare cheats. But she also touches on a number of concrete ways Hasidic community leaders have, in fact, worked to improve the "quality of life" of Jews in Crown Heights—as when Rabbi Fogelman tried to secure state aid for Jewish homeowners who had lost their garages. She thus raises the thorny question of inequity in city services. Her accusations echo the charges of Black community leaders since the 1970s that Hasidim receive "preferential treatment" from the police and other state agencies—treatment that may, in fact, help "the poorest Jew [live] like a middle-class Black person in Crown Heights."

Over the past few decades, Lubavitch leaders and organizations have often worked to secure subsidies and services for Jews in Crown Heights—and, to a lesser extent, for the community as a whole. In his 1969 speech encouraging Jews to stay in Crown Heights, the Rebbe called on his community to strengthen the infrastructure of their neighborhood, and in the years since his Hasidim have responded to his call.[48] In the 1970s, for example, the Crown Heights Jewish Community Council collaborated with a number of Hasidic real-estate developers to organize Chevra Machazikei Hashchuna, or the Coalition to Strengthen the Neighborhood. Chevra (as it was commonly known) brought in millions of dollars in government funds for housing development and renewal, low-income rental subsidies, and job training—dollars that went disproportionally to Lubavitch Hasidim (and to Chevra board members). A group of investors affiliated with Chevra also purchased private homes from Jews leaving the neighborhood, and resold them to Hasidim. Their efforts may account for the presence of relatively low-income Jews in relatively high-income areas of Crown Heights, and for the impression of many Black Crown Heights residents that Jews "live in all them newly renovated places."

Of course a number of local Black churches, and other Black institutions, have also sponsored real-estate developments tailored to suit the needs of their communities. But Chevra took such favoritism a number of troubling steps further. In 1978, New York's City Council released a report detailing fraud and mismanagement at Chevra, including the misuse of public funds, and allegations of harassment against Black tenants in buildings Chevra hoped to renovate—with federal subsidies—for Hasidic Jews.[49] Equally, if not more, disturbing was the apparent complicity of federal Housing and Urban Development officials in Chevra's discriminatory projects. HUD consistently approved Chevra's explicitly stated plans to "affirmatively market" federally subsidized housing to Hasidic Jews, in an attempt to redress what Chevra termed a "racial imbalance in the community."[50] The FBI investigated Chevra's fiscal irregularities and Mayor Ed Koch cut its city funding, but no legal actions were ever taken. Chevra collapsed, however, in the mid-1980s.[51] In the years since, Lubavitch community organizations and private Hasidic developers have continued to build and renovate subsidized housing for both Blacks and Jews. These developments have sometimes been controversial—as in 1989, when the kosher-style double sinks in a city-subsidized building raised eyebrows among local Black leaders—but in recent years, Hasidic developers have increasingly tried to build partnerships with local Black organizations.[52]

In addition to such housing and economic development initiatives, Hasidic leaders and organizations have devoted a great deal of energy to allaying their community's fears of crime.[53] Indeed, the first organized Hasidic response to the demographic transformation of Crown Heights in the 1960s was the formation of a controversial community crime patrol known as the Maccabees—an organization accused of vigilantism by Black Crown Heights residents.[54] The Maccabees were disbanded in the early

1970s, but were later replaced by a longer lasting community patrol known as Shmira—which has often been subject, rightly or wrongly, to the same accusations. Like the Afro-Caribbean woman quoted above, many Black Crown Heights residents are deeply suspicious of the Hasidic community's "twenty-four hour watch from Kingston on down."

Lubavitch leaders have also worked to maintain relationships with the local 71st police precinct, and with city- and borough-wide police brass. For a number of years in the 1970s, the 71st precinct kept a patrol car stationed around the clock in front of 770 Eastern Parkway. Although this controversial practice was halted in 1978, it seems to linger in the minds of many neighborhood residents, like the Afro-Caribbean woman who complained above about "the cops over there on Eastern Parkway and Kingston, patrolling that church they got over there." Moreover, the lack of a patrol car in front of 770 did not necessarily signal the end of the relationship between Hasidim and police. Not long after it was removed, local police began escorting the Rebbe on his frequent visits to the graves of his wife and father-in-law—a service that had complex consequences following the death of Gavin Cato.[55]

These policies and practices have been criticized for decades by Black Crown Heights residents and community leaders, who see them as evidence of a troubling double standard in policing and city services—or even as evidence, in the words of one prominent activist, of a "deliberate and calculated collusion by officials to promote the interests of the Hasidim."[56] These charges may or may not be accurate, but they are hardly far-fetched. Unequal state subsidies for predominantly White communities are not a new or surprising phenomenon in New York City or the United States as a whole. Indeed, the government funding at stake in debates over "preferential treatment" in Crown Heights pales in comparison to the massive state investment in the predominantly White suburban communities now home to many of the Jews who left Crown Heights in the 1960s.[57] In this context, it's not hard to imagine a subtle bias in favor of the Lubavitch Hasidim, without any "deliberate and calculated collusion."

Yet it is extremely difficult to say whether the subsidies and services secured by Lubavitchers constitute preferential treatment from the state. With the exception of Chevra's unethical real-estate dealings, it may be impossible to distinguish the hard-won fruits of community organizing from the ill-gotten gains of deceitful politicking. Jews in Crown Heights often point out—and Blacks often acknowledge, with grudging admiration—that their leadership has been able to demand services from local and national politicians because Hasidim consistently vote in higher percentages than their neighbors. When the Rebbe was alive his personal blessing guaranteed thousands of Lubavitch votes, and many politicians—Black, Jewish, or what-have-you—were eager to court such a reliable voting block. Local Black leaders are divided as to whether such political organizing strategies constitute an attack on their neighborhood's Black majority, a model of community empowerment to emulate, or a bit of both.

MY GOAL HERE is not to settle this question, but simply to highlight some of the ways Lubavitch community leaders have worked to preserve the "decent homes and decent lives" of Jews in Crown Heights. By now, I think, we can better understand Rabbi Fogelman's efforts to secure state aid for the Jews of Montgomery Street—to fix the wall that held up their garages, and shore up the fragile class distinction separating them from "the end of the world" just "eight blocks away." Garages matter, because for New Yorkers at least (to paraphrase Stuart Hall), real-estate is the modality through which class is lived. Spatial patterns in the built environment often index socioeconomic differences, but they may also foster perceptions of difference where none actually exists—as in the misleading geographic correlation between Jews and wealth in Crown Heights. These real and imagined class distinctions have helped define the boundaries of "Crown Heights" and its "Jewish neighborhood."

We must not, however, get too caught up in garages and other material things, lest we forget what Hasidim consider the defining feature of Crown Heights: the fact that this is the Lubavitcher Rebbe's neighborhood—the site, according to some, where the messiah will soon be revealed, and the redemption of God's creation will commence.

Religious Spaces: "The Rebbe's Daled Amos"

For the Lubavitch Hasidim, a "Jewish neighborhood" is more than merely a euphemism for, or ethnic variety of, a White middle-class neighborhood. It is both of these things, but it is also a specifically religious space, home

to the many institutions a community needs to live by the commandments
of the Torah—synagogues, ritual baths, yeshivas, a rabbinic court, kosher
grocers, Jewish book stores, and so on. For Hasidim, these religious institutions define the boundaries of "Crown Heights" every bit as much as the
neighborhood's racial and socioeconomic geography. The religious space
of Hasidic Crown Heights overlaps in crucial ways with spaces defined by
race and class, but it is shaped by a different geographic logic.

For example, the locations of synagogues shape the conceptual maps
and settlement patterns of Lubavitch Hasidim. Their "Crown Heights"
extends west to Nostrand Avenue, in part because there is a synagogue in
the Beis Rivka school building on Crown Street between New York and
Nostrand. It extends east to Rochester Avenue, although very few Jews live
east of Utica, because a synagogue and mikvah continue to thrive on President Street between Utica and Rochester. And it extends south to Maple
Street, sort of, because every Saturday morning a devoted group of Hasidim walks from all over the neighborhood to hold services at the otherwise defunct Maple Street Shul. Thanks to a geographic imagination
shaped by communal religious life—and the practical limitations of rabbinic law, which restricts Hasidim to traveling by foot on Shabbos and
most holidays—these synagogues help mark the boundaries of the Lubavitch community.

Although the boundaries of the community may be defined by any
orthodox synagogue, its center is defined by the synagogue the
Previous Rebbe established at 770 Eastern Parkway. Hasidic community
and geography—like Hasidic most everything else—is structured around
the Rebbe. To Lubavitch Hasidim, their Rebbe's presence has always been
the defining feature of Crown Heights, and this remains the case today
despite his death in 1994. Lubavitchers often mark their Rebbe's geographic centrality by referring to Crown Heights as "the Rebbe's daled
amos," a phrase that draws metaphoric significance from the technicali-
ties of Jewish law, where it refers to the minimum required breadth of a
private home—four cubits, or *daled amos.* To describe Crown Heights as
"the Rebbe's daled amos" is to define the entire neighborhood as the
Rebbe's home—a private Jewish space, and a uniquely holy place for his
Hasidim. In this section I will show how the boundaries of "Crown
Heights," and the neighborhood's central position within the global

Lubavitch community, have been shaped by this religious imagination of
social space.

AS I DISCUSSED in the introduction, most Hasidic Jews are fervently devoted to their Rebbes—charismatic leaders whom Hasidim see as interme-
diaries between God and the community, and representatives of God's will
on earth. The spiritual and political centrality of each Hasidic community's
Rebbe has generally been reflected in the social and geographic centrality
of the Rebbe's court, which serves as a pilgrimage site for Hasidim and a
source of inspiration and authority. Indeed, most contemporary Hasidic
communities are known by the name of the city or town where their
Rebbes first established a dynastic court—the Lubavitchers from Lubavitch (in today's Belarus), the Bobovers from Bobov (in Poland), the Bo-
stoners from Boston (yes, in Massachusetts), and so on. The Lubavitch
community, however, has shifted this traditional Hasidic pattern by working to spread Hasidism throughout the Jewish world, thereby asserting the
authority of their Rebbes as leaders of world Jewry as such. Lubavitchers
thus tend to imagine Crown Heights—which the Rebbe rarely left during
his four decades of leadership, except to visit the Previous Rebbe's grave
in Queens—as nothing less than the spiritual center of the Jewish people.

Crown Heights thus echoes, and to some extent supplants, the Holy
Land of Israel. Although most Lubavitchers fervently await the messianic
ingathering of the Jews in their ancient homeland, and many hold ultra-
nationalist views of contemporary Israeli politics, they nevertheless imagine a Jewish world centered firmly around their Brooklyn neighborhood.
For example, a Lubavitch rabbi once told me a remarkable story about a
disciple of the Baal Shem Tov (the eighteenth century founder of Hasidism)
who yearned to visit the Holy Land, but realized—after a series of symbolically charged dreams—that the center of Jewish life lay at his master's court
in Poland, rather than at the ancient temple in Jerusalem. My Hasidic acquaintance summed up the moral of the story by telling me, bluntly,
"Crown Heights is the center of the world."[58]

This sentiment is widely shared among Lubavitchers, in Crown
Heights and elsewhere, but it is expressed particularly fervently by those
Hasidim who believe that their Rebbe is—or was, or could have been—the
messiah. For the messianists within Lubavitch (a large and influential mi-

nority of the community), the Rebbe's singular redemptive role adds cosmological depth to his geographic centrality. They often point out that according to Hebrew numerology, "770" is equivalent to "Beis Moshiach" or "House of the Messiah," and claim it was thus no accident that the Previous Rebbe settled in Crown Heights, so his son-in-law could announce the redemption of creation from Eastern Parkway. One fervent messianist described Crown Heights as "the event horizon"—the physical site on the cusp of time's progress toward the end of history. And another (a community leader who has been active in Brooklyn politics) told a group of relatively secular Jews on a week-long program at a Crown Heights yeshiva:

> Here you are. For a little while, a short while, you have a chance to drink at the well-springs of Melech HaMoshiach [The King Messiah, the Rebbe]. You should know where you are. There's nothing like this anywhere in the universe. Nothing. Nothing, anywhere. . . . It's such an incredible gift that for some reason God likes you—loves you!—enough to send you here, to this seemingly crazy little corner of Brooklyn. Who would ever believe it! . . . Look where we are over here, this little ten square-block area. The anthropologist here [that is, me] is gonna tell us that this is weird! . . . Okay, it's very strange, but in the midst of this run-down corner of Brooklyn, that most of the rest of New York City writes off, and doesn't even know exists—from this place, the light goes forth to the universe.

This Hasid's spiritual vision of "Crown Heights" rearticulates the social marginality of his working-class immigrant neighborhood through the cosmological centrality of his Rebbe, The King Messiah, whose well-springs sustain creation.

Such visions may not be dismissed as mere flights of rhetorical fancy. Indeed, the religious imaginations of the Lubavitch Hasidim have transformed the social geography of Crown Heights in concrete ways. As we will see, the Rebbe's presence in 770 has been both a centripetal and centrifugal force on his "Jewish neighborhood"—drawing it together in a concentrated pattern of settlement, while opening it up to a web of interconnected global spaces.

Because orthodox Jews only travel by foot on Shabbos and most holidays, there has always been a great incentive for Lubavitchers in the New

York area to live within walking distance of 770. Until a stroke left him unable to speak in 1992, the Rebbe's farbrengens on Shabbos and holidays were central to the religious life of the community, and only those Hasidim living, or visiting, in or near Crown Heights were able to attend. Even since the Rebbe's death in 1994, many of his Hasidim—though by no means all—like to pray in 770 on Shabbos and holidays, where they feel his continued presence. Their desire for spiritual intimacy with their Rebbe, combined with the practical limitations of rabbinic law, has put a premium on homes around 770—the closer to the Rebbe, and his memory, the better.[59] In the 1970s and 1980s, some Hasidim approached Black homeowners in the area with unsolicited offers to buy their homes, often with cash offers well above market value—and sometimes, critics charged, with threats and harassment against Blacks who wouldn't sell. A 1987 survey found that 60 percent of Black homeowners in south Crown Heights had been approached, at some point, with such an unsolicited offer. Of those who could recall the identity of the potential buyer, 85 percent said they were Jewish or Hasidic. One Black homeowner and survey respondent reported a Hasid offering him a blank check if he would move out within a week.[60] These inflammatory practices angered some local Blacks and Black community leaders, one of whom accused the Lubavitch Hasidim of "Zionist expansion" in a 1978 letter to the *New York Amsterdam News*.[61] Along with the discriminatory practices of real-estate developers like Chevra Machazikei Hashchuna, these aggressive efforts to buy homes near 770 help account for the high percentage of Hasidim on the residential blocks straddling Kingston Avenue. Lubavitchers have thus reshaped their neighborhood according to Jewish law and Hasidic theology—to fit within the boundaries of "the Rebbe's daled amos."

At the same time, however, under the Rebbe's leadership the Lubavitch community has expanded around the world at a truly astounding rate. In the years following World War II, Lubavitch refugees and émigrés formed substantial communities in a number of major cites, including Los Angeles, Montreal, Buenos Aires, London, Paris, Johannesburg, Sydney, and Kfar Chabad (a Tel-Aviv suburb founded by Lubavitchers). And since the 1950s, as an element of their community's outreach campaigns, thousands of Lubavitchers have moved around the world as "emissaries" of the Rebbe—establishing synagogues, schools, and community centers in small and large Jewish communities, in order to promote orthodox Judaism. As a result of this organized and ideologically driven global migration, there are now Lubavitchers (and non-Hasidic Jews affiliated, in varying degrees, with Lubavitch) in at least forty-three of the United States, and in forty-six other countries (including, for example, Thailand, Uzbekistan, and the Democratic Republic of Congo).[62] All told, there are over 100,000 Lubavitchers living in hundreds of communities around the world, forming a sprawling transnational network with Crown Heights at its spiritual and institutional core.[63]

This network instantiates Lubavitch visions of the Rebbe's world leadership, but it stretches the homey intimacy of his "daled amos" to its global breaking point. Like their Afro-Caribbean neighbors and many other contemporary migrants, Lubavitchers in Crown Heights inhabit a transnational or diasporic community, with friends and relatives living in—and shuttling between—points around the globe.[64] They strive to create a bounded "Jewish neighborhood" within walking distance of 770, yet conduct their daily lives in social spaces that transgress the boundaries of neighborhood and nation-state. What happens to "Crown Heights" in the global sprawl of the Lubavitch community? Lubavitchers around the world have addressed this question, in part, by building full-sized replicas of 770 in Kfar Chabad, Los Angeles, Jerusalem, Melbourne, Buenos Aires, and elsewhere.

The flow of Hasidim between Crown Heights and its far-flung diaspora has had significant effects on the social geography of the neighborhood. When the Rebbe was alive—and especially as his community's messianic fervor grew in the 1980s and 1990s—thousands of Hasidim came on pilgrimage to 770 for Shabbos and holidays. Although the Jewish population of Crown Heights was about 12,000 in the early 1990s, there were probably as many as 15,000 Hasidim in the neighborhood each and every weekend, and up to 20,000 during major holidays—staying in the homes of friends, relatives and strangers, in over-crowded yeshiva dormitories, and in a run-down hotel on Crown Street. Since the Rebbe's death, his Hasidim have continued coming to Crown Heights, in lesser numbers, for major holidays, and to visit their Rebbe's grave (which lies next to his predecessor's, in Queens). Hasidim living in the neighborhood greet these visitors with open arms, but some worry that the presence of so many foreign Hasidim

may exacerbate local tensions between Blacks and Jews. One Hasid, a
Brooklyn native in his thirties, complained about the hundreds of young
yeshiva students who come from abroad each year to study at 770. He described the Israelis, in particular, as troublemakers who can't get along
with non-Jews. "Y'know," he said angrily, "they can come here, they can
mess things up, and they can go back home. I gotta live here!"

DESPITE SUCH COMPLAINTS, the hospitality that Hasidim in Crown
Heights show to Jewish pilgrims from around the world stands in stark
contrast to their trenchant criticism of non-Jewish "outsiders" from
around the corner. In Lubavitch eyes, the Rebbe's presence makes Crown
Heights a center of the global Jewish diaspora, while sealing it off from Al
Sharpton's "Christian walk." The boundaries of Crown Heights are thus
painstakingly drawn—and selectively permeable—by spatialized religious
difference.

Multiple Geographies, Multiple Identities

I argued, in the introduction to this chapter, that the equation of space
and identity expressed in the popular image of a "Jewish neighborhood"
must be understood as a contingent product of history and politics, not
taken for granted as a natural fact. The subsequent sections have shown,
I hope, that the Lubavitch community's ties to Crown Heights have been
produced by three rather different, though intersecting, histories: the history of racial segregation in America's cities, which shaped the growth
and decline of a White ethnic neighborhood; the history of urbanization
and real-estate development, which shaped the uneven distribution of
brownstones and tenements; and the history of a global religious movement, shaped by a beloved charismatic leader. These histories are inter-
related in complex ways, and they have coalesced to define a fifty-odd
square-block area of north-central Brooklyn. But they are by no means
identical, and their spaces are not quite coextensive. They don't always
refer to the same "Crown Heights."

Indeed, they don't always refer to the same "Lubavitch community."
Each of these spaces—defined by race, class, and religion—is linked to one
of many strands in the collective identity of the Lubavitch Hasidim, and to

one of many differences between Lubavitchers and their neighbors. As I have argued at length, these identities and differences are inextricably tied together—co-constituted within a broader process of identity formation. Yet they are often, nevertheless, in tension with each other. Like the spaces that help define them, they are not identical or coextensive. The Lubavitch Hasidim nearly always describe themselves as a "Jewish community" living in a "Jewish neighborhood," but in different contexts this "Jewishness" can connote racial Whiteness, middle-class propriety, or religious observance—criteria that sometimes complement yet sometimes complicate each other. Lubavitchers thus inhabit a number of intersecting but conflicting geographies of difference. The diverse spaces of their social lives don't quite coincide to form a single or unified place-based identity.

Yet Lubavitchers, like most people, tend to insist on the seamless unity of their various identities—describing themselves as White middle-class Hasidim, with little or no sense of tension or contradiction. And the popular perception of a "neighborhood" as a clearly defined place on a map, rather than a fluid set of social relations, helps them to do just that. The reification of "Crown Heights"—the substitution of a physical place for the social processes that produced it—allows Lubavitchers to conflate the diverse histories and geographies mapped in this chapter. In lieu of the overlapping spaces I have traced, Lubavitchers imagine a single "neighborhood" defined, for nearly a century, by the presence of Jews living in middle-class homes. Never mind the shifting boundaries of the neighborhood from the 1920s through the present day, or the fact that the Jewish "alrightniks" of the past may have had far more in common with today's Caribbean immigrants than with the Hasidim. When these fragmented spaces and identities are envisioned as expressions of a single, enduring place, they are unified in the physical and conceptual medium of brick and brownstone.

The idea of "Crown Heights," as a place on a map, thus helps Lubavitchers neutralize the tensions between race, class, and religion—producing a complex form of Jewishness through a complex sense of place. The equation of a "place" and a "people" lends a sense of coherence to the geographies of difference that produced them both.

3

Kosher Homes, Racial Boundaries

The Politics of Culinary and Cultural Exchange

As we learned in chapter 2, Crown Heights is a remarkably well integrated neighborhood, in at least some senses of the word. Although part of south Crown Heights is widely perceived as a "Jewish neighborhood," this area is hardly a Jewish enclave. Indeed, the densest area of Jewish settlement in Crown Heights is approximately 60 percent Black. Blacks and Jews live side by side in south Crown Heights, sharing the streets of a community that can't be easily defined in racial or religious terms. Yet perceptions of Jewish spatial difference remain. Blacks and Jews alike tend to see the Lubavitch Hasidim as "a people that dwells apart" (Numbers 23:9) in the midst of a diverse Brooklyn neighborhood. And these perceptions endure for good reason. Despite the geographic integration of Crown Heights, Blacks and Jews in the neighborhood live largely segregated lives. They live side by side—sharing crowded streets and city services—but they spend their days in parallel social worlds, at an intimate distance, with little or no interaction bridging the divide.

As we will see in this chapter, most Lubavitchers are perfectly content with this combination of geographic integration and social segregation. The Torah, as they understand it, commands them to keep their social distance from Gentiles, and most see no reason to forge closer ties—either personal or political—with their Black neighbors. Indeed, many view such relationships with Gentiles as a threat to the religious life of their community. However, many Black Crown Heights residents and local public officials see the social divide between Blacks and Jews as an ethical and political problem that must be overcome if Crown Heights is to avoid further

conflict in the future. Multicultural civic life, as they understand it, requires us all to break down the barriers of racial segregation, and build
mutual understanding across our differences.

For example, the Reverend Clarence Norman, Sr.—a prominent local
pastor and social activist who has worked, intermittently, with Lubavitch
community leaders since the 1960s—expressed his frustration at the segregation of Black and Jewish lives by drawing a distinction between the
reality of "integration" and his goal of "intergration." He described Crown
Heights as a bellwether for the rest of Brooklyn, or perhaps for the United
States as a whole:

> If we can't make integration—*inter*gration—work in Crown Heights,
> it can't work anyplace. Because Crown Heights is the only truly in-
> tegrated neighborhood in Brooklyn. The only one! . . . Here you
> have families, children, old people, young people, living side by
> side. But the tragedy is, we're living side by side—two communities
> living side by side—with no interrelation, no relationship with each
> other, except when there's an explosion. That's the only time we
> talk, or dialogue, is when something happens. . . . I continue now—
> and always will—to try and have dialogue with the Jewish commu-
> nity, to urge our people to work with them, and see what we can do
> to bridge these gaps. But it's difficult, and it's frustrating.

Frustrating, that is, when Blacks and Jews must balance the demands of
racial integration and religious purity.

Indeed, the efforts of Reverend Norman and others to "intergrate"
Crown Heights in ways that go beyond physical co-presence will most
likely continue to be frustrated by the rather different view of "community" held by most Lubavitch Hasidim. One Hasidic woman—a grandmother and activist who participated, with increasing frustration, in many
of the Black-Jewish dialogues organized in the early 1990s—cast doubt on
the basic premises of such efforts. I asked her if Crown Heights residents
would benefit from an "open and honest dialogue," and she replied:

> We don't want it. They don't want it either. There's no point in it.
> Because the issues that we have, that are problems, are not issues
> that are gonna be solved that way. For instance . . . I've heard, at

different things that I've gone to, y'know: "You don't eat in my house" or "You don't say hello to me" or "You won't let my kids play." So what? *So what!?* So what if I don't let my children play with your children? My children and your children don't have anything in common. I don't want them to play. Does that make me a bad person? No. It just makes me a person who doesn't want my children to play with your children. It doesn't make you less, or me more. It just means that we're different. . . . Y'see that's what also makes me upset, that there really is no respect for diversity, that there's always a lot of pressure on the Jews to come across, and be open, and share. But that's not—if we lived in Great Neck [a predominantly White suburban community] we'd be the same way! . . . We're not interested. We're just insular. You don't like my being insular, that's your problem. It's not my problem. And the pressure from the city and from different agencies, to try and overcome that, is insulting!

To this woman, like most Lubavitchers, Reverend Norman's work toward "intergration" is an "insult" to her way of life as a Jew. She answers his call for "dialogue" with a resolute refusal to "come across, and be open, and share." She thus raises a number of fundamental questions about Black-Jewish relations in Crown Heights—and the bewildering diversity of American society. Is it, in fact, a "tragedy" for Blacks and Jews, or others, to live "side by side . . . with no interrelation"? Must we "bridge these gaps" if we wish to build a multicultural society? Must Crown Heights residents eat and play together if they wish to live together in peace? Like many Lubavitch Hasidim—though for somewhat different reasons—I think the answer to these questions may be no.

This chapter will explore these questions in a number of different but overlapping ways. In the following section I will discuss some of the practices, beliefs, and institutions that help maintain a social divide between Blacks and Jews in Crown Heights, by examining Hasidic concerns with the boundaries between public and private—or Black and Jewish—space. In subsequent sections, I will discuss the efforts of government agencies and community organizations to bridge these boundaries through programs for "dialogue" and "cultural exchange." I will explore the relationships between race, religion, and the concept of "culture," then focus on moments when Black and Jewish cultures have been defined by distinctive cuisines, and cultural exchange thus linked to the sharing of food.

Many Americans have come to associate the experience of cultural diversity with the consumption of diverse foods, but this popular equation of culture and food was extremely problematic in Crown Heights, as it placed the political project of cultural exchange in tension with Lubavitchers' adherence to the dietary laws of *kashrus*—laws that make it difficult, according to most Hasidim, for Blacks and Jews to eat together. By examining the differences between "cultural food" and "kosher food," I will ultimately show how the social divide between Blacks and Jews reflects the competing demands of two different systems for the production—and consumption—of collective identity.

The Private Space of the Jewish Home

Day-to-day relationships between Blacks and Jews in Crown Heights tend to be circumscribed by the boundaries of the private home. Simply put, Blacks and Jews rarely enter each other's homes. When they do, it is almost always for some specific purpose—as employer and employee, or customer and client. They almost never socialize. As Roslyn Malamud explained to Anna Deavere Smith: "I don't love my neighbors. I don't know my Black neighbors. There's one lady on President Street—Claire—I adore her. She's my girlfriend's next-door neighbor. I've had a manicure done in her house, and we sit and kibbitz and stuff. But I don't know them. I told you we don't mingle socially because of the difference of food and religion and what have you here."[1] This is the everyday reality behind Reverend Norman's claim that "the tragedy is, we're living side by side—two communities living side by side—with no interrelation, no relationship with each other." And this reality is tied, as I will show in this section, to the place of the "Jewish home" in Lubavitch understandings of Jewishness, as well as the place of the private home in American understandings of urban space.

MOST LUBAVITCH HOMES are marked as "Jewish" in countless overt and subtle ways. The doorposts of all Lubavitch homes, like those of many other Jews, are adorned with small or large *mezuzahs*—decorative cylinders containing scrolls inscribed with verses of the Torah. Passing through the front door, visitors and family members often touch the mezuzah then kiss the hand that did so. Upon entering the home, one is immediately surrounded by images of Jews and signs of Jewishness. The living rooms and dining rooms of most Lubavitch homes are decorated with portraits of the Rebbe, his predecessors, and his beloved wife. These are often accompanied by other Judaic images or family photos, and far less often by secular works of art. In most Lubavitch homes, the dining room is dominated by a long wooden table, to accommodate large families and frequent Shabbos guests. The living and dining room walls are often lined with towering bookshelves filled with Hebrew and Yiddish texts, as well as ritual items like kiddush cups and candlesticks. Taken together, these design elements and consumer goods saturate most Lubavitch homes with Jewishness.

The daily round of family life is also defined, in large part, by Jewishness. Like other orthodox Jews, Lubavitch Hasidim follow religious laws that shape nearly every aspect of their lives. Moreover, the quotidian details of religious observance have profound spiritual significance to many Hasidim. Since the eighteenth century origins of the movement, Hasidism has always sought to infuse the material world with transcendent spirituality—to "sanctify the concrete," in Hasidic terms. In keeping with this fundamental principle, most Lubavitchers place domestic life at the heart of Jewish practice and identity. And in keeping with the gendered division of space and labor that they share, to a large extent, with many other Americans, most view such domestic matters as the distinctive province of Jewish women.[2] For example, in a well-known 1964 letter to a Lubavitch women's organization, the Rebbe wrote:

> As the *Akeres Habayis*—the foundation of the home—the Jewish mother is largely responsible for the perpetuation of the very foundations of Jewish existence: Taharas Mishpocho [the laws of "family purity" governing sexual relations between husbands and wives], Kashrus, the sanctity of Shabbos and Yom Tov [holidays], the education of the children—the whole set up of the home and of all the members of the household, to maintain the continuity of the Jewish way of life and the very existence of the Jewish people.[3]

One Lubavitch woman I know expressed a similar sentiment in more concrete terms, by comparing a cheesecake to the Torah itself. In the spring of 1998 I was a guest in her home for the holiday of Sh'vuos—a holiday commemorating the giving of the Torah at Mount Sinai, which Ashkenazic orthodox Jews mark by reading the Ten Commandments in synagogue then eating a special dairy meal. Our holiday meal was centered around the traditional cheese and potato blintzes, and topped off by the best cherry cheesecake I've ever had. As she served desert, our host told the family and friends gathered around her table: "This is the essence of Sh'vuos. You thought it was about the Aseres HaDibros [the Ten Commandments], but really it's all about the cheesecake." Of course she was speaking with tongue partly in cheek—and her husband was quick to reinterpret her comment as a metaphor for Lubavitch understandings of the relationship between spirituality and materiality. But still, I'm sure she meant what she said—not literally, perhaps, but in some important sense.

Indeed, since the Lubavitcher Rebbe's death in June of 1994, the ritual and spiritual significance of the Lubavitch home has increased, while the significance of the synagogue has in some sense declined. While he was alive, the Rebbe stood at the uncontested center of ritual life in the Lubavitch community. On Shabbos and most holidays, many Lubavitch men and a fair number of women would rush through a cursory meal at home, then flock to the main synagogue at 770 Eastern Parkway to attend the Rebbe's farbrengens. Since the Rebbe's death, however, Shabbos and holiday meals—in the intimate space of the home—have taken precedence over public ritual. Synagogue services are still required of all Hasidic men, and popular with many women, but the center of Lubavitch religious life now lies at the Shabbos table, where Hasidim often sit for hours at a time, talking with family and friends, eating customary foods, drinking a few toasts, singing Hasidic songs, and listening to the words of their Rebbe, as recounted from memory and written texts.

GIVEN THE SIGNIFICANCE of the home in Lubavitch ritual practice and collective identity, it is hardly surprising that many Hasidim draw a sharp distinction between their homes and the streets—between private and public space. This distinction is marked, of course, in the built form of the modern city (and in many other architectural traditions), but it is also elaborated in the cultural imaginations of many Hasidim. The ingrained habit of touching a mezuzah, for example, marks one's passage in and out of a space defined by the Torah scrolls the mezuzah holds. And in the eyes of many Lubavitchers, the Jewishness of the home is mirrored by the Blackness of the surrounding streets. The boundaries of the home—the doorway, the stoop, the windows and walls—thus define performative spaces, in which racial and religious differences are staged and perceived.

The difficulties, both real and imagined, of crossing the divide between private and public are illustrated in one of the funniest monologues in *Fires in the Mirror*. A Hasidic woman told Anna Deavere Smith how the peace and quiet of her Shabbos rest were interrupted late one Saturday afternoon when her baby accidentally turned on the radio, and "all of sudden came blaring out, at full volume, sort of like a half station, of polka music. But with the static—it was blaring, blaring."[4] She was in a bit of a bind, because religious law forbids orthodox Jews from turning electricity on or off (or even touching a radio) during Shabbos, so there were hours to go before her family could get rid of the blaring polka without violating the Torah. After trying unsuccessfully to ignore it, then waiting to see if the baby would turn it off (children under three are allowed to violate the laws of Shabbos, as long as an adult does not tell them to do so), she went outside to find a non-Jew who could turn it off for her. Gentiles are not bound by the laws of Shabbos, but Jews cannot ask them directly to perform tasks that would violate these laws. They must choose to do so of their own free will. And so, as our increasingly frantic Lubavitch matron explained to Smith:

> I went outside and I saw a little boy in the neighborhood, who I didn't know and he didn't know me. Not Jewish. He was Black. And he wasn't wearing a yarmulke—because you could be Jewish if you were Black, but I figured with these two things [that he wasn't]. So I went up to him and I said "My radio is on really loud and I can't turn it off." And he looked at me a little crazy, like "Well?" And I said "I don't know what to do." So he said "Okay." So he followed me into the house and he hears this music so loud and so unpleasant, and then he goes over to the stereo and he says "You see this little button here that says 'on' and 'off'? Push that in, and it turns it off." And I just sort of stood there looking kind of dumb, and

then he went and pushed it. And we just laughed that he probably thought "They say Jewish people are supposed to be really smart, and they don't know how to turn off their radios!"[5]

The Jewish home appears in this wonderfully comic, self-reflexive narrative as an alternate reality, set apart from the streets by more than spatial or social difference. Simply by crossing the threshold between public and private, the Hasidic protagonist and her young accomplice move between two seemingly different worlds—between Saturday and Shabbos, or Blackness and Jewishness. Unlike the streets that surround them, Hasidic homes are structured by the Torah—by a comprehensive legal regime that grants distinctive meanings to everyday objects and classes of people, like radios and babies or Blacks and Jews.

For many Lubavitchers, and other Jews, the social order and spiritual quality of the Jewish home are exemplified, above all, by the dietary laws of kashrus. Indeed, orthodox Jews often equate the "Jewish home" with the "kosher home." As I will discuss in detail below, the laws and customs of kashrus shape nearly every element of Hasidic culinary practice, and touch upon many other aspects of everyday life in a Hasidic home. Kashrus thus distinguishes Lubavitch homes from the surrounding streets as surely as it distinguishes meat from milk. As with the gap between Saturday and Shabbos, the distinctive patterns of family life in a kosher home mark the boundaries between Blacks and Jews in Crown Heights.

Moreover, the laws of kashrus provide many Lubavitchers with a symbolic register for describing other differences between Blacks and Jews. Hasidim often describe the Gentile world as unkosher, or *treif*, in its entirety, and link the opposition between "kosher" and "treif" to a broad opposition between order and disorder in social and moral life. They tend to imagine the streets around their homes as amoral spaces, polluted by the behavior of their Gentile neighbors—by "unkosher" forms of consumption and sexuality. And for many Lubavitchers, these perceptions are crystallized in condemnation of the Labor Day Carnival, an event that fills the streets of Crown Heights with Afro-Caribbean music, sexually suggestive dancing, scantily clad performers, and exuberant public drunkenness. Lubavitchers tend to see Labor Day, of all days, as a day to remain in a kosher home.

In 1997, I spent Labor Day morning at a yeshiva on Eastern Parkway, on the Carnival route itself, where morning prayers were troubled by a sense of impending danger. As we began to hear whistles and crowd noises outside, one Hasid hurried to close every window, then turned up the air-conditioners to drown out the sound. Later, when prayers were over, he went downstairs and locked the front door. I asked him if there had been a problem in previous years with Carnival-goers coming inside, and he warned me: "You've got two million schvartzes, they're all drunk, everyone's got to use the bathroom—anything could happen. You never know."[6] Even with the windows closed and the doors locked, Carnival still disturbs many Lubavitchers. One woman who used to live on Eastern Parkway shuddered when I raised the topic in an interview: "Uch," she exclaimed, "don't even—I don't want to talk about it, because I find it the most repulsive thing in the entire universe, that parade. I despise it so intensely." I asked why, and she responded with sarcasm: "Because I just love to watch people urinating in the street and hopping around half-naked—oh yes, that's really such a pleasant experience. And the music . . . my walls vibrated. It's not normal!" Playing devil's advocate and cultural relativist, I suggested that the music and dancing may be perfectly normal to people from the Caribbean. "Who cares?" she replied, with a distinctive mixture of tolerance and intolerance. "What do I care what they're doing? I just don't want them to do it in front of my house!" Here again, we see Black Crown Heights from the distinctive perspective of a Jewish home.

Hasidic perceptions of their neighbors are not limited, however, to such images of immorality and excess. Lubavitchers often speak fondly of specific Black neighbors with whom they exchange greetings, or perhaps even chat, as they take out the garbage or work in the garden. But these more positive exchanges are also structured by the distinction between private and public space. For example, a Lubavitch community activist recalled a bonding moment with one Black neighbor:

> People are people . . . there's such a thing as the *human* experience, y'know, which all people can relate to on some level. . . . I remember once, standing on my stoop in the middle of winter, freezing, and smoking a cigarette in the morning. And I saw this Black guy walking down the block on his way to the subway—at seven in the

morning, or whatever, y'know. And we just looked at each other, y'know, and thought, "Wow, man." Y'know here we are, both of us, freezing our behinds off, early in the morning, going to work, to make a living. And it was like a human contact, y'know. That's a human experience.

In its own way, this "human experience" represents an important recognition of Black-Jewish commonality—especially coming from a man who tended to stress the unbridgeable difference between Gentiles and Jews, and told me a few minutes later that, "There's no reason to have a closer relation [with our Black neighbors]. If we come into contact with them in our workplace, and like that, okay. But socially, we don't—we are forbidden to socialize with non-Jews." The bond he shared with his neighbor was real and moving, though fleeting. It was typical of the momentary bonds New Yorkers often form with strangers they meet, in passing, on the streets.[7] But it was not the simple "human contact" he took it to be. It did not transcend the social order of today's Crown Heights. Their common humanity could not bridge the divide between private and public space—between a Hasid's stoop and the sidewalk below.

THIS INSULARITY MAY SET Lubavitchers apart from their Black neighbors, but it doesn't necessarily set them apart from "mainstream" American norms. Indeed, Jews in Crown Heights are acting much like other New Yorkers when they avoid their neighbors and retreat into their homes. Lubavitchers know this, and while they often stress the specifically Hasidic reasons they cannot socialize with Gentiles—"the difference of food and religion and what have you"—they also contextualize their distant relationships with their neighbors within broader patterns of urban life.

Nearly every time I asked them about the social divide between Blacks and Jews, my Lubavitch acquaintances asked me in turn: "When you were growing up in Park Slope"—the gentrified neighborhood just across Prospect Park—"did you know any of your neighbors?" Not really, I had to admit—just a few, after living in the neighborhood for years, and many were other Jews my family met at a local synagogue. I grew up playing with other kids on the block, but as in Crown Heights these social ties rarely entered the private sphere. I mentioned to one Hasidic friend that my parents had recently moved to a co-op apartment on Manhattan's Upper West Side: "Do you think they know their neighbors?" she asked. "They walk the same halls, and ride in the elevator, but I bet you they've never been inside their apartments." No, I had to admit, they hadn't.

Like my own home in Park Slope, Lubavitch homes in Crown Heights are shaped by a history of popular discourses, social practices, and architectural forms that have defined the American home as a private sphere for the family—set apart from the workplace, and from the supposed chaos of urban life. In a survey of this history, Tamara Hareven argues that the private home, as most Americans now imagine it, first developed in the early nineteenth century, as a result of the Industrial Revolution. When industrialization removed productive labor from most homes, "the household was recast as the family's private retreat . . . a specialized site for the family's consumption, child-rearing, and private life," and a "utopian retreat from the outside world."[8] Indeed, many of the social trends Hareven locates at the origin of the American private home also characterize life in today's Crown Heights. She argues that "The idealization of the home as a haven was a reaction to the anxiety provoked by rapid urbanization, resulting in the transformation of old neighborhoods and the creation of new ones, the rapid influx of immigrants into urban areas, and the visible concentration of poverty in cities."[9] For today's Hasidim—like the nineteenth-century bourgeoisie—maintaining the boundaries of a "utopian retreat" means living in selective ignorance of one's neighbors.

The resulting patterns of social distance and insularity are hardly unique to Crown Heights. Indeed, the physical co-presence of total strangers—set apart by anomie and alienation, as well as race and class—has long been seen as a hallmark of the modern city. In 1916, for example, the pioneering sociologist Robert Park described the city as a place "where thousands of people live side by side for years without so much as bowing acquaintance," where "The anarchist and the club man, the priest and the Levite, the actor and the missionary who touch elbows on the street still live in totally different worlds."[10] Similarly, the anthropologist Sally Engle Merry described the "neighborhood of strangers" where she conducted fieldwork in the 1970s as "a series of distinct, unconnected social networks occupying the same geographical space."[11] Few Lubavitchers have

read these authors in urban studies, but many voice similar critiques—
and celebrations—of the anonymity of urban life. Once, while discussing
the lack of neighborliness in Crown Heights, a Lubavitch rabbi who was
raised as a secular Jew in the suburbs of Dallas told me of his pleasant surprise when he visited his family in Texas, and was confronted by subur-
banites on lawn-mowers calling out "Hello Rabbi!" as he walked to
synagogue on Shabbos. It's a shame, he said, that no one in Crown Heights
says hello to their neighbors, but when he tried to do so himself—upon his
return from Texas—the first Black guy he greeted asked him for money in
return. He thus described the social divide between Blacks and Jews in
Crown Heights as a product of life in New York: "Y'know," he reminded
me, "Crown Heights isn't a ghetto. It's not so separate."

But Lubavitch homes in Crown Heights aren't quite the same as Reform Jewish homes in Park Slope, or suburban homes outside Dallas. Perhaps above all, Lubavitchers' homes aren't always as "private" as the
homes of other Americans. Or rather, the private space of the Lubavitch
home is not always restricted to family alone. On Shabbos and holidays—
moments at the heart of Hasidic home life and domestic ideology—many
Lubavitchers open their homes to a wide variety of guests. These guests
may come for a meal, or stay the night. They may be family or friends from
around the corner or around the world, yeshiva students and other young
singles without families of their own, or total strangers sent to Crown
Heights by one of the Lubavitch community's outreach programs for non-
orthodox Jews. Of course, there are some Lubavitchers who don't open
their homes to guests, but many will welcome anyone with an interest in
Hasidism or Jewish orthodoxy—anyone, that is, whom they perceive as
Jewish. This ethic of hospitality, and agenda of outreach, opens Lubavitch
homes to the Jewish world, while closing them off to Black Crown Heights.

Nevertheless, the comparisons I've drawn between Lubavitch homes
and other private spaces suggest that Jewish resistance to "intergration"
in Crown Heights is not simply a matter of Hasidic insularity. Rather, it is
tied to far broader trends in American life. The roots of the problem—if
one sees it as such—lie not only in Hasidic interpretations of religious
law and local patterns of Black-Jewish relations, but in the process of industrialization, the architectural form of the private home, the American
ideology of individualism, and the social ecology of urban space. These

interwoven histories shape daily life and community relations in Crown
Heights and throughout the United States.

MY BRIEF DISCUSSION of these broader histories brings us back to the
question of "intergration," but from a somewhat different perspective.
Rather than simply asking why Blacks and Jews in Crown Heights do not
socialize, we must ask instead—or as well—why this fact has become so
politically charged. Why should Crown Heights residents get to know their
neighbors when so few other New Yorkers do? Why have the boundaries of
their homes become such hotly contested spaces? Why does it matter who
eats with whom?

The simple—yet far too simple—answer to these questions lies in the
fact of Black-Jewish difference in Crown Heights, and the history of communal conflict in the neighborhood. Unlike most homes in Park Slope or
Dallas, homes in Crown Heights sit on the front-line of a conflict that has
politicized the boundaries between public and private space. In the wake
of the violence of 1991, Blacks and Jews in Crown Heights cannot simply
coexist in casual neighborliness or benign neglect. Their social relations—
or lack thereof—have taken on broader political significance.

But these seemingly simple truths belie the complexity of Black-Jewish
difference in Crown Heights. What exactly is the broader significance of the
Hasidic community's insularity? Blacks and Jews often disagree, and their
disagreement ultimately stems—like so many other bones of contention in
Crown Heights—from an underlying dispute over the nature of their difference. As I have noted, most Black Crown Heights residents see their Jewish neighbors' insularity as a form of racial segregation, while most
Lubavitchers see it as a commandment of the Torah that has nothing to do
with race. As one Lubavitcher argued above, "if we lived in Great Neck
[with other White people] we'd be the same way!" The distinction is crucial because racial segregation is generally considered a social pathology—
or at least, in Reverend Norman's words, a "tragedy"—while religious
beliefs are generally granted the protection that accompanies a "respect
for diversity."

The space between "integration" and "intergration" is thus crosscut
by conflicting discourses of difference. The social divide between Blacks
and Jews in Crown Heights is linked to an underlying divide between

divergent understandings of collective identity and social reality. In the following sections, I will examine the efforts of some Crown Heights residents to bridge these divides through the concept of "culture" and the sharing of food.

Race, Religion, and Culture

In the years following the violence of 1991, a number of government agencies and community organizations tried to transcend the tensions between race and religion—and bridge the divide between Blacks and Jews—by describing Black-Jewish difference as a matter of "culture." These organizations established forums for Black-Jewish dialogue, and more often than not encouraged participants in these forums to embrace the "cultural diversity" of Crown Heights by sharing their "customs" and "traditions" with their neighbors. "Culture" was invoked, in the wake of violence, as a mediating and depoliticizing term—in between race and religion. Activists and officials hoped that Blacks and Jews would exchange recipes and rituals, rather than accusations of racism and antisemitism. Drawing on the conceptual model of "multiculturalism" that has often shaped state interventions into community relations, as well as educational programs in public schools, universities, and elsewhere, many felt that ritualized discussions of foods, music, holidays, or what-have-you would bridge the divide between Blacks and Jews, and help to ameliorate conflict in Crown Heights.

For example, on September 27, 1991—barely a month after the cessation of violence in Crown Heights—the Brooklyn borough president and the Crown Heights Coalition (a group of community leaders the borough president's office had just organized) invited 150 Black public school students to visit a *sukkah* erected by a Lubavitch community organization. Every fall during the holiday of Sukkot, Lubavitch Hasidim (like many other Jews) build outdoor booths, or sukkahs, where they eat their meals for eight days. Sukkot brings the private sphere of the Jewish home out in public for a week, filling the streets of Crown Heights with the sounds of Hasidic melodies and the smells of kosher foods—and generating no little curiosity among Black Crown Heights residents. The Crown Heights Coalition and the borough president's office saw this as an ideal opportunity to bridge the gap between Blacks and Jews. While visiting the sukkah, the children learned about the ancient harvest festival of Sukkot, and had a snack of soda and cookies. Longtime borough president Howard Golden then exhorted the children—and no doubt their hosts—with words of multiculturalist wisdom. He told them:

> So much of bias and bias-related violence stems from fear and ignorance. We can break down these barriers by learning about the cultural traditions of our neighbors. The joyous holiday of Sukkot—marking a new harvest, a new beginning—is the perfect time for the people of Crown Heights to work towards a unified and peaceful future.[12]

For an anthropologist like myself, it is tempting to imagine that the concept of culture—a concept at the heart of American anthropological thought—might provide a conceptual and political common ground for Crown Heights residents divided by race and religion. But some in the audience did not share Golden's enthusiasm for "learning about the cultural traditions of [their] neighbors." One Lubavitcher I knew, whose family had been attacked in the violence of the previous month, attended the event and was horrified by what she considered kowtowing to antisemitism. Years later she asked me rhetorically, "We should invite them into our sukkahs, and give them snacks so they won't kill us?"

   Though I cannot pass judgment on her anger, given the violence she suffered in August of 1991, I do not intend to endorse this Hasid's bigoted generalizations about "us" and "them." But I do intend to take her concerns seriously, and listen to them with a sympathetic ear. As we have already seen, her reluctance to invite Black schoolchildren into a Jewish ritual space reflects a broad Lubavitch concern with the boundaries of the Jewish home. And as we will see in this section, her resistance to the process of cultural exchange raises far-reaching questions about the concept of culture, and the role of this concept in American politics.

OVER THE PAST few decades, a number of intersecting social movements and trends have placed "culture" close to the heart of American political life. These have included, among others: the African American civil rights struggles of the 1950s and 1960s; the turn toward Afrocentrism in the

Black Power movement of the late 1960s, and the subsequent "ethnic re-vival" among many White Americans; the concurrent emergence of "sec-ond wave" feminism, gay liberation, and similar social movements; the dramatic increase in migration to the United States that followed the 1965 reform of U.S. immigration law; and perhaps above all, the increasing commodification of "culture" and "heritage" throughout the world. As a result of these tumultuous trends, "multiculturalism" has emerged as a dominant model for understanding the diversity of the United States.[13] Minority communities defined by politicized differences are now gener-ally believed to possess autonomous "cultures" that shape their relation-ships with American society. As the anthropologist Verena Stolke has noted in a somewhat different context, "the notions of culture and cul-tural difference, anthropology's classical stock-in-trade, have become ubiquitous in the popular and political language in which [social] con-flicts and realignments are being phrased."[14]

Multiculturalist definitions of culture, like that invoked by former Borough President Golden, differ from anthropological ones in a number of crucial ways. Perhaps above all, most contemporary anthropologists describe "culture" as a fluid and contentious process that transgresses the boundaries of clearly defined communities—as, for example, when di-verse Americans debate the very meaning of the "American culture" they nevertheless somehow share, or diverse peoples throughout the world read radically different meanings into Hollywood films. Multicultural pro-grams, however, all too often gloss over such complexities, and instead take static objects—like distinctive clothing, holidays, or foods—as self-evident signs of membership in homogeneous "cultural" groups. Blacks and Jews in Crown Heights, for example, may be distinguished as easily as Kwanzaa is from Hanukah, dreadlocks from yarmulkes, or jerk chicken from gefilte fish—without making an effort to understand the meanings of Black and Jewish lives.[15]

On a fundamental level, however, both anthropologists and multicul-turalists tend to imagine culture as a universal conceptual language—a theoretical Esperanto—bearing the promise of mutual understanding across all forms of difference. The intellectual and political projects of ethnographic description and cultural exchange each rest on a founda-tional, and rarely questioned, assumption that the heterogeneous practices

and beliefs of diverse communities throughout the world may be subsumed within, or at least translated by, the concept of culture. "Culture"
is thought to be a neutral medium, or Cartesian grid, within which differences of race and religion, nation and ethnicity, gender and sexuality, and
so on and so forth, may all be located and defused. Like the Belizean
beauty pageants described by the anthropologist Richard Wilk, culture
creates a "global system of common difference" that "standard[izes] a vo-
cabulary for describing difference, and provide[s] a syntax for its expression . . . making wildly disparate groups of people intelligible to each
other."[16] Jerk chicken and gefilte fish may be exchanged in a Black-Jewish
dialogue, or compared in the pages of an anthropological text, because
both are considered equivalently "cultural." It is thus hardly surprising
that Borough President Golden and others looked to the "cultural traditions" of Crown Heights residents to bridge the divide between Blacks and
Jews. The concept of culture contains, at its core, a utopian promise of
universal understanding—even between people who won't enter each
other's homes.

   This well-meaning universalism remained relatively uncontested as
long as "culture" remained within the ivory tower, structuring scholarly
accounts of social life, rather than social life itself. The term's global
reach is belied, however, by its mixed reception as a popular concept in
Crown Heights and elsewhere. Over the past thirty or forty years, in diverse communities around the world, growing numbers of people have
begun to describe themselves in terms of "culture."[17] Many others, however, have been reluctant to do so, and their reluctance casts doubt on
the universal promise—or pretensions—of the term.

   For many Black Crown Heights residents, discussions of "culture"
and "tradition" form potent rhetorics of self-making and community-
building—rhetorics closely linked to racial Blackness, though not quite
identical with it. And for Afro-Caribbean immigrants, more specifically,
Caribbean "cultures" define enduring links to ethnic communities and an-
cestral homes. This enthusiastic embrace of the concept of culture seems
to stem, in part, from the specific social history of the African diaspora.
Celebrations of "African culture," for example, help to refute the longstanding charge that Black Americans were stripped of all autonomous
traditions in the course of plantation slavery.[18] But these celebrations also

reflect the ties between contemporary discourses of "culture" and the checkered history of "race." Although the concept of culture was initially developed (by the pioneering anthropologist Franz Boas and his students) as a critique of racial determinism, current discussions of culture, in the United States and elsewhere, often link the concept to essentialist understandings of race and nation.[19] Black Crown Heights residents generally view culture as a matter of "nurture" rather than "nature," and this distinction establishes a fundamental tension between culture and race in definitions of Blackness. But when "culture" is imagined as a static object—when traditional practices and beliefs, or clothing and foods, are thought to be passed unchanged from generation to generation—it may easily take the place of "blood" as a marker of ostensibly immutable difference. This racialized vision of culture is central to the identities of many Black Crown Heights residents.

Few Lubavitchers, however, have embraced such understandings of cultural difference. For many Jews in Crown Heights, "culture" remains a more or less alien way of thinking about social life. Lubavitchers certainly imagine immutable identities and differences, but unlike their neighbors, they construct them in terms that have little to do with culture. In a certain sense of the word, the Lubavitch Hasidim do not have a culture. They don't experience themselves as "having a culture"—they don't objectify their culture—in the same ways many of their neighbors do. Lubavitchers experience themselves as having commandments from God that govern nearly every aspect of their lives, and this is substantially different from "having a culture." Indeed, the concept of culture generally implies a historical perspective on one's practices and beliefs that is fundamentally inimical to the transhistorical truths claimed by many sectarian religious communities. No matter how it may be objectified, culture is nearly always seen as a product of social forces, while the word of God is thought to transcend the constraints and considerations of the social world. One's commandments from God may not, therefore, be "exchanged" with one's neighbors in quite the same way one's culture may be. According to Lubavitchers, Kwanzaa and Hanukah have nothing in common—one was enjoined by God, while the other is merely a "cultural tradition." Dreadlocks and yarmulkes are in no sense equivalent, because the practices and beliefs of God's chosen people are categorically unique.[20] It is thus difficult to

incorporate Lubavitch understandings of Jewishness into a multicultural
or anthropological concept of culture.

"Culture" was not, therefore, the neutral term that activists, officials,
and some Crown Heights residents hoped it would be following the violence of 1991. Hasidic resistance to "cultural exchange" complicated the
process of Black-Jewish dialogue, as will be clear when we examine the
tensions between cultural and kosher food.

Cultural Food, Cultural Exchange

Multicultural programs tend to locate "culture" in a broad range of objects and practices—music and arts, language and literature, holidays and
hairstyles, to name just a few—but they often establish a particularly intimate connection between culture and food. From university dining halls
to national folk-life festivals, street-corner take-out joints to haute cuisine fusion menus, many Americans have come to equate the experience
of cultural diversity with the consumption of diverse foods. With the rise
of multiculturalism and the increasing commodification of culture, people around the world have come to see "cultural foods" as symbolically
charged vessels for collective identity.

Of course, culinary differences have long been used to define social
solidarities and distinctions. It is, as Richard Wilk has noted, "an anthropological truism that food is both substance and symbol," providing "a
particularly potent symbol of personal and group identity."[21] The exchange of food, or commensality, plays a nearly universal role in con-
structing and cementing social relationships. As the pioneering scholar of
religion William Robertson Smith argued in his famous *Lectures on the Religion of the Semites*, "those who eat and drink together are by this very act
tied to one another by a bond of friendship and mutual obligation," while
"those who do not eat together are aliens to one another, without fellowship in religion and without reciprocal social duties."[22]

Contemporary understandings of "cultural food" clearly draw upon
these ancient and widespread patterns. But the static link between food,
culture, and identity seems to be a rather recent development. Wilk notes,
for example, that when he first conducted field research in Belize in the
early 1970s, most people told him there was no such thing as "Belizean

food." But by the early 1990s: "A Belizean cuisine has appeared, first in ex-
patriate Belizean restaurants in New York and Los Angeles, then in the
form of a 'Belizean Dish of the Day' at tourist hotels. Belizean cookbooks
were produced by the Peace Corps, and today almost every eatery [in Be-
lize] which isn't Chinese is advertising 'authentic Belizean food.' "[23] In
twenty short years, writes Wilk, "dishes that were once markers of rural
poverty [have] been converted into national cuisine."[24] According to Wilk,
this new understanding of "authentic Belizean food" has been popularized, in large part, by educated elites self-consciously attempting to construct a national culture. Somewhat similarly, I would argue, American
understandings of "cultural food" have been popularized by authors and
activists working to promote racial harmony and cultural diversity.[25] Yet
even in this class-specific milieu, these newfound culinary identities leave
a funny taste in many mouths. The legal scholar Patricia Williams recalls,
for example, being invited to a book party:

> The book was about pluralism. "Bring an hors d'oeuvre represent-
> ing your ethnic heritage," said the hostess, innocently enough. Her
> request threw me into a panic. *Do I even have an ethnicity?* I won-
> dered. It was like suddenly discovering you might not have a belly
> button. I tell you, I had to go to the dictionary. . . . What are the
> habits, customs and common traits of the social group by which I
> have been guided in life—and how do I cook them?[26]

Williams concludes that out of her various "ethnic heritage[s]," her West
African ancestry has probably had the greatest impact on her life in
America's racialized society—a decision that highlights the ties between
race and culture in American multiculturalism. But unfortunately, she
writes: "I haven't the faintest idea what they do for hors d'oeuvres in West
Africa."

ALTHOUGH SOME BLACK Crown Heights residents undoubtedly share
Williams's reservations, many seem to have embraced the concept of
"cultural food." Black children are taught, from a young age, to link food
and identity by the curricula of local public and private schools. For example, at the Crown Heights Youth Collective (a more or less Afrocentric
private school and influential community organization, led by the activist

and educator Richard Green), an elementary school science class on seeds and germination was organized around a student project to grow collard greens—an archetypically "Black" food in popular imagination. Green began the class by reminding his twenty or thirty African American and Afro-Caribbean students that the collards they were going to grow "had a big part to play in our whole mission as a people," because "back when we were slaves, whenever our great-great-grandmothers had to make a meal they went outside and collected collard greens."

The intersections of race and culture around foods like collards allow Black Crown Heights residents to articulate a range of culinary identities. For example, one Black woman (a member of the Black-Jewish women's group Mothers to Mothers, which I will discuss in detail below) drew on her favorite foods to define herself as a "Black American" rather than an "African American"—an identity she considered too stridently separatist. Although she echoed the rhetoric of popular Afrocentrism when she told me, in an interview, that the heritage of ancient Africa was "in [her] bloodline"—claiming "it's in the bloodstream that we were kings"—she insisted that she does not consider herself "African" in any way: "Because of my culture and the way I'm brought up—I been brought up in America. My culture is American, Southern American. Okay? I cook with pork. I season with fatback. I don't make chicken, 'cause I ain't crazy 'bout no chicken, but I eat ham. I make collard greens, candy yams. All of that's part of my cultural food."[27] This woman thus defines herself as one sort of Black person rather than another by drawing a distinction between her circulatory and digestive systems—a distinction that reflects the tension between race and culture in the construction of Blackness. Yet she nevertheless imagines her "cultural food" as comparable, in many ways, to her African blood. Although she describes her culture as American rather than African, and links it to "the way [one is] brought up" rather than one's "bloodline," she still imagines it, like race, as a collective inheritance from the past—a static object passed down through the generations, from her ancestors in the South to her childhood in Bed-Stuy. Through a process of cultural objectification, or reification, her "cultural food" stands in for this complex history.[28] The legacy of slavery in the American South is collapsed into collard greens and fatback, just as Jewish life in

Eastern Europe may be stuffed (in Yiddish, *gefilte*) into a fish patty topped with horseradish.

This transformation of history into recipe facilitates cultural exchange across communal boundaries by distilling identities into portable and edible objects—locating culture in products rather than processes, on the plate rather than in the kitchen. Just as "an hors d'oeuvre representing [one's] ethnic heritage" may be brought to a book party, these "cultural foods" are made to be shared. Indeed, the process of exchange is often central to their status as "cultural." The historian Donna Gabaccia has shown, for example, that many of the foods associated with American ethnic groups only took on their "ethnic" character through interethnic exchange. Bagels, she writes, "became firmly identified as 'Jewish' only as Jewish bakers began selling them to their multi-ethnic urban neighbors."[29]

A century or so later, in multi-ethnic Crown Heights, my African American and Afro-Caribbean acquaintances often took pride in their knowledge of "Jewish" foods, and expressed pleasant surprise that I had heard of—let alone ate and enjoyed—"Black" foods. An Afro-Caribbean woman I once chatted with in a grocery store almost fell down laughing when I told her I was buying ingredients for a curry—then made me promise I'd come visit her in Trinidad. The Haitian cook at a Lubavitch yeshiva smiled mischievously as he told me that the yeshiva students would soon start speaking Creole, thanks to the (strictly kosher) rice-and-peas he was serving them for lunch every day. In these and countless other cases, Black Crown Heights residents saw "cultural foods" as ingredients in their collective identities, yet took pleasure in sharing both food and identity with others.

Many thus see culinary exchange as an exemplary form of cultural exchange—and an ideal way to foster racial harmony. For example, an African American community activist I spoke to recalled, with giddy nostalgia, the meals he had shared with secular Jewish friends as a child growing up in Brownsville in the 1950s. He described his Jewish friends coming to his home for collard greens, then rattled off a long list of the "Jewish foods" he used to eat in their homes: bagels, gefilte fish, white fish, kugel, pastrami, tongue, matzah-ball soup, and many more I can't remember. His voice rose and his smile widened as he built to a crescendo recalling all these foods—until finally he slapped his knee, burst out laughing, and cried with delight: "A lot of times when I shitted, I shitted Jewish! And they shitted South!"

THIS HEARTFELT VISION of Black-Jewish unity through collards and kugel was at once shared and coopted by the activists and officials who developed programs for Black-Jewish "dialogue" after the violence of August 1991. Borough President Golden's 1991 Sukkot speech marked the beginning of a concerted effort on the part of city agencies, museums, local and national organizations, and a few neighborhood residents, to bridge the divide between Blacks and Jews by teaching Crown Heights residents about "the cultural traditions of [their] neighbors." The programs developed by these organizations took the salutary effects of "cultural exchange" for granted, and often—though not always—linked culture to food.

Over the course of the 1990s Crown Heights residents witnessed, and occasionally even participated in, far more programs for dialogue and exchange than I can describe. Some programs—like the basketball games, discussion groups, and "unity concerts" planned by the community organization Project CURE—had little or nothing to do with food. In some— like the joint Hanukah-Kwanzaa celebrations held for a number of years at the Crown Heights Youth Collective, or the ambitious series of museum exhibits and public programs known as the Crown Heights History Project—food was one topic of discussion and exchange among many. And some—like the community barbecues I will describe below, the "holiday party" held each December by members of Community Board Nine, and the 1998 grand opening of the Crown Heights Community Mediation Center—were centered around the sharing of food, but did not dwell on the links between food, culture, and identity.

These links were often highlighted, however, in the programs and publications of the Crown Heights Coalition. The coalition, as I noted above, was organized by the Brooklyn borough president's office days after the violence of August 1991, and it brought together a broad range of Black and Jewish community leaders—rabbis and pastors, educators and activists, elected officials, community board members, and the directors of local nonprofit organizations. The coalition's programs, however, were largely conceived by staff members and consultants of the borough president's Office of Ethnic Affairs, rather than by Crown Heights residents themselves. And these pluralism professionals often drew on multiculturalist models of cultural food and exchange.[30]

For example, the coalition's committee for "Cultural Awareness and Interaction" published and distributed a glossy booklet for neighborhood youth, entitled *Who Are My Neighbors? Answers to Some Questions about the Many Cultures of Crown Heights.* At the beginning of the chapter on "Culture," the booklet's anonymous authors explain to their young readers that, "Culture is the way that you, your family and friends do things. It includes the foods you eat, the holidays you celebrate and the languages you speak."[31] After discussions of Kwanzaa and a number of religious holidays (which, oddly enough, are not included in the previous chapter on "Worship and Religion"), the authors turn to the links between culture and food. They tell their readers that, "Every Caribbean country has national dishes which form the regular diet of its people," and give examples of "special Caribbean foods" like jerk chicken (from Jamaica), roti (from Trinidad and Guyana), and fried pork (from Haiti). They then ask, with disarming simplicity, "What kinds of things do Jewish people like to eat?" and answer: "Many Jewish people in Crown Heights have family roots in Europe, so foods that originated in Poland, Hungary, Germany, Russia and other Eastern European countries are very popular." They give examples of "Jewish foods" like gefilte fish, chicken soup, and kugel.[32]

This booklet was just one part of a broader educational campaign. Coalition members visited local public schools and yeshivas, making "cultural heritage presentations" and answering students' questions.[33] As I have described, the coalition hosted a group of Black public school students visiting a Lubavitch sukkah. And finally, the coalition itself met on April 15, 1992, for a Passover "Seder of Reconciliation" in which Black and Jewish leaders "shared in the traditional Jewish meal of matzah and bitter herbs to celebrate the story of the Jews fleeing oppression in Egypt."[34] The goal of these programs was to educate Crown Heights residents about the lives and beliefs of next-door neighbors they did not know or understand—in the hope that "cultural exchange" would bridge the divide between Blacks and Jews. As Borough President Golden told the children of Crown

Heights in his preface to *Who Are My Neighbors*, "The more we know about each other, the better we will understand each other. This is our greatest hope for the future."[35] Inspired by this multiculturalist ideal, and guided by the popular equation of culture and food, the coalition hoped that by breaking bread—or matzah—together, Crown Heights residents might learn to live in peace.

There was a fundamental asymmetry, however, in the Crown Heights Coalition's programs for cultural exchange. Black school children visited a sukkah, but Lubavitch yeshiva students never attended, say, a tent revival. The Passover "Seder of Reconciliation" was not followed by an Easter "Feast of Renewal." Black Crown Heights residents were eager, or at least willing, to sample their Jewish neighbors' "cultural food," yet Lubavitchers would not, or could not, do the same. To understand this resistance to culinary and cultural exchange we must examine Lubavitch understandings of kosher—rather than cultural—food.

Kosher Food, Kosher Selves

Lubavitch participation in culinary and cultural exchange is limited by Lubavitchers' careful adherence to the dietary laws and symbolic principles of kashrus, which tend to require boundaries between both foods and communities—milk and meat, Jews and non-Jews. Indeed, many Hasidim in Crown Heights see the requirements of kashrus as a primary explanation of the social distance between the neighborhood's Blacks and Jews. As Roslyn Malamud explained above, "we don't mingle socially because of the difference of food and religion and what have you here."

The social segregation of Jews and Gentiles is, in fact, a longstanding element—and explicit goal—of the laws of kashrus. According to the Torah, kashrus is a crucial dimension of the Israelites' holiness, and the Hebrew word for "holy" means, in essence, "set apart." The laws of kashrus are thus specifically intended to set the Jews apart from their neighbors.[36] The Babylonian Talmud, for example, justifies the rabbinic law against drinking wine that has been handled by a non-Jew as a measure to discourage the sort of intimate relationships that might eventually lead to intermarriage.[37] Some 1,500 years later, a Lubavitch rabbi echoed this analysis when he explained the significance of kashrus to me by invoking

the specter of unkosher sex: "A Yid and Goy," he warned, "if they work together, and go to the same restaurant, then they have a few drinks, and
then who knows?" More broadly, he said, "We shouldn't be in a position
where we might learn from [non-Jews], and then we begin to act like
them. A Yid should act like a Yid, not like a Goy." To maintain this purity,
he emphasized, Jews must observe the laws of kashrus down to the smallest detail.

In an interview with Anna Deavere Smith, Rabbi Shea Hecht—an influential but controversial Lubavitch leader—highlighted the role of
kashrus in maintaining communal boundaries, and touched upon some
of the legal details that limit Black-Jewish commensality in Crown Heights.
Although Hecht played a leading role in many of the Black-Jewish dialogues that followed the violence of 1991, he told Smith bluntly: "My goal
is not to give anybody a message that we [in Crown Heights] plan on working things out by integrating our two things."[38] Like most Hasidim, he argued that integration is impossible given the difference between Blacks
and Jews. "Number one," he said, "we're different, and we think we should
and can be different." He argued that although Blacks and Jews must
grant each other mutual respect as "children of God,"

> That does not mean that I have to invite you to my house for din-
> ner, because I can't go back to your home for dinner, because
> you're not going to give me kosher food! And I said, so, like one
> Black said "I'll bring in kosher food." I said "Eh-eh." We can't use
> your ovens, we can't use your dishes. It's not just a question of buy-
> ing certain food, it's buying the food, preparing it in a certain way.
> We can't use your dishes, we can't use your oven![39]

Indeed, as Hecht notes, Hasidic observance of kashrus is "not just a question of buying certain food." As we will see, the laws of kashrus constitute
a complex and far-reaching code governing dishes, ovens, and many other
aspects of orthodox Jewish life.

THE HEBREW BIBLE establishes the foundations of kashrus in two main
ways. First, a broad range of animals are described, in Leviticus 11 and
elsewhere, as "abominations" unfit for Israelite consumption. Best known
among these forbidden foods are all varieties of pork and shellfish.[40] And

second, the Israelites are told, in Exodus 23:19 and elsewhere, not to "boil a kid [a young goat] in its mother's milk." This prohibition was later interpreted by the Talmudic sages to outlaw the mixing of milk (and other dairy products) with meat (a category that includes cattle and poultry but not fish), and to require the use of separate utensils for dairy and meat meals. A kosher kitchen thus has two sets of dishes, cutlery, pots, pans, Tupperware, tablecloths, and most everything else—and four sets of many items, including milk and meat utensils for the holiday of Passover, during which orthodox Jews may not eat leavened bread. Sinks, appliances, refrigerator shelves, and counter spaces must be segregated by meat and dairy, and some kosher kitchens have two of each of these big-ticket items. Any lapse in kashrus—a dairy plate rinsed in the meat sink, for example—may require destruction of the items involved, or a potentially expensive process of cleaning and purification. Moreover, as I have noted, the laws of kashrus extend far beyond the kitchen, shaping a "kosher home" in countless subtle ways. Hasidic children, for example, are not allowed to play with representations of nonkosher animals, like bears, so a Lubavitch toddler's room is often home to a surprising number of bright yellow stuffed chickens.

These laws also govern the entire process of food production—from slaughterhouse to supermarket, farm and factory to corner deli. The Talmudic sages and later rabbinic authorities established detailed procedures for the slaughter of kosher animals, and defined a number of physical imperfections that make otherwise kosher animals unkosher, or treif (literally, "torn"). They established strict requirements for foods deemed particularly holy, and thus particularly subject to impurity. Milk, for example, must be produced under the supervision of an orthodox Jew. And wine, as I have noted, may not be handled by a non-Jew—unless it is first boiled, which reduces its sanctity. Most orthodox Jews do not keep such stringent standards of kashrus, but Lubavitchers and other Hasidim do. While most kosher foods are available in any supermarket (if one knows how to spot a reputable kosher certification), a number of specialized companies supply Hasidim with strictly kosher products like supervised milk, known as *chalav Yisroel* (literally, "Jewish milk"). Finally, most Hasidic communities have their own semi-independent industries for ritual slaughter, or *shchita*, to produce kosher meats according to their own distinctive standards. Many Lubavitchers, though not all, only eat "Lubav-itcher shchita" meats—just as other Hasidim eat their own communities' meats—and therefore cannot eat meat meals in the homes of most other orthodox Jews.

This intricate web of law and custom lies behind Rabbi Hecht's skep-ticism of his neighbor's offer to "bring in kosher food." Indeed, with the (sometimes crucial) exception of packaged foods bearing kosher certifica-tions, Lubavitchers simply cannot eat in their Black neighbors' homes—or most anywhere else outside of their community. But the significance of kashrus in Hasidic life is by no means limited to these practical consider-ations. For most Hasidim, as I have noted, the everyday practice of cook-ing and eating is tied to broader concerns with personal and communal purity.

ACCORDING TO HASIDIM the social boundaries established by kashrus help secure the very essence of Jewishness, because kosher food creates kosher, observant Jews, while nonkosher food creates nonkosher, apos-tate Jews. A Lubavitch rabbi summed up this point during an informal kashrus course for newly orthodox Jews by telling me, simply, "We are what we eat." This seeming cliché is, in fact, tied to fundamental princi-ples of Lubavitch theology and social thought. And as we will see, these re-ligious principles tie the laws of kashrus to the construction of Jewishness, in a way that parallels—yet diverges from—the ties between food and "culture" outlined above.

My kashrus course was arranged, in February of 1997, by the Kashrus Committee of the Lubavitch Women's Organization, which makes such classes available to newly orthodox Jews in Crown Heights. Their goal is to teach formerly secular Jews the day-to-day basics of kashrus—the kinds of things they never learned by osmosis while growing up in a kosher home. The rabbi who taught the course thus focused, above all, on practical is-sues like spotting reputable kosher certifications, setting up a kosher kitchen, and so on. But before we got to these details, he made some gen-eral points about the significance of kashrus. He began his presentation by reminding me, "You know the famous saying, of course: 'We are what we eat.' So the same thing goes with food, and the same thing especially with kosher food."

He stressed the significance of this fact by telling me what he described as "a famous story." He recounted how some years ago, a non-Hasidic orthodox family called on a prominent Lubavitch rabbi, Nissan Mangel, to ask his help with their son, who was getting involved with Jews for Jesus. Rabbi Mangel agreed to study Torah with the boy, in order to debunk the Christian literature he'd been reading. He asked the boy to come to his house in Crown Heights, and told him he could bring all the Christian books he wanted—though he insisted he would not read these books himself. After a year of study, I was told, the boy "was finally convinced that whatever he was involved in was full of baloney. And they had made up a deal that if he is convinced that this is full of baloney, he's gonna take every single book, every single pamphlet, and burn it. The whole suitcase full, everything. So that's what he did. He went home—they lived in an apartment building—and he took everything he had, and he went to the incinerator, and he threw everything down there. But while he was doing it, he was crying hysterically." Unfortunately, according to my narrator, the young boy was irresistibly drawn to heresy. Although "he under[stood] logically that . . . the Torah is the true way of life," he still had an inexplicable "feeling" for Christianity.

At this point, Rabbi Mangel decided to write to the Lubavitcher Rebbe, to ask for his advice and blessing. The Rebbe responded that the boy's family should be careful in their observance of kashrus, and though Rabbi Mangel was reluctant to broach the topic with the boy's father—whom he knew to keep kosher "one thousand percent"—he felt compelled to convey the Rebbe's message. When he told the boy's father what the Rebbe had said, the father immediately started to cry. He confessed that although his family still kept kosher in every other way, not long before his son's troubles began they had started drinking regular milk instead of chalav Yisroel—buying it at a local deli, instead of "schlepping from Flatbush to Boro Park to buy a bottle of milk." Following this revelation, however, his family immediately returned to drinking chalav Yisroel, and his son soon returned to yeshiva. As my narrator reassured me, "The whole story straightened out."[41]

This narrative establishes a series of symbolic links between the laws of kashrus and other aspects of Jewish life—in Rabbi Mangel's insistence that his wayward student come to his (kosher) home; in the rabbi's reluctance to consume Christian literature that is "full of baloney" (and surely not kosher baloney); and in the boy's promise to throw this literature in a fire (a ritual act that resonates with the central role of flame in koshering tainted kitchen utensils). But beyond such symbolic associations, the story also envisions a concrete, causal link between kosher food and Jewish observance. An orthodox family stops drinking chalav Yisroel, and their son strays from the Torah. By drinking unkosher milk, he sinks into unkosher Jewishness. He never makes a conscious choice to believe in Jesus, but is forced into this belief inexorably, like an addict, by the unkosher milk he's been drinking.

When the protagonist of the story, Rabbi Mangel, told his own version in a lecture to a class of newly orthodox yeshiva students (later marketed by the yeshiva on a cassette tape called "You Are What You Eat"), he situated the plight of the wayward yeshiva boy in a far broader historical and theological account of the significance of kashrus. Mangel began by recounting a dramatic decline in Torah observance over the past two hundred years. He argued that this shift in Jewish practice and identity, which academic historians often attribute to "modernity," has in fact been caused by unkosher food. He explained that despite their intellectual justifications, the real reason contemporary secular Jews fail to keep the laws of the Torah is that their souls have been "defiled" by unkosher food:

> The only reason so many Yidn [Jews] now don't accept Torah and mitzvahs [commandments]—it's not because they're so sophisticated, they're so intellectually enlightened. They say "Why should we be like old fashioned people 500 years ago?" But the truth is the only reason they don't accept it is because their neshoma [soul] became contaminated with trefa [unkosher] food.

Even the seemingly minor transgression of drinking what Mangel describes as "goyishe [non-Jewish] milk" can have disastrous consequences: "You can't imagine how many Jews, precisely for this reason, either they marry shiksas [non-Jewish women], or become dope addicts, or become—all of the mishegas [craziness] they went through in the 60s and 70s—precisely for this reason: because they did not use chalav Yisroel!"

In sum, according to Mangel and other Lubavitchers, nonkosher food is a "virus" that "contaminates" the Jewish soul—and thus the entire Jewish people. But this threat of pollution is balanced by the promise of purity. Kosher food, by contrast, helps Jews fulfill their God-given mission as a chosen people. As the editor of a popular kashrus manual for newly orthodox Jews reminds her readers, "the kosher diet . . . is designed to bring refinement and purification to the Jewish people. . . . [W]hen one eats kosher food one's receptivity to G-dliness is enhanced."[42] Indeed, she quotes from the great sage Rashi to promise her readers that "meticulous care in kashrus will bring redemption in our time."[43]

This link between kashrus and Jewish peoplehood rests, in part, on a central theme of Hasidic thought: the distinctively Hasidic emphasis on the spiritual dimensions of everyday life, on the ability of average Jews to commune with God through food and drink, work and leisure, sex and social life. Like much of Hasidic thought, this "sanctification of the concrete" builds on the kabbalistic theology of Isaac Luria, a famous sixteenth-century mystic. In Lurianic cosmology, creation is shot through with "sparks" of divine energy, exiled from their source and trapped in the "shells" of material things by a cataclysmic shattering of the cosmic order that followed its creation. According to both Lurianic and Hasidic thought, the God-given purpose of the Jewish people—the essence of their chosenness, and their unique contribution to the messianic re-demption of the cosmos—is to liberate these sparks of godliness from the physical world and return them to God. Jews may accomplish this task by using material objects for spiritual purposes, according to the standards of religious law—for example, by slaughtering a cow in a kosher way, keeping its flesh separate from dairy products, saying the proper blessing before consuming it, then using its sustenance for prayer and Torah study.[44]

However, these sparks of divine energy enter the material world in different ways, and they don't all maintain the purity of their source. Kosher and nonkosher foods—like Jews and non-Jews, for that matter—are all created and sustained by the energy of God, but the divine energy of kosher foods enters the world from an elevated spiritual realm, close to the essence of God, while the divine energy of nonkosher foods enters the world from an impure realm, far from its ultimate source. According to

Hasidim, the body absorbs these pure and impure energies when one eats. As Rabbi Mangel explains:

> It's not the potato itself, or the chicken itself ... but the Word of God, which comes from the mouth of the Abeshter [The One Above]. This divine energy, this nitzus eloki [godly spark], this spark is in the food. And this food—this divine energy—is what can influence a person. . . . When a person eats, every organ takes out the particular things which the body needs. But what does the neshoma [soul] need? It doesn't take out Vitamin C, or Vitamin B, or Vitamin E, or the carbohydrates and proteins and so on—it takes out this nitzus eloki. Just like the physical body takes out from food the chemical ingredients the body needs, the neshoma takes out the spiritual ingredients in the food.

The impure energy found in nonkosher food thus led to "all of the mishegas [secular Jews] went through in the 60s and 70s," while the godly energy found in kosher food will help orthodox Jews "bring redemption in our time."

THESE THREATS AND PROMISES demonstrate the widespread Hasidic belief in the power of food to produce and sustain—or pollute and undermine—Jewish identity and community. In Lubavitch eyes, nothing a Jew eats or does can make them a non-Jew, but the food one eats can still influence the nature of one's Jewishness in far-reaching ways. There are a number of important parallels between this Hasidic understanding of kosher food and Black Crown Heights residents' understandings of cultural food. The claim, quoted above, that collard greens "had a big part to play in our whole mission as [Black] people" resonates with the claim that kosher food "is designed to bring refinement and purification to the Jewish people." Much as fat-back and candied yams mark the difference between a "Black American" and an "African American," chalav Yisroel marks the difference between a yeshiva student and a Jew for Jesus. As signs and performances of authenticity, both cultural and kosher foods help construct collective identities. They may not make a Black person White, or turn a Jew into a Gentile, but they do shape one's relationship to Blackness or Jewishness. In each case, "We are what we eat."

But these parallel links between food and identity function in substantially different ways. For Lubavitch Hasidim and other orthodox Jews, the "Jewishness" of kosher foods generally inheres in the preparation and consumption of the food according to religious law, not in the food itself. Again, as Shea Hecht noted, "It's not just a question of buying certain food, it's buying the food [and] preparing it in a certain way." There are a number of foods that are inherently nonkosher and non-Jewish, but no food is inherently kosher or Jewish. A hamburger, or jerk chicken, or Peking duck, can all provide the godly energy needed to sustain a Hasid's Jewish soul if the meat is slaughtered, prepared, blessed, and consumed appropriately. And a bowl of cholent (a "traditional" and highly symbolic stew eaten on the Sabbath) can pollute one's Jewish soul if accompanied by a glass of milk.

By contrast, according to many Black Crown Heights residents—as well as the government agencies and community organizations promoting "cultural exchange" in Crown Heights in the 1990s—foods like jerk chicken and cholent crystallize and inculcate collective identities, more or less regardless of how they are prepared and consumed. Distinctive techniques and ingredients are no doubt required to make a "Haitian" fried plantain, for example; but once it is produced, this "Haitianness" is independent of the codes that governed its production. A kosher chicken soup, however, will most likely become tainted—and lose its "Jewishness"—if it is removed from a kosher home, or served with Haitian plantains. Kosher food, in short, is inextricably tied to social practices and institutional structures that cultural food is designed to transcend.

The Blackness and Jewishness of cultural and kosher foods are thus produced by two comparable, yet divergent, systems of objectification—two different systems for the production and consumption of identity. In each case, elements of everyday life are transformed into symbols of collective identity. But cultural foods are created when specific culinary *objects* are taken to represent the histories that produced them and the people who eat them, while kosher foods are created when specific culinary *processes* are taken to represent the authority of religious law and the cosmological significance of God's chosen people. As the preface to the kashrus manual quoted above reminds its newly orthodox readers, a Hasidic Jew must not confuse "the true meaning of eating Jewishly" with "nostalgic images of chicken soup with matzah balls, or blintzes with sour cream."[45] The difference is crucial in today's Crown Heights, because the definition of "cultural food" in terms of portable, edible objects facilitates culinary and cultural exchange across communal boundaries, while the definition of "kosher food" in terms of an intricate web of standards and practices inhibits just such exchange.

Blacks and Jews at Barbecues

Yet as I have noted, over the course of the 1990s a number of Crown Heights residents worked to overcome these social and conceptual differences by sharing meals of various kinds. In addition to one-time programs like those hosted by the Crown Heights Coalition, two annual events have brought Blacks and Jews together for meals: a large picnic sponsored by a local police precinct, and a more intimate backyard barbecue organized by the Black-Jewish women's group Mothers to Mothers.

These meals complicated, though never erased, the lines between Black and Jewish communities and cuisines. Their organizers worked to negotiate the tensions between kashrus and culture, and these negotiations often revealed unexpected complexities in each culinary system. The barbecues demonstrated, for example, the role of "American" food in bridging the gap between Blacks and Jews, and the role of kashrus in defining distinctions among different types of Jews.

EVERY SUMMER SINCE 1995, the 71st Precinct has sponsored the "Crown Heights Family Day" picnic on a Sunday afternoon in June. This well-funded and highly publicized event usually brings thousands of neighborhood residents out to a local park for carnival rides and information booths, speeches by politicians and community leaders, a police officer DJ spinning pop hits and disco classics, and loads of free food. Lubavitchers are always well represented in proportion to their share of the local population, but the crowd is nevertheless mostly Black, and the entertainment generally reflects this demographic imbalance. Although Hasidic children love face paints and balloons as much as anyone, the Electric Slide just doesn't appeal to most Hasidic teens and adults. Religious laws against mixed-gender dancing make this a thoroughly unkosher activity.

When it comes to the food, however, the picnic organizers strive to be as inclusive as possible, guaranteeing kosher meals for all Hasidim who attend. Nonkosher hot dogs and hamburgers are donated each year by a range of local merchants, while kosher hot dogs are always supplied by a Hasidic caterer who only uses "Lubavitcher shchita" meats. When I first attended the picnic in 1998, kosher juices and teas were provided by Snapple, and the deserts included both ice cream pops and flavored ices—for Hasidim who could not eat ice cream with hot dogs. Black and Jewish children could thus share their love of junk food, while avoiding the "cultural foods" of their neighbors.

Yet despite the good times—and ketchup stains—shared by all, the Family Day picnic does not really address the thorny issue of culinary exchange between Blacks and Jews in Crown Heights. The picnic is held in a public park, and thus skirts the troublesome boundaries of Crown Heights residents' homes, allowing Blacks and Jews to share a festive occasion on neutral ground, with no need to enter anyone else's space. This is, in fact, precisely the point. The result, however, is an event that stands outside of—and does not really impact—the familiar patterns of neighborhood life. Crown Heights residents need only come to the park and bring their appetites. They need not make space for their neighbors in their everyday lives, or contribute anything toward the meal. By avoiding both cultural foods and private homes, the Family Day picnic allows Crown Heights residents to meet, once a year, on the shared terrain of "American" food.

Moreover, when it comes time to cook their state-sponsored meal, Blacks and Jews remain segregated in their own outdoor kitchens. The kosher foods and utensils must not come in contact with nonkosher ones, so the picnic organizers set up two separate areas for cooking and serving. In 1998, the kosher hot dogs were grilled a few at a time on inexpensive disposable grills (see figure 11), while the nonkosher ones were grilled en mass on huge grills made from bisected steel drums—like those often used to make Caribbean foods for the Labor Day Carnival and other festive occasions (see figure 12). While the Hasidim struggled to light their coals in the rain, their neighbors were engulfed in a haze of excitement and greasy smoke. This arrangement worked well enough in 1998, when the turn-out was low thanks to the rain. In 1999, however, tempers flared

FIGURE 11 The kosher barbecue grills at the 1998 Crown Heights Family Day Picnic.
(Photo by the author.)

and angry words were exchanged when the Hasidic cooks—running out of
food, because they hadn't anticipated such a large crowd—announced
that the kosher hot dogs were for Jews alone.

This culinary segregation is a reasonable response to a practical concern, but it nevertheless shows that the Family Day picnic fails to bridge

FIGURE 12 The nonkosher barbecue grills at the 1998 Crown Heights Family Day Picnic. (Photo by the author.)

the social divide between Blacks and Jews in Crown Heights. By serving state-sponsored hot dogs cooked on segregated grills, the picnic offers Crown Heights residents separate meals in close proximity—just as Blacks and Jews live separate lives in close proximity the rest of the year. A truly shared meal requires cooperative planning, as we will see by examining the backyard barbecues organized by Mothers to Mothers in the 1990s.

MOTHERS TO MOTHERS was founded in 1992 by a Lubavitch woman named Henna White and an Afro-Caribbean woman named Jean Griffith Sandiford, each of whom saw the group as a response to the violence of 1991.[46] Over the next four or five years, the group grew to include some fifteen to twenty Black and Jewish women. Most of the women, though not all, lived in or near Crown Heights, and most of the Jews, though not all, were Lubavitch Hasidim.

The Mothers (as they often called themselves, though they weren't all mothers) began meeting each month and talking—about religion, politics, and above all family life. They met, at first, in the neutral space of a conference room at the Brooklyn district attorney's office (where Henna White works). And they continued meeting, on and off, for a decade, until their membership flagged in 2002. They invited guest speakers to facilitate discussion on topics ranging from the violence of August 1991 to child welfare policy. But one African American member told me the conversations that had the greatest impact on her were:

> The ones where we got to share our cultures, and the [Jewish] women sharing their culture, which is wrapped around their religion. . . . Y'know, like I was telling them about when I was a little girl, and I had to chop and pick cotton—and they probably had never heard of cotton! And with them just sharing their culture and religion, that helped me understand some things [about the Hasidic community]. And just being around, y'know, different people.

Over time, personal friendships took the place of formal dialogue. And in the summer of 1993, after a year and a half spent building trust, the Mothers decided to hold the first of their annual barbecues. Given the common symbolic association of women with domestic life—and the Mothers' own claims that their shared experiences as women helped them transcend the divide between Blacks and Jews—they considered it uniquely meaningful and appropriate to share a meal.

Like the Family Day Picnic, the Mothers to Mothers barbecue generally avoided Black and Jewish "cultural foods." Rather than serving jerk chicken or pickled herring, they met on the shared terrain of hamburgers and potato chips. But unlike the police officers planning a picnic for thousands, the Mothers went out of their way to make sure every member could contribute to the meal. The barbecue was usually hosted by a non-Hasidic orthodox woman living in a suburban-style neighborhood south of Crown Heights (where homes tend to have big backyards) but everyone who came brought food if they wanted to. And this, of course, raised questions of kashrus. I asked Henna White how the Mothers overcame these concerns, which so many Hasidim consider impossible, and she replied: "Well it wasn't very complicated . . . the [Black] women had to learn about kashrus. So everyone had to buy potato chips with a [kosher certification] on it, and nobody had a problem with it." Another Hasidic member, who coordinated the barbecue for a number of years, told me there was never a problem with kashrus. She described the planning process: "I called up—I think Ann [an African American member] was bringing pickles this year—and she asked me 'Ben's Pickles [a brand] OK? I think it's got [a kosher certification].' And y'know, like, everybody knows already! We've learned about each other's cultures, and everybody respects it. Nobody—there was not one person, and we've been doing this a number of years—has brought anything that they shouldn't have." I asked this woman what she thought when other Lubavitchers explain Black-Jewish tensions by claiming that "We can't eat together," and she replied simply, "That's garbage."

Indeed, at the barbecue I attended in July of 1998, a dozen or so Black and Jewish women sat comfortably in a Brooklyn backyard—chatting and laughing while enjoying hot dogs and hamburgers, potato and macaroni salads, vegetables, tabouli, pickles, chips, soda, and beer. But the culinary divide between Blacks and Jews still lingered beneath the surface of this bucolic scene, shaping the barbecue menu in subtle but significant ways. Take, for example, the meat: As I have noted, many Lubavitchers only eat meats slaughtered by their community's distinctive standards. But these meats aren't readily available outside of Crown Heights, so some summers the Mothers relied instead on a more widely available brand that isn't officially "Lubavitcher shchita," but is certified kosher by a well-known Lubavitcher. Few Hasidim would trust a non-Jewish consumer, no matter how well intentioned, to make such subtle distinctions among different kosher meats, so a Jewish member of Mothers to Mothers always brought the hamburgers and hot dogs for the barbecue—the symbolic equivalent of bringing the turkey on Thanksgiving, as opposed to, say, the cranberry sauce.[47] As in every meal shared by Blacks and Jews in Crown Heights, culinary authority and decision making ultimately had to rest with the Jews. Blacks had no choice but to accept the requirements of kashrus, and learn how to buy the right pickles and chips.

Most of the Black women in Mothers to Mothers were more than happy to do just this, out of respect for their Hasidic friends' dietary requirements—and perhaps for their "culture." But some weren't entirely thrilled with the arrangement. The same woman who told me, above, that her "cultural food" includes "pork" and "fat-back" said she understood, from her reading of scripture, why the Jews in Mothers to Mothers refused to eat these nonkosher foods, but she was nevertheless frustrated by what she saw as their stubbornness in planning the barbecue. "It's all kosher food," she complained, "so in a sense you feel that—well it's a one-way street when it comes to food."

THIS WAS NOT, however, the only culinary divide that shaped the Mothers to Mothers barbecue. Though the Black women in the group were willing—if not always happy—to abide by the standards of kashrus, the Jewish women didn't always agree just what those standards were. Indeed, Henna White explained that the hardest part of planning the barbecue, in the first few years, was negotiating the differences among Jews who keep kosher in different ways. These differences were actually more difficult to resolve than the culinary divide between Blacks and Jews because, as White told me, "There's more of a sensitivity when someone says 'Oh, I don't eat that meat' and the other one says 'I do.' "

This sensitivity reflects a complex history of intra-Jewish kashrus politics. While the laws of kashrus have often marked boundaries between Jews and Gentiles, differing interpretations of those laws have just as often marked boundaries among Jews. The slaughter of kosher meat, in particular, has long divided Jewish orthodoxy—distinguishing Hasidim from other orthodox Jews, setting Hasidic communities apart from each other, and occasionally marking factional divides within these communities. In 1787, for example, a rabbinic court in White Russia (where the Lubavitch community was founded) passed a decree against all meats prepared by Hasidic slaughterers, who agreed with the rabbinic authorities on most aspects of kosher slaughter but used a different sort of blade. The court declared in no uncertain terms: "What their slaughterers kill may not be eaten, it is carrion. The dishes they use are polluted and forbidden."[48] And in 1997, when a faction of Lubavitch community leaders opposed to the rabbinic court of Crown Heights announced plans to market a competing variety of Lubavitcher shchita meats (plans that were never fulfilled, as far as I know), a leading supporter of the rabbinic court received a rousing round of applause at a public meeting in 770 when he told his opponents: "There are enough McDonald's here, you don't need shchita! Any meat you bring into this neighborhood is treif."

Mothers to Mothers steered clear of such debates by serving Lubavitcher shchita or a close equivalent. (Fortunately for them there were not, in fact, two factional versions of Lubavitcher shchita.) But this wasn't always enough to guarantee Hasidic participation in the annual barbecue. Kashrus is not, as we've learned, "just a question of buying certain food," and though a backyard barbecue served on disposable plates avoids a number of thorny kashrus concerns, many Hasidim still won't eat in (or behind) a house they consider treif. One long-time member of Mothers to Mothers told me, with some regret and discomfort, that she'd never been to the annual barbecue because she could not eat in the home where it was held. The problem, she said, was that the barbecue's hosts were non-Hasidic orthodox Jews—observant enough to keep what they consider a kosher home, but not nearly enough to meet her own kashrus standards. If, she explained, the barbecue were held at a non-Jewish home, she would be happy to go, hang out and chat, and decline any food. But at the home of another orthodox Jew her reluctance to eat would be a terrible insult. And so, she said, she had never attended the barbecue—thanks to the culinary differences among orthodox Jews, rather than those dividing Blacks and Jews.

This Hasid was hardly alone, however, in her kashrus concerns about fellow Jews. In July of 1998, as the other members of Mothers to Mothers sat chatting at the barbecue she could not attend, their conversation turned to a similar problem they had faced together not long before. In the fall of 1997, a number of the Mothers traveled to Washington, D.C., to receive a "Heroes Against Hate" award from the Anti-Defamation League, a nationally known Jewish organization devoted to fighting antisemitism and racism. The award was presented at a banquet, hosted by the ADL at the prestigious Kennedy Center. But the event was "a disaster," in one Mother's estimation, because the ADL served them nonkosher food. I heard a number of slightly different narratives of this event, so I can't be sure exactly what happened, but it seems that the Mothers attending the banquet were already seated and about to eat, when a waiter—or an intern, or a low-level staff member—snuck up and told them, just in time, that the food wasn't kosher, or at least not kosher enough. He offered to get them kosher take-out, which they ate by themselves in a separate room before returning to attend the rest of the ceremony.

The Black and Jewish women of Mothers to Mothers—dressed to the nines to be honored at the Kennedy Center for their "heroic" effort to bridge the divide between their communities—thus sat together sharing kosher take-out, while a Jewish organization held a nonkosher banquet in the next room. This moment complicates a number of widely shared assumptions about the role of kashrus in shaping communal boundaries. The laws of kashrus undoubtedly contribute to the social divide between Lubavitchers and their neighbors, but the meals I've described show that the effects of kashrus cannot be reduced to the popular wisdom that Blacks and Jews cannot socialize "because of the difference of food and religion and what have you."

THESE INTRA-JEWISH KASHRUS POLITICS return us, by a somewhat circuitous route, to the fundamental differences between kosher and cultural food. While the multiculturalist concept of culture assumes a fairly simple equation between "cultural foods" and the communities who eat them—taking collards and kugel, or fat-back and chicken soup, as symbols of Blackness and Jewishness as such—the details of kashrus allow for subtle distinctions, and acrimonious debate, between and among different groups of Jews. Each culinary system constructs identities and boundaries, but "culture" generally does so by objectifying ostensibly homogeneous communities, while kashrus generally does so by legislating an endless proliferation of differences.

We thus see, once again, that the social divide between Blacks and Jews reflects an underlying divide between Crown Heights residents' understandings of self and other, community and society. The problem in Crown Heights—if one sees it as such—is not simply that Blacks and Jews rarely eat together, socialize, or visit each other's homes. The problem is that Crown Heights residents interpret these facts in substantially different ways.

Intergration and Pollution, Multiplicity and Reduction

I have explored a number of overlapping topics in this chapter—from the spatial boundaries of Lubavitch homes to the multiculturalist concept of culture, from the culinary habits of Crown Heights residents to the activism of state agencies and community organizations. But these wide-ranging discussions have all revolved around one central fact: most Lubavitchers are perfectly happy to have no social contact with their non-Jewish neighbors, while many Black Crown Heights residents and elected officials see such contact as an essential step toward building a harmonious and peaceful community.

This difference of perspective ultimately reflects the tensions among a number of different discourses of Black-Jewish difference. Reverend Norman calls for "intergration" to combat the evils of racial segregation, but Lubavitchers refuse to "be open, and share" because the Gentile world threatens religious pollution. Borough President Golden works to "break down these barriers" by teaching Crown Heights residents about the "cultural traditions of [their] neighbors," but his efforts are thwarted by Lubavitch reluctance to have a "culture" or eat "cultural foods." Race, religion, and culture thus struggle to account for the social divide between Blacks and Jews.

Although they imply different understandings of Crown Heights politics, these discourses of difference share at least one thing in common: each marks an effort to reduce the multiplicity of Black-Jewish difference to a single, uncontested axis of difference. The advocates of each tend to claim—or simply assume—the conceptual and political priority of their own understanding of collective identity. They invoke "race," "religion," and "culture" as totalizing metalanguages, in Evelyn Brooks Higginbotham's terms, capable of accounting for—or subsuming—all other forms of difference.[49] Reverend Norman and other Black activists place race over religion when they call for "intergration" in Crown Heights without acknowledging the real constraints Hasidic interpretations of rabbinic law put on relationships between Jews and Gentiles. At the same time, however, Lubavitch Hasidim place religion over race when they claim that their insularity is nothing more than a matter of rabbinic law. It may be true, as one Hasid told me, that "If we lived in Great Neck we'd be the same way," but Crown Heights isn't Great Neck, and in Crown Heights their fear of religious pollution is inexorably tied to racial segregation. Finally, in the wake of the violence of 1991, the activists and officials led by Borough President Golden placed culture over race and religion alike when they asked Blacks and Jews to exchange recipes and rituals, rather than discuss the everyday realities of life in Crown Heights.

The well-meaning universalism of "cultural exchange" captures both the promise and pitfalls of all such attempts to reduce the multiplicity of difference. By translating the different differences of Crown Heights residents into a single system of common difference, the concept of culture may very well foster a superficial form of mutual understanding. The Blacks have their collard greens and jerk chicken, the Jews have their matzah-balls and gefilte fish, and even if they don't usually eat together—or think of themselves in such reductive terms—they can at least conceptualize each other's lives. In a place like Crown Heights, where dramatically different people share busy streets, limited housing, and overtaxed public facilities, a bit of mutual intelligibility may go a long way. Yet I worry that this act of translation may ultimately subsume the idiosyncratic identities of Crown Heights residents, and others, within a state-sponsored regime of mandated difference—forcing Blacks and Jews, and everyone else, to define their identities and communities in equivalent ways. I worry that the deeply held beliefs of Crown Heights residents will be supplanted, in time, by a sanitized vision of their "cultural traditions."

I have therefore followed a rather different strategy in my analysis of the divide between Blacks and Jews in Crown Heights. I've made no effort to reduce the irreducible multiplicity of Black-Jewish difference. Rather than privileging either race or religion as the "real" explanation of contested social facts, I've allowed these discourses of difference to coexist in an unresolved tension—an unstable dialectic with no simple synthesis; an ongoing process of conceptual and political give-and-take that can't be transcended through an appeal to "culture" or any other totalizing term. This, I would argue, is the kind of process Crown Heights residents must undertake together if they wish, in Borough President Golden's words, "to work towards a unified and peaceful future."[50]

4

White Skin, Black Hats, and Other Signs of Jews

One of the first things I noticed when I moved to Crown Heights were the gazes and glances that often followed me as I walked down Eastern Parkway and other busy blocks. Like many New Yorkers, Crown Heights residents are avid people-watchers. The streets of the neighborhood are shot through with lines of sight—with looks that carve up social space—as Blacks and Jews check each other out, looking for anyone who doesn't fit in, does something unexpected, or somehow catches their eye.

Of course, as a White secular Jew who often wore a yarmulke and other signs of Jewishness, but never grew a beard or looked the part of a Hasid, I was a textbook case of "doesn't fit in." And to some extent, I'm sure, my sense of being followed by the prying eyes of my neighbors was a projection of my own anxiety about doing ethnographic research. Yet I gradually realized that furtive glances and brazen stares like those I encountered on the streets of Crown Heights play a significant role in the everyday lives of many neighborhood residents. In a neighborhood where Blacks and Jews live segregated lives on integrated blocks, Crown Heights residents spend much of their time surrounded by oddly intimate strangers. This combination of proximity and anonymity is a defining feature of urban life, but it takes on added significance in Crown Heights, where a history of conflict has left many area residents somewhat wary of their neighbors. Crown Heights residents keep an eye on each other from across a politically charged divide—wondering about each other's lives, trying to make sense of each other's actions, and looking for clues to the identities of strangers.

This chapter will explore the visual (and other) signs that catch the eyes and imaginations of Crown Heights residents as they walk the streets of their neighborhood. How, I will ask, do Blacks and Jews experience and interpret their neighbors' identities on an everyday basis? How, above all, do they try to tell—and understand—a Jew when they see one? My analysis will show how the streets of Crown Heights are cross-cut by intersecting axes of visible difference.[1]

While the previous chapters have often drawn relatively clear distinctions between "racial" and "religious" perceptions of difference, this chapter will survey a more complex terrain. Blacks and Jews on the streets of Crown Heights do not look solely for visual signs of race or religion. Their gazes tend to flit back and forth between phenotype and fashion, hats and skin, noses and necklaces, hairstyles and textures, dreadlocks and beards. Race and religion mix and mingle on the surface of the body, often intersecting in unpredictable ways. A visual sign like a woman's dreadlocks may (or may not) mark a complex combination of racial Blackness, Caribbean descent, and Rastafarian beliefs. A man's black hat and beard may (or may not) mark the Whiteness beneath. In Crown Heights, as elsewhere, most Jews are White and most Blacks are Gentiles. But they don't always look the parts they are playing, or play the parts their neighbors expect of them. Men and women, for example, perform Blackness and Jewishness in dramatically different ways. And Black Jews perform both Blackness and Jewishness in ways that confuse most everyone else. Taken together, signs of race and religion define complex perceptions—and misperceptions—of difference.

Moreover, Blacks and Jews often articulate different views of the relationship between these external signs and the inner selves they are thought to mark. Although Black Crown Heights residents often identify Hasidim by their distinctive clothes—speaking, as we will see, of "the people in the long black coats"—many doubt whether such ephemeral signs can truly alter the racial Whiteness beneath. One African American community leader expressed this common sentiment when he told me that racism is more debilitating than antisemitism because Jews, unlike Blacks, can always escape prejudice by changing their appearance: "A Jewish guy can take off his yarmulke, cut his side-burns, change his last name, and now he's White! A Black person—I can't take off my yarmulke, I can't take off the color of my skin, can't cut my side-burns, can't change my last name—I'm still Black." But most Hasidim do not view their observance of the religious laws and customs that shape their distinctive dress as a negotiable or disposable aspect of their selves. Indeed, one Lubavitch leader told a journalist that he could "identify with the Black plight" precisely because, "What they say is we, the Blacks, can never assimilate here in America, and that's just the way I feel. The bottom line is, you can't change your color, and I can't take my yarmulke off. I can't take my beard off."[2]

In Crown Heights and elsewhere, the relationship between dress and the body lies somewhere between these two polarized claims. Ethnic, religious, and subcultural dress is not merely an ephemeral supplement to a racially fixed body, but neither is dress always fixed in itself.[3] Clothing and bodies form reciprocal relationships, and each may be transformed through articulation with the other. Black Crown Heights residents "can't take off the color of [their] skin," but they can choose to wear business suits or track suits, dreadlocks or jheri curls. Hasidic men "can't take [their] yarmulke[s] off," but they can choose to wear them under baseball caps or black fedoras. Stylistic choices like these mark, and help define, distinct varieties of Blackness and Jewishness. Individuals may thus be identified in a number of sometimes contradictory ways, as elements of dress mix and mingle with aspects of the body—accentuating and undercutting racial and religious identities. Blacks and Jews in Crown Heights therefore appear, to themselves and each other, as complex composite figures.

I will explore these multifaceted perceptions of identity by examining the ways Crown Heights residents attempt to spot a range of Jews—Black and White, male and female, orthodox and otherwise. First, however, I will explore the ambiguous place of American Jews within the social history of racial visibility.

Jews, Race, and Visibility: "It Just Shines Out"

On a Friday afternoon in the spring of 1997, I stood in Washington Square Park, in Manhattan's Greenwich Village, with a group of students from a yeshiva in Crown Heights, as they did the kind of outreach work Lubavitchers are known for worldwide: asking passersby if they're Jewish, giving out tracts to encourage orthodox observance and Lubavitch beliefs, providing Shabbos candles for Jewish women, and helping Jewish men put on tefillin. As a colorful cross-section of the Village swirled around us—college kids with book bags and sunglasses, high school kids looking for "smoke," businessmen in suits and a rush, tourists with cameras and bewildered looks, tattooed skate-punks, dreadlocked Rastas, and more—I asked a few of the Hasidim how they decided whom to ask, "Excuse me, are you Jewish?" They couldn't ask everyone, so how did they tell who might be a Jew? I had asked other Hasidim the same question before, and heard a broad range of answers, but this time a young man who had only recently become a Lubavitcher tried to explain: "It's just something up here," he said, gesturing toward his face. "It's just a look." He then held up a hand in front of his forehead, with his fingers outstretched like beams of light, and told me: "It's the neshoma [the Jewish soul]. . . . It just shines out."

In the luminous world of Hasidic thought, the soul of a Jew is fundamentally different from that of a Gentile. Its spiritual roots lie in a wholly different realm of godliness—a higher realm that contains a greater degree of God's pure light, the *Or Ein Sof* (literally, "the light of infinity"). According to Lubavitchers, as I noted in the introduction, this "godly soul" ties Jews directly to their God and his Torah. And according to some, it exudes a spiritual radiance that makes every Jew, quite literally, "a light unto the nations" (Isaiah 42:6). Lubavitchers don't see Jews as a "racial" or "ethnic" group, or even as a "religion" really, so their Jewishness cannot necessarily be spotted by a yarmulke, a Star of David pendant, or a stereotypical nose. Rather, they are bearers of a unique soul that was created by God, from the core of his being, before he even created the world. Their Jewishness rests on this soul and nothing more, so if they are visible, as a group, it must be by some unique quality of the soul. Regardless of what Jews may look like—whether they're secular or orthodox, male or female, Ashkenazic or Sephardic, Black or White—according to some Lubavitchers their soul "just shines out."

In practice, of course, things aren't so simple. As they look for Jews in Washington Square Park and elsewhere, Lubavitchers often rely on social distinctions that have nothing to do with Jewish souls—making racial distinctions between "Black" and "White," and more subtle distinctions

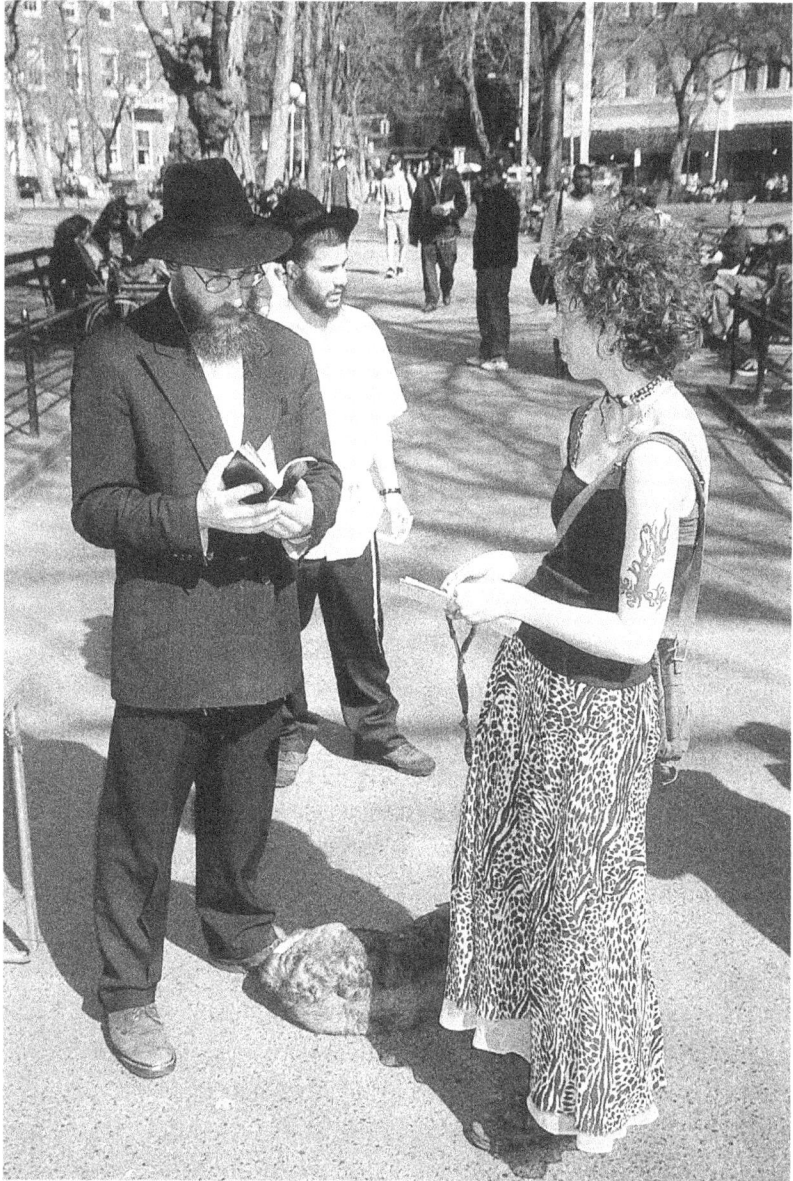

FIGURE 13 A Lubavitch yeshiva student doing outreach work with a passerby in Washington Square Park. If her Jewish soul "shines out," it does so in spite of her clothing and tattoo, which transgress Hasidic understandings of Jewish law. (Photo by the author.)

by other visual signs. One Black orthodox Jew I met in Crown Heights complained that they never ask him if he's put on tefillin, although of course he does so every morning in synagogue. And a secular Jewish acquaintance of mine said that they always ask if he's Jewish when he's wearing glasses, but never when he's wearing contacts. At times, these Lubavitch outreach campaigns resemble a Shakespearean comedy of errors—an endless parade of mistaken identities, accompanied by a-thousand-and-one snappy answers to, "Excuse me, are you Jewish?" And yet, this yeshiva student's vision of a shining Jewish soul is a testament to the clarity most Lubavitchers attribute to Jewish identity and difference.

This vision is rooted in the esoteric details of kabbalistic thought, but it's not quite as exotic—or culturally distant—as it may initially sound. Indeed, it resonates with a widely shared assumption about race and visibility. In the course of their daily lives, Americans tend to assume that the racial identities of strangers are visible at a glance. This assumption may be belied, at times, by various forms of ambiguity and "passing," but most Americans still believe that an individual's race is more or less obvious through a range of visible signs. As Michael Omi and Howard Winant note in their influential analysis of race in America: "One of the first things we notice about people when we meet them (along with their sex) is their race. We utilize race to provide clues about *who* a person is."[4] This leap from visible signs to inner truths—from the color of a person's skin, the texture of their hair, and the shape of certain facial features, to a set of assumptions about their ancestry, social position, and cultural heritage— helps to secure the social reality of race by tying it to physical realities that seem somehow indisputable. As Robyn Wiegman has argued: "[T]he visible has a long, contested, and highly contradictory role as the primary vehicle for making race 'real' in the United States. Its function, to cite the body as the inevitable locus of 'being,' depends on a series of bodily fictions assumed to unproblematically reflect the natural meaning of flesh."[5] Indeed, the thoroughgoing racialization of American society often depends on the seemingly straightforward visual operation of telling someone's race by bodily signs. In countless overt and subtle ways, "race" requires visible difference.[6]

Contemporary American Jews are not generally considered racially distinct from Gentiles, but from the mid-eighteenth to mid-twentieth centuries Jewishness—like Blackness or Whiteness—was thought to lie in "the natural meaning of flesh." As historians like Sander Gilman and Matthew Jacobson have shown, Jews were widely seen as marked by swarthy and diseased skin, large crooked noses, flat feet, nasal voices, and a number of other external signs that hinted at their "impure" blood.[7] In 1775, for example, Johann Blumenbach—the influential theorist of biological race who first divided humanity into "Caucasoid," "Negroid," and "Mongoloid" races—argued that the long-term stability of these physical types was illustrated by the enduring "racial face" of the Jews. The Jews, he argued, "under every climate, remain the same as far as the fundamental configuration of the face goes," and can thus "be distinguished at the first glance even by those little skilled in physiognomy."[8] In 1893, an author in the *New York Sun* agreed that, "The Jewish face and character remain the same as they were in the days of the Pharaoh. . . . Usually a Jew is recognizable as such by sight. In whatever country he is, his race is always conspicuous."[9]

This self-evident clarity faded quite a bit over the course of the twentieth century, as American Jews (like other European immigrants) assimilated into an unmarked racial Whiteness. The racialization of Jewishness is still echoed in signs like the "Jewish nose"—a mark of difference that Gilman argues "came to be the sign of the pathological Jewish character for Western Jews, replacing the pathognomic sign of the skin, though closely linked to it."[10] Indeed, one Afro-Caribbean Crown Heights resident blended race with religion when she told me that the Bible confirms the distinctive Jewish nose. She assured me that, "Jesus told us how to know the Jews—by the nose." I was startled by her claim, but she promised, "Yes! Read your Scriptures, you'll find it. You can know them by the nose." However, most Americans are no longer so sure of their ability to distinguish Jews by sight. Indeed, despite her invocation of the authoritative biblical text, this Caribbean woman didn't have a particularly clear eye for the distinctive Jewish nose. She assured me I had one, but I suspect her certainty rested on the yarmulke I was wearing at the time. In fact, our entire discussion stemmed from a story she told me about a Jewish woman she mistook for Italian. She may thus claim to "know them by the nose," but in the course of her everyday life she—like most Americans—is more likely to see Jews and Italians as indistinguishably White.

Hence the importance, to some Lubavitch Hasidim, of the luminous Jewish soul—an ostensibly incontestable mark of a Jewish identity no longer grounded in "the natural meaning of flesh." Lubavitch imaginations of this spiritual radiance are equivalent, in many ways, to secular imaginations of racial phenotype. The visual signs may be somewhat different, and to most Americans the signs of race are a bit more clear, but the perceptual operation is fundamentally the same. In either case, one's inner self "just shines out."

THIS ASSUMPTION IS BELIED, however, by the complex economy of Jewish visibility in Crown Heights. Not all Jews are equally visible, as Jews, in all social contexts. Popular assumptions about race and gender work to reveal or obscure the inner truth of Jewishness. We may begin to chart these dynamics by contrasting two scenes of Jewish visibility—two different Jews in two different moments, only one of whom was actually seen as a Jew.

On August 19, 1991, at about 11:20 P.M., shouts rang out at the corner of President Street and Brooklyn Avenue. As I described in chapter 1, Charles Price saw Yankel Rosenbaum walking on President Street, saw that he was a Jew, and marked this fact with a chilling sense of certainty: "There's one! Get him!" he reportedly cried, "There's a Jew! Get the Jew!" Without diminishing the tragedy and brutality of this murder, I'd like to pose a question that may seem trivial or obtuse: How, exactly, did Charles Price know that Yankel Rosenbaum was a Jew? In the dim light, muggy air, and chaotic din of a riot in progress, what made Rosenbaum's Jewishness visible?

Even in the absence of a luminous soul or unmistakable physiognomy, the answer seems simple. As the attorney who led the 1997 prosecution of Charles Price and Lemrick Nelson noted in her opening statement to the court: "Yankel Rosenbaum was an orthodox Jew and he was readily identifiable as Jewish by his beard and yarmulke"—and, I would add, by the White face between them. Rosenbaum's Jewishness was clearly marked because he, like most Jewish men in Crown Heights, bore a number of specific visual signs: a full beard and light skin; a large black yarmulke; black pants and a button-down shirt (light blue in Rosenbaum's case), with his *tzitzis* (the fringes of a ritual undergarment) hanging down over his belt.

This was not exactly the "typical" dress of a male Lubavitcher—and in fact Yankel Rosenbaum was not a Lubavitcher—but it was pretty close. It was, more or less, the visual image Charles Price had in mind when he set out to "Get the Jew."

The significance, and specificity, of this "Jewish" image will become clearer if we compare the murder of Yankel Rosenbaum to another act of violence against an orthodox Jew in Crown Heights. On May 29, 1988, on a lazy Sunday afternoon, children were playing on the sidewalk of President Street between Utica and Schenectady Avenues, just half a block from the scene of the accident that would kill Gavin Cato three years later. An eight-year-old Black girl snatched a ball from a Hasidic toddler and—as happens all too easily in Crown Heights—violence escalated from this innocent exchange. The toddler's father shoved the young Black girl to the ground, and the girl's fifteen-year-old cousin came to her aid, confronting the Hasidic man. He then shoved and punched this teenage girl, knocking out one of her teeth. But the Hasid didn't and couldn't know—Or could he? And if not, why not?—that the teenager he punched was an African American orthodox Jew, an honor student at a high school affiliated with Yeshiva University.

Ten years later, I discussed this incident with a sister of the girl who was punched, showing her an article in the *New York Amsterdam News* that described the assault.[11] She spoke of it passionately, and remembered "like it was yesterday" how her sister ran upstairs to their apartment, bleeding from the mouth and carrying a tooth in her hand; how her father held her back as she ran downstairs to seek revenge; and how the Hasid who punched her sister apologized profusely when it was all sorted out. "I'm so sorry!" he told her family repeatedly, "I didn't know she was Jewish! I'm so sorry! I didn't know!"[12] The ostensible clarity of an identity that "just shines out" has thus fractured into a jarring disjuncture between "There's one! Get him!" and "I'm so sorry! I didn't know!" One Jew was attacked on the streets of Crown Heights because his Jewishness was clearly visible, while another was attacked because hers was not. What are we to make of this difference, and the tensions it highlights in Jewish identity and visibility?

The anthropologist Daniel Segal raises similar questions about our perceptions of Jewishness (and other identities) in his discussion of the museum exhibit, *Too Jewish? Challenging Traditional Identities*.[13] Segal compares one work of art critiquing the idea of the "Jewish nose" with another celebrating the "Jewishness" of certain noses, and asks: "So which is it? Can you tell a Jew when you see one?" He suggests:

> A common sense way of dealing with this tension would be to answer: "Well, you can't always tell a Jew when you see one, but much of the time you can." . . . In this common sense approach to the problem, visual clues and the underlying, knowable facts of Jewish identity are two separate variables that are said to be robustly, if imperfectly, correlated, so that Jewish looks are a fairly reliable indication of being Jewish. In this view, it is an empirical fact about Jews that, more often than not, they look Jewish.[14]

In other words, there may not be a distinctive soul—or distinctive nose—shining out of every Jew, but there's still a distinctive Jewish "look" that often enough allows one to spot them. This "common sense" view seems intuitively correct, and especially so in today's Crown Heights, where the predominantly White Lubavitch Hasidim live in a predominantly Black neighborhood, and take a number of steps to make their Jewishness more visible. It's not so hard to spot a "typical" Jew on the streets of Crown Heights, and Yankel Rosenbaum looked the part, while the Black orthodox girl who was punched did not. Yet Segal is right to argue that:

> This common sense way of thinking [about identities] is both mistaken and pernicious. In my view, the never perfect correlation between observable signs of Jewishness and the knowable facts of Jewishness is not an empirical fact about the population of Jews in the world. Rather, this correlation is better understood as a property of the way visual typifications of Jews, on the one hand, and the knowable facts about Jewish identity, on the other, are socially forged or constituted.[15]

Whatever correlation may or may not exist between the "observable signs" and "knowable facts" of Jewishness is a product, in other words, of culturally specific perceptions and performances—ways of seeing and being Jewish that have complex histories.

In today's Crown Heights, the "never perfect correlation" between Jewish signs and Jewish selves has been "socially forged" at the intersection of race, religion, and gender. Rather than seeking the seductive clarity of a shining soul—or the seductive simplicity of a facile claim that some Jews "look Jewish" while others just don't—the following two sections will chart the signs that marked the Jewishness of a White man in a beard and yarmulke, but failed to mark the Jewishness of a Black girl in casual clothes.

Black Coats and Modest Skirts:
Signs of Some White Jews

More than any other item of material culture, the black suits, hats, and coats worn by many Hasidic men have become a visual icon of Hasidic Brooklyn. In Crown Heights and other neighborhoods, long black coats mark the presence of Hasidim. Although some observers may not recognize them as signs of Jewishness (I once heard a young Black child in the Brooklyn Botanic Garden ask his father "Are they Amish?" as a Lubavitch family walked by), to many the black coat represents a certain something—whether spiritual mystery or rigid conformity—close to the heart of Hasidic life. For example, in the very first line of her popular account of Lubavitch community life, Lis Harris uses the well-worn image of a well-worn coat to capture the "strange spectacle" of Hasidic men celebrating the holiday of Simchas Torah. "In the small hours of a cold fall morning," she writes, "when most of Brooklyn was asleep, some five thousand bearded, dark-hatted men, wearing nearly identical dark suits and coats, danced around a decrepit synagogue, arms clasped."[16] The dancers remind Harris of an image she had once seen in a box of family photographs, a picture "of a fierce-looking, bearded old man, wearing the sort of fur hat and long black coat that Hasidic men wear."[17] So she heads to Crown Heights, in search of her roots, yearning for the warmth of this "long black coat."

Like many New Yorkers, Harris projects a preconceived image of Hasidic life onto the ready-made screen of a long black coat: "they" all look alike, and so different from "us"; like somebody's great-grandfather,

FIGURE 14 Lubavitch men celebrating the holiday of Lag B'Omer in front of 770.
(Photo by Miriam Rubinoff. Reprinted by permission of the photographer.)

escaped from a sepia-toned photograph. Of course, Brooklyn's Hasidim
are not actually survivors of another time. In their own distinctive ways,
they are very much a part of twenty-first-century American life. But, as
Harris notes, they don't dress quite like other Americans. And to some

extent, they do tend to dress alike. There is a broad range of dress within each Hasidic community, and dramatic differences between different communities, but there is still a certain Hasidic "look."

Lubavitchers have never dressed in the elaborate garb typical of many Hasidim in Williamsburg and Boro Park. Even in the nineteenth century, they dressed a bit less distinctively than other Hasidim, and a bit more like the surrounding Gentile communities. Lubavitch men do not wear the stockings, knickers, and slippers that some other Hasidic men wear (in the fashion of eighteenth-century Polish nobles, according to some scholars).[18] Very few Lubavitch men wear the long *peyos*, or side-locks, that are typical of most Hasidim—and fascinating to secular observers. Even on Shabbos and holidays they don't wear *streimels*, the lavish round fur hats favored by most Hasidim. Indeed, Lubavitchers are often criticized by other Hasidim for being too "liberal" and "modern" in their dress, and much else.[19] But there's still a fairly distinctive Lubavitch look, to which many Lubavitch men conform or aspire. Following the lead of their Rebbe, most Lubavitch men wear simple black fedoras on top of their black velvet yarmulkes. Some make a point of denting the crowns of their fedoras just so, so they fold in a triangle rather than a straight line—just like the Rebbe's (see figure 15). They wear solid black suits in all weather, usually single-breasted and always buttoned with the right side over the left, as the right hand represents God's mercy while the left represents God's judgment, and one always wants mercy to win out over judgment. Most wear plain white dress shirts under their suits, usually with stiff buttonless collars and rarely with ties. And most wear the fringes, or tzitzis, of their ritual undergarments hanging over their black slacks, rather than tucked in. Like other Hasidim, most Lubavitch men grow long, full beards, as they interpret the Torah to forbid trimming them in any way. Yet despite his full beard, and his strict observance of rabbinic law and Hasidic custom, the "typical" Lubavitch man looks more like an American businessman of the 1950s than a Polish nobleman of the 1750s.

And of course, Lubavitch men often depart from this "typical" image in more or less subtle ways. Many younger men wear fashionable suits in gray or muted colors, but still buttoned right over left. In the summer, while vacationing in the country, some are even rumored to wear short

FIGURE 15 A young Lubavitcher aspires to look like his Rebbe. (Photo by the author.)

pants and T-shirts—although the Rebbe himself found this a bit scandalous.[20] Some men trim their beards slightly, and a few wear no beards at all (removing them with depilatories or electric razors, so as not to break the unequivocal law against shaving). Some wear dark green or blue fedoras, or other hats, and a few wear no head covering beyond their yarmulke. A neighbor of mine when I lived in Crown Heights owned a big black cowboy hat, which he wore to see the country music star Garth Brooks play in Central Park, and joked he would one day wear to synagogue—much to his wife's chagrin. As in all communities, religious and secular, there are substantial (though hardly unlimited) variations on many Lubavitch norms, including norms of dress. And there's plenty of room for idiosyncratic adaptations of "traditional" norms to "modern" life. Consider, for example, the Crown Heights tailor who offered, with a sly smile, to switch the buttons to the other side of my black leather jacket, so I could button it right over left "like a Hasid."

But these creative variations on the Lubavitch look are limited to relatively private spheres of social life (and evidently concerts in Central Park). The more one is acting as a part of the Lubavitch community, in public ritual settings, the more one is expected to look the part. Nearly all

Lubavitch men, regardless of how they dress during the week, have an out-fit set aside for Shabbos and holidays—a newer black suit, a nicer black hat, and a clean white shirt. Indeed, the item of clothing that most clearly defines Hasidic masculinity is only worn in these ritual contexts. The *kapote* (pronounced "kaputuh") is a knee-length black coat made from lightweight fabric, often silk, that is worn over one's suit and tied around the waist by a belt of black thread called a *gartel*. Only married Hasidic men wear kapotes, with very few exceptions, so this quintessential long black coat distinguishes Hasidim from other orthodox Jews—or at least it seems to, by imposing a simple visual opposition on a communal boundary that is far more complex. In Crown Heights synagogues, on Shabbos and holi-days, one sees an ocean of men in fedoras and kapotes—performing an image of solidarity and uniformity that doesn't quite hold during the rest of the week.

THE SOCIAL SIGNIFICANCE of these hats and coats has taken shape gradu-ally, through a history of debate over Jewish dress and identity. For cen-turies, Jews and others have used distinctive clothes to mark Jewish difference. In medieval Europe—as in contemporary Brooklyn—Jews who adhered to strict interpretations of religious law often chose to wear dis-tinctive clothing, following rabbinic decrees based upon the Torah's com-mandment (in Leviticus 18:3) not to follow the ways of the Gentiles.[21] Less observant Jews often tried to assimilate into the broader society by wear-ing clothing like that of their Gentile neighbors, but medieval Christian monarchs sometimes required both Jews and Muslims to wear distinctive clothes or colored badges, to prevent them from passing into European Christendom.[22] American society, however, has encouraged Jewish as-similation to mainstream norms of dress (and most everything else). Eu-ropean Jews arriving in the United States in the nineteenth and twentieth centuries faced pressure from Jewish and Gentile authorities—not to mention their own aspirations and desires—to conform to American fashions.[23]

This process of assimilation was hardly as simple or inevitable as im-ages of America's "melting pot" would have us believe. But by 1940, when the Previous Rebbe settled in Crown Heights, the vast majority of New York Jews had adapted American styles of dress. Even the orthodox had

crafted distinctively American forms of observant Judaism that, in the
words of the historian Jenna Weissman Joselit, "[kept] outwardly distinctive practices to a minimum." As Joselit notes: "The absence of distinctive
dress was a hallmark of [Jewish New York between the World Wars]."[24]
Crown Heights at this time was largely home to an immigrant elite that
was better off and more assimilated than Jews in other Brooklyn neighborhoods. In this milieu, the handful of Hasidim in the neighborhood
must have stuck out like a proverbial sore thumb. Indeed, the art historian
Linda Nochlin, who grew up in Crown Heights in the 1930s and 1940s, recalled the uncanny image Hasidim presented to her assimilated eyes:
"There weren't many Hasidim around in those days, before World War II
brought them in droves to my old neighborhood. But I remember quite
early peering down into a kind of basement assembly room below street
level and seeing Them crowded together, like black beetles, bowing and
mumbling, little men wearing odd, identifiable garments, so different
from my emancipated doctor grandfather's white linen summer suit and
jaunty straw boater."[25] The "odd, identifiable garments" of Hasidic men
thus distinguished Crown Heights Hasidim from their neighbors—and
made them an object of secular curiosity and fantasy.

By 1951, when Menachem Mendel Schneerson became the Lubavitcher Rebbe, Crown Heights was even more densely Jewish than it had
been in the 1930s. Hasidim had settled there because it was a "Jewish
neighborhood," but they entered a community where the distinctive dress
of Hasidic men marked them as exotic and disturbing interlopers, or perhaps even "black beetles" whose humanity seemed in doubt. In this context, the new Rebbe—who, it was sometimes rumored, had refused to wear
a long black coat when he studied at the Sorbonne in the 1930s[26]—
devoted his energy to encouraging Jewish observance among his Hasidim
and other Jews. The Rebbe often pointed out that according to the Talmudic sages, the Israelites had only merited redemption from Egypt because
they refused to change their traditional names, language, and dress.[27] And
so, he argued, distinctive "Jewish" clothes must remain an integral part of
the distinctive Jewish community he would build in Crown Heights.

Following the White flight of the 1960s, Lubavitchers in Crown
Heights may generally be identified as the only "White" people in a predominantly "Black" neighborhood. But even in this context, they are

often still identified by the distinctive dress of Hasidic men. Long black coats continue to define the difference between Lubavitchers and their neighbors, shaping Black Crown Heights residents' perceptions of Jews, for both better and worse. For example, James E. Davis—an African American minister, police officer, and politician, who was born and raised in Crown Heights and served the community on New York's City Council from 2001 until his tragic death in 2003—described the profound effect that the Lubavitcher Rebbe had on him as a child.[28] Davis told me (and anyone else who would listen, as he ran for various offices in the late 1990s) how the "Grand Rebbe" used to walk by his home every Saturday afternoon, and how his father would encourage him to go outside and say "Shalom Rabbi." He described his view of the Rebbe, as a Black child growing up in the 1960s and 1970s: "We didn't know the Grand Rebbe was the Grand Rebbe. We just knew there was this older gentleman—who, as he got older, took smaller steps—coming around the corner . . . and if you wait about thirty seconds, you would see approximately ten thousand bearded men in black suits following him home." This image of the Rebbe's entourage as "bearded men in black suits" mirrors Linda Nochlin's image of Hasidim in "odd, identifiable garments," but where Nochlin recalls seeing "Them crowded together" as an animalistic horde, Davis recalls an image of solidarity under the Rebbe's leadership—a solidarity Davis worked to instill in Black Crown Heights residents as well.

Unfortunately, however, as Black-Jewish relations worsened in the late 1970s, some African American leaders used images of long black coats to paint a more malevolent picture of the Lubavitch community. One of the first communal conflicts in Crown Heights broke out in June of 1978 following the Hasidic beating of a Black teenager, whom Hasidim alleged had accosted or assaulted an elderly Hasid.[29] In demonstrations that summer, Black activists often accused the neighborhood crime patrols that Hasidim had organized since the 1960s of anti-Black vigilante attacks. The Reverend Herbert Daughtry cofounded the "Black Citizen's Patrol," and predicted— or perhaps threatened—violence between these Black and Hasidic patrols. On June 19, according to the *New York Times*, Daughtry told a crowd of demonstrators on Eastern Parkway: "When the people in the long black coats meet our men, let us see what will happen." Jewish leaders were horrified, however, when the *New York Post* reported that Daughtry said: "We

will get the Jews and the people in the long black coats." Daughtry vehemently denies this more provocative version, yet it is clear—regardless of
his wording or intent—that he saw the Lubavitch community as a threat to
Blacks in Crown Heights, and imagined this threat wearing "long black
coats."[30]

As the conflict of June 1978 proceeded through the courts, some
Lubavitchers found ways to turn this popular image to their advantage.
In the 1979 trial of two Hasidic men charged in the assault that had sparked
the conflict, the suspects chose to sit in the court gallery (rather than with
their attorneys) surrounded by other Lubavitch men—all of whom wore
black suits and full beards. This defense strategy made it difficult for witnesses to identify the accused, and most likely contributed to their acquittal on all counts. But their attorneys had claimed from the start that the
suspects were innocent passersby, arrested by police who couldn't tell the
difference between one Hasid in a black suit and another. Either way,
their black suits and beards shaped the outcome of their trial, and their
role in Crown Heights politics.[31]

A decade or so later, similar visual images shaped the roles of various Crown Heights Jews in the violence of August 1991. Although Yankel
Rosenbaum wasn't wearing a coat when he was stabbed to death, his yarmulke and beard helped mark his Jewishness in the eyes of the young men
who attacked him. And Isaac Bitton's "typical" Hasidic dress—black hat,
black suit, full beard, and all—made him an object of violence (as I described in chapter 1), although he is a Moroccan Sephardic Jew, with dark
"olive" skin, who has sometimes faced prejudice from White Lubavitchers.
Fortunately for Bitton, however, he was able to leave Crown Heights the
following day, by hiding in the back seat of a car driven by his neighbor—
an African American orthodox Jew who doesn't dress like a Hasid, and was
not recognized as a Jew by the rioters breaking the windows of Jewish-
owned cars.

Finally, the power of these popular images of Jewishness was at once
confirmed and subverted in the murder of Anthony Graziosi on September
5, 1991, about two weeks after the violence in Crown Heights. Graziosi—a
sixty-seven-year-old Italian American businessman from Queens—had
stopped his car at a red light in north Crown Heights when he was attacked, out of the blue, by four Black men, one of whom shot him to

death. The only man tried for the murder was acquitted, so his killers' intent will never be clear. But his family's attorneys claimed Graziosi was killed because his full beard and black suit made him look like a Hasidic Jew. Even in the absence of a Jewish soul, a long black coat may still "shine out."

BUT BLACK COATS and beards clearly don't mark the Jewishness of *all* Jews in Crown Heights. To the contrary, this popular image of a "typical" Hasid obscures the reality of a Jewish community that is actually far more diverse. The same assumptions that led four Black men to mistake Anthony Graziosi for a Hasidic Jew also lead non-Hasidic observers to overlook the Jewishness of many Jews in Crown Heights—including, above all, Lubavitch women. Unlike the black coats of Hasidic men, the modest skirts of Hasidic women have rarely been objects of public fascination or commentary. Lubavitch women thus tend to be less visible, as Jews, than Lubavitch men. On the streets of Crown Heights, a White woman in a long skirt is typically seen as a Hasid, but in other social contexts her Jewishness may be invisible.

Lubavitch women do wear their own distinctive styles of dress, which are regulated by the standards of *tznius*, or modesty, codified in rabbinic law and Hasidic custom.[32] The laws of tznius require women to show humility before God, and to shield their bodies from the eyes of men, so Lubavitch women and girls tend to dress quite conservatively—wearing long skirts or dresses, stockings to cover whatever part of their legs might otherwise show, and loose tops with long sleeves and high necks. Married women generally follow these standards more carefully than single women or girls, and they are also required to cover their hair, which is thought to incite sexual desire in men. Married Lubavitch women rarely shave their heads, as many other Hasidic women do, but most cut their hair short—two inches or less—and wear wigs in public. As with Hasidic men's fashions, there is a broad range of more or less acceptable "tzniusdik" styles. And like Lubavitch men, Lubavitch women often dress in styles somewhat closer to the American mainstream than other Hasidim do. Indeed, some young Lubavitch women follow secular fashion closely—looking for just the right balance between tznius and Soho—and a few wear clothes that follow the letter of rabbinic law while flouting Hasidic custom through

FIGURE 16 A Hasidic woman and her children on the beach at Coney Island. (Photo by Miriam Rubinoff. Reprinted by permission of the photographer.)

public displays of sexuality. But all Lubavitch women and girls are concerned, in their own ways, with tznius, and young girls are often reprimanded when they fail to dress appropriately.

The tzniusdik styles of Lubavitch women are closely scrutinized by Lubavitchers themselves, and by other Hasidic Jews. Indeed, Hasidim often read the smallest details of tznius—the seam of a stocking, the slit of a skirt, or the length of a sleeve—as signs of a woman's religiosity, and marks of social distinction among the various Hasidic communities.[33] Yet despite the central role of tznius in marking intra-Hasidic differences, the wigs and modest skirts of Lubavitch women have rarely been taken as signs of Jewishness by the secular Jews and Gentiles with whom Lubavitchers have always shared Crown Heights. While Hasidim may tell a Lubavitcher from a Bobover by their skirts and stockings, to outsiders they both may be indistinguishable from other women in conservative clothes (see figure 16).

The social forces contributing to this symbolic invisibility are themselves somewhat difficult to see. The appearance of most Lubavitch women does seem less distinctive than that of most Lubavitch men. A well-tailored business suit with a skirt just covering the knees, or a cable-knit sweater and denim skirt down to one's ankles, or a colorful long-sleeved sun dress—these are all tzniusdik styles that mark their wearers as Hasidim only to practiced and careful eyes. And a wig—especially an expensive one—may look just like a woman's hair, in almost any color or style. Hasidic women can thus "pass" as Gentiles far better than Hasidic men. But visual distinctions between Jews and Gentiles—or Blacks and Whites, for that matter—have always rested on fantasies of difference, and never simply on "objective" facts. Indeed, women have often been marked as Jews by far less than modest skirts and wigs, so we can't explain the relative invisibility of Hasidic women by the facts of their appearance alone.[34] Perhaps their relatively limited role in public ritual and community politics has kept their appearance out of the public eye and the popular imagination.[35] Perhaps, for example, if women had been active in the Lubavitch community's neighborhood crime patrols, Herbert Daughtry would have targeted his anger at "the people in the modest skirts" as well.

Regardless of its causes, the relative invisibility of Hasidic women's Jewishness sometimes has significant effects on their relationships with Gentiles in the public sphere. For example, one Lubavitch woman—a prominent behind-the-scenes activist, businesswoman, and grandmother in her fifties or sixties—told me of an incident during the violence of 1991 that helped to spark her activism:

> I was walking in [Manhattan] after I had an appointment, and I was carrying an attaché case. I will never forget this. Two Blacks, delivery guys, right off Fifth Avenue . . . I heard these two guys saying: "Hey man, did you hear about what happened in [Crown Heights] last night? . . . You heard what they did to that guy? Hey man, he deserved it." And I was just livid . . . and I reacted in the worst possible way that you can. I actually stopped dead in my tracks, I turned around, and I eyed them as though, y'know, if looks could kill they would die. . . . So they saw me—it was very obvious—and one of them said: "She must be a Jew," or "She must be one of them," or something like that. I guess my anger was really written on my face.

In Manhattan, then, a Lubavitch woman dressed for a business meeting, "carrying an attaché case," may be invisible as a Jew. The Black men discussing the murder of Yankel Rosenbaum couldn't tell she was "one of them" until she "eyed them as though, y'know, if looks could kill they would die." Only at this point was her Jewishness, along with her anger, "written on [her] face." This brief interaction was a transformative experience for my Hasidic acquaintance, pushing her from fear to political engagement. And the experience was predicated, in an important sense, on her invisibility as a Jew.

The gendered nature of her experience is clear when compared to her husband's experiences of antisemitism. He told me he often hears comments like "Heil Hitler" on the subway, and said it shocked him at first because he never heard such things when he was growing up in a small midwestern town. His wife then interrupted to explain: "There's reasons for that. Number one, when he was in a small town he didn't look like he was particularly Jewish. And when he was here, he was noticeably Jewish, because he wasn't orthodox then and now he is. So that's partly the reason. In other words, the orthodox Jew brings out this red flag, and somehow [Gentiles] feel they have to . . . we're singled out!" Yes, I agreed, as we kept chatting—but singled out in ways that are substantially different for women and men. In most non-Jewish eyes, the Jewishness of Hasidic women does not "shine out" like that of Hasidic men.

Colored Kippahs and Dreadlocks:
Signs of Some Black Jews

Though Hasidic women may often be seen as White rather than Jewish, few observers find this combination of identities startling or contradictory. Their Jewishness might not be visually obvious, but it does not pose many perceptual problems. Blacks, however, are typically assumed *not* to be Jews. Few observers seem to notice, or acknowledge, the Jewish souls "shin[ing]" out" of Black bodies—or the yarmulkes and beards framing Black faces. And when Crown Heights residents actually notice Black Jews, they—both Blacks and Jews—tend to view them with a mix of surprise and discomfort. Black Jews in Crown Heights are caught in a perceived contradiction between race and religion. Their Jewishness is rendered nearly invisible by racialized assumptions about the appearance of a "typical"

Jew. Their predicament is summed up well by Ralph Ellison's famous meditation on African American invisibility, "I am invisible, understand, simply because people refuse to see me."[36]

THERE HAS NEVER BEEN an especially large number of Black orthodox Jews in Crown Heights, but there has been a small community—or perhaps a network of families—since at least the early 1970s. Black Jews were drawn to Crown Heights, some told me, by the unique opportunity to live in a predominantly Black neighborhood that also offers the institutions and services, from kosher butchers to ritual baths, required to live by the laws of the Torah. Their numbers have fluctuated over the years, from about twenty families in the late 1970s to a half-dozen families today. For a few years in the mid- to late 1970s an African American rabbi named Avraham Coleman led an interracial but predominantly Black synagogue and yeshiva on Crown Street, and published a magazine that proclaimed itself "The Voice of America's Black Jews."[37] Since the closing of this synagogue in 1978, Black Jews in Crown Heights have attended a number of synagogues and prayer groups that are known in the neighborhood as predominantly Sephardic. While I was conducting fieldwork, from 1996 to 1998, a few of the neighborhood's Black orthodox Jews attended Sabbath services in a small Sephardic synagogue housed in a yeshiva for secular Jewish men who wish to become Hasidim. In addition to these Black orthodox Jews, the synagogue's congregation included a few Sephardic Lubavitchers, a few non-Hasidic Sephardim who lived nearby, and an occasional White Hasid.[38]

Despite their longstanding presence in Crown Heights, these Black Jews have remained invisible to most Lubavitchers. When they are seen— or noticed—on the streets of the neighborhood they are often met with startled reactions, sly glances, or brazen stares. For example, when I asked one African American Jew raised in Crown Heights about her day-to-day experiences growing up as a Black Jew, she answered immediately, "Oh, you mean like everyone staring at us when we walked to shul, and they saw my father wearing his [prayer shawl] on Shabbat?" Fleeting moments like this may seem trivial or insignificant, but other Black Jews I spoke to described the profound effect of their Hasidic neighbors' failures to recognize them as Jews—the pent-up anger that threatens to surface when yet another Hasid seems to ignore one's neighborly greeting of "Good Shabbos."

This misrecognition is rooted, above all, in the popular equation of Jewishness with Whiteness, but this racialized view of the Jewish body is also tied to assumptions about Jewish dress. Black Jews in Crown Heights are rarely seen as Jews, in part, because few wear clothes seen as distinctly "Jewish." There is one well-known family of Black Lubavitch Hasidim in the neighborhood, who follow Lubavitch customs in dress and all else. The father of the family, Rabbi Yisroel Francis, was profiled as a "Man of Faith and Color" in a 1992 article in the *Daily News*, and the author noted that "Walking the streets of Crown Heights, with his wispy beard and wearing the long, dark coat, suit and full-brimmed black hat traditional to male Lubavitchers, Francis is a familiar but curious figure."[39] But unlike Rabbi Francis, most of the Black orthodox Jews in Crown Heights identify as modern orthodox and/or Sephardic, and they tend to dress accordingly—in clothes that may or may not visibly distinguish them from non-Jewish Blacks. The men wear business suits, slacks, or jeans. Some of the women also wear slacks or jeans (which are forbidden to women by Hasidic understandings of tznius), while others wear dresses and skirts that don't always fit Hasidic styles. Some Black orthodox men wear beards, but some do not. Most wear their tzitzis tucked inside their pants, and some wear brightly colored and patterned yarmulkes based on Sephardic styles. These distinctive yarmulkes are generally intended, and sometimes perceived, as statements of Sephardic Jewish identity, but they are often confused with the "African" cuffees worn by some Black Muslims and secular Black nationalists.

One Black Jew in Crown Heights—who doesn't consider himself a Hasid, though he is married to a White Hasidic woman—complained that he is sometimes mistaken for a Lubavitcher on Shabbos because he usually wears a kapote, yet is mistaken for a Muslim during the rest of the week because he wears a Sephardic yarmulke, or kippah: "Because of this particular type of kippah, not the little small one or the beanie . . . they feel, uh, [most people] don't say 'Oh, are you Jewish?' Now some do, but [most say] 'You've got to be Muslim.' Again, that's because of the kippah." He told

me, with dignity and patience, that he has learned to overlook these misperceptions as he has grown in his identity as an orthodox Jew. But he wor-
ries about his teenage sons, who aren't so observant and want to wear
mainstream fashions. While he understands their desires, he still demands of them: "Wear your tzitzis. Put your kippah on your head. At least
look like a Jew." He tells his sons it isn't enough for them to wear baseball
caps that cover their heads (as modern orthodox teenage boys often do).
As Black Jews, he says, "You have to look even more like a Jew—because of
your color."

Some Black Jews in Crown Heights have done just this, taking steps
to increase the visibility of their Jewishness, in a conscious or uncon-
scious effort to overcome assumptions about Jewish Whiteness. For example, although he was not Hasidic, Rabbi Avraham Coleman (the leader
of the Black synagogue described above) felt a spiritual bond with the Satmar Rebbe of Williamsburg, and often dressed for Shabbos like a Satmar
Hasid. He wore a wide fur streimel, and a kapote brocaded with richly colored velvet—a far more traditional Hasidic style than the black fedoras
and kapotes of his Lubavitch neighbors.[40] And in the spring of 1998, during the holiday of Passover, Rabbi Yisroel Francis took the unusual step of
posting a personal "Pesach Message of Deliverance" on bulletin boards in
Crown Heights synagogues. The text emphasized Lubavitch interpretations of the holiday, while a photo emphasized Francis's Jewish identity by
showing him dressed in a black suit and fedora, standing in front of a
bookshelf lined with Hasidic texts.

Yet despite such efforts to increase their visibility, Black Jews in
Crown Heights generally remain invisible as Jews. When they dress in
ways that mark their Jewishness, they often face startled looks from Hasidim who see their visual signs of race and religion—black skin and
black hats—as walking contradictions. A Lubavitcher I knew once told
me of a time he stopped to chat with a Black Jewish acquaintance on a
street corner in Crown Heights. A young Lubavitch boy walked by, saw a
bearded White man in a black suit and fedora talking with a clean-
shaven Black man wearing a yarmulke, and could hardly believe his eyes.
The boy stopped in his tracks and stared at them, gawking, until finally the Black Jew turned and asked, as his acquaintance later recalled:

"What's the matter? You never seen a Black Jew before? Here I am! See, I'm Jewish!"

THERE ARE, HOWEVER, other ways to see Black Jewishness that have little to do with yarmulkes or beards—and other Black Jews in and around Crown Heights who have little to do with the Lubavitch Hasidim. Since at least the early twentieth century, a small but substantial number of African American and Afro-Caribbean people have declared themselves to be the true descendants of the biblical Israelites, and thus the "true Jews" of today. Such claims of Black Jewish history and genealogy are expressed most clearly by the Black Hebrew Israelites, Rastafarians, and other Black nationalist religious sects, but they are shared, in varying degrees, by a broad range of Black Crown Heights residents (including at least some Black orthodox Jews, many of whom nevertheless distance themselves from what they consider the inauthentic Judaism of the Hebrew Israelites). I will discuss the Hebrew Israelite movement in detail in chapter 5, when I explore Black and Jewish Crown Heights residents' claims of Israelite descent. Here, however, I will examine how Hebrew Israelites and Rastafarians reinterpret racial Blackness to make their Jewishness visible in everyday life.

Most Black Crown Heights residents who claim Israelite descent have ambivalent relationships with both Blackness and "race." They tend, in Robyn Wiegman's phrase, to "cite the body as the inevitable locus of 'being' "—grounding their Israelite identities in ostensibly incontestable biological facts and ostensibly obvious phenotypic signs.[41] Yet they nevertheless disrupt popular understandings of race by locating the spiritual meaning of Blackness in the words of the biblical text. For example, the early Black Israelite minister Fleming Aytes set out to demonstrate the Israelite origin of Black Americans in his 1927 book, *The Teaching Black Jew.* Among other scriptural proofs, Aytes quotes the prophet Isaiah's threat that the Lord will strike any Israelite who disobeys him with "burning instead of beauty" (Isaiah 3:24) and the psalmist's threat that "God shall wound the head of His enemies, and the hairy scalp of such a one as goeth on still in his trespasses" (Psalms 68:21, as Aytes cites it from the King James Version). He then explains the present-day relevance of these scriptures:

Now, those curses have put a mark on the Jews, so that they can be easily distinguished from all other nations. . . . Because if the Jews' hair has been cursed, and their comeliness has been cursed, then the Jews are an ugly, bad-haired nation. And if the Jews are an ugly, bad-hair nation, they are black people.[42]

Following the "Black is beautiful" aesthetic of the 1960s and 1970s, and the accompanying celebration of racialized features like nappy hair, few contemporary Black Israelites would describe themselves as "an ugly, bad-hair nation." But the interpretive method of tying bodily signs to biblical texts is still used in a number of different ways. Hebrew Israelites, Rastafarians, and Afrocentric Christians often cite King Solomon's self-declaration: "I am black, and comely" (Song of Songs 1:5) as evidence of his African descent.[43] Some ask how Moses could have passed as a grandson of Pharaoh (Exodus 2:10) if he himself was not a Black African—as Black nationalists generally take the ancient Egyptians to be. And some look to the birth of the patriarch Jacob and his vilified brother Esau (of whom we will hear much more in chapter 5), tying the Bible's description of Esau as "red" and "hairy all over" (Genesis 25:25) to the pink skin and relatively thick body hair of many White Americans, a connection intended to prove—by way of a manichean contrast between "Black" and "White"—that Black Americans are the descendants of Jacob, or children of Israel.

Orthodox Jewish commentators and secular Bible scholars offer rather different interpretations of each of these passages. But these Black Israelite readings of the biblical text draw rhetorical authority from at least two important streams of American cultural and religious thought. They rest, above all, on the binary logic of race in the United States— reading the contemporary contrast between Black and White into the sacred history of the scriptures. And they rest on the literalist hermeneutic that has characterized American interpretations of the Bible since at least the nineteenth century.[44] Orthodox Jews may base images of Jewishness on centuries of rabbinic law and tradition, but given the racial logic of American society and scriptural logic of American Protestantism, Hebrew Israelites may call these images into question through a "plain sense" reading of King Solomon's claim to be "black."

Much as Hebrew Israelites resignify their skin through biblical narrative, Rastafarians resignify their hair through biblical law. Many devout Rastafarians wear matted dreadlocks and full beards, following the biblical injunction, "Ye shall not round the corners of your heads, neither shalt thou mar the corners of thy beard" (Leviticus 19:27), as well as the law that requires a Nazarite, who pledges to remain holy before God, to "let the locks of the hair of his head grow" (Numbers 6:5). Rastafarianism is an extremely diverse, decentralized movement, and not all Rastas see their dreadlocks as signs of Israelite identity, but it is a very common interpretation.[45] In the fall of 1991, for example, a journalist spoke with a dreadlocked Trinidadian Crown Heights resident who explained he grows his dreads following the same biblical passage that leads Hasidic men to grow their beards. "We are the real Jews," the Rasta concluded from this. "We are the Israelites. . . . It's in the Bible, mon."[46]

Finally, in addition to resignifying racialized bodily features, Rastafarians and Hebrew Israelites often wear distinctive clothing that accentuates their Jewish or Israelite identities. For example, members of the prominent Rasta sect the Twelve Tribes of Israel assume tribal affiliations that are based on their birthdays and marked by distinctive colors. Twelve Tribes Rastas born in October mark their membership in the tribe of Dan by wearing blue, while those born in July mark symbolic descent from Judah by wearing brown, and so on.[47] Hebrew Israelites sometimes mark their descent from Jacob with yarmulkes and fringed undergarments similar or identical to those worn by orthodox Jews, with a range of distinctive Judaic jewelry, or with white turbans adorned with Star of David pendants. Members of the Israeli Church of Universal Practical Knowledge, a Hebrew Israelite sect known for preaching racial apocalypse in Times Square and elsewhere, sometimes wear ornate flowing robes seemingly patterned on Hollywood images of the ancient Israelite priesthood. Many Hebrew Israelites, however, wear no distinguishing garments in everyday life—passing simply as Black, just as mainstream Jews often pass as White (see figure 17).

Like the seam of a Hasidic woman's stockings, these somatic and sartorial signs of identity speak to relatively limited audiences. When they notice them at all, Lubavitchers tend to disregard these unexpected signs of unorthodox Jewishness. But if one takes such visual signs seriously, it

FIGURE 17 Members of the Israeli Church of Universal Practical Knowledge preaching near Times Square. The man on the right wears clothing that marks him as an "Israelite," while the man on the left passes as "Black." (Photo by the author.)

becomes increasingly difficult to tell, at a glance, just who is a Jew on the streets of Crown Heights.

JUST HOW DIFFICULT became clear to me late one Friday afternoon, in the fall of 1997, as I sat by the side of Prospect Lake, in a section of Prospect Park bordering on Crown Heights. I was talking with a Jamaican Rasta I'd known for a little while—a spiritual leader of sorts—and a number of his informal disciples, who had come to the park to "reason" together and enjoy the beautiful day. The leaves were turning fall colors, matching the red, gold, and green of the Rasta flag my acquaintance had hung from a nearby tree, and the lake was shimmering in the late afternoon sun—in warm Brooklyn light, like a Hopper or Vermeer. We'd been talking for a couple of hours about the history of ancient Babylon, the Pope's war against Haile Selassie, and other dread topics, when I stood up to go, anxious to get home before the siren that marks the beginning of Shabbos in Crown Heights.

But before I could leave, my acquaintance stopped me to ask: When could he come study with me at the "Jewish churches" in Crown Heights? I'd studied with him, learning about Selassie, and I was always welcome—he stressed clearly—but I'd yet to reciprocate. He knew I was an anthropologist, not a Hasid, but he wasn't interested in academic scholarship. He wanted to study Torah with the Lubavitch Hasidim. Well, I tried to put it gently, I'm not sure if they would accept you. He sensed my equivocation and replied: What do you mean you're not sure? Is it yes or no? No, I said, the Lubavitchers don't let anybody study with them who they don't think is Jewish. He laughed, and flashed a mock indignant scowl—not that he was surprised or angry, but he surely disapproved. He then stepped back a bit and shifted his weight on to one foot, extending his arms at his sides, with his palms up—striking a pose, opening himself to my gaze—and declared: "They kyan [can't] look at me an' tell me I'm not a Jew."

A simple statement of fact, in his eyes. But how did he look, in this moment, as both Rasta and Jew? What were the signs? Bathed in magic-hour light, his blood-shot eyes gleamed orange and his dark brown skin glistened a bit. Chin-length dreadlocks and a wispy beard accentuated the sharp angles of his sunken cheeks (he was something of a mystic, and ate only fresh fruits and vegetables, which may have accounted for his rail-thin face and body). He wore blue-jeans, ripped at one knee, and a blue denim shirt unbuttoned over a white T-shirt. A number of pendants hung down to his chest on red, gold, and green beaded strands: a large metal Ethiopian cross and a wooden elephant, among others. A silver Lion of Judah pin was affixed to one collar, and his breast pocket bulged with a half-dozen pens and pencils, including highlighters for marking up biblical texts, and countless scraps of paper. This was Rasta the Nazarite—natural mystic and Bible scholar. This was the pose he struck, outlined in Brooklyn light: "They kyan look at me an' tell me I'm not a Jew."

Of course they can, and do. But many Black Crown Heights residents disagree, claiming—and performing—unorthodox Jewish identities. Jewishness in Crown Heights thus takes on a number of different visual forms, depending on one's point of view, and one's position at the intersection of race and religion.

Walking and Spitting: Jewishness in Motion

The signs of Jewishness I've discussed thus far are predominantly visual and relatively static—snapshot images of identity and difference Crown Heights residents extract from the flow of everyday life. But these signs, and the people marked by them, are often experienced through a range of senses, and nearly always experienced in motion. Crown Heights residents frequently catch, and recall, glimpses of gestures and movements they see as distinctively Black or Jewish. They overhear, or imagine, snippets of conversation that offer tantalizing clues to the intentions of strangers. Like skin, hair, and clothing, these evanescent signs are thought to provide evidence of Black and Jewish selves.

For example, I once stopped to listen to a Hebrew Israelite preacher speaking in a pedestrian plaza in Flatbush, just south of Crown Heights, and he decided—as such preachers often do—to incorporate my Whiteness into his sermon. He told the fifteen or twenty Black Brooklynites gathered around him that he would "show [me] from the Bible that [me] and [my] White race are the source of all the wickedness on this earth," then proceeded to do so by equating my pink skin with Esau's, by way of Genesis 25:25. I turned to leave, fresh out of ethnographic endurance, and he proclaimed to the crowd in an exultant voice: "Just like it says in the Psalms, 'The wicked flee, while the strong stand like a lion!'" (actually a paraphrase of Proverbs 28:1). He explained that my cowardly flight shows the wickedness of the so-called White people, while his stalwart preaching proves that so-called Blacks are in fact descendants of the tribe of Judah, which the scriptures often compare to a lion. Our actions spoke as loudly as our skin, revealing our identities as descendants of Jacob and Esau.

Although this is, no doubt, a particularly dramatic (and carefully staged) example, it highlights the ways that Crown Heights residents, and others, assess the behavior of strangers on the street. They tend to take actions as signs of identities, muddying the conceptual distinction between what one *is* and what one *does*. Fleeting images and overheard comments fuse with popular stereotypes and attributed intentions to form multilayered perceptual phenomena. Race and religion are perceived as dynamic qualities—endowed, for better or worse, with direction and movement.

IN THE EYES of both Black and Jewish Crown Heights residents, the embodied style of everyday Hasidic sociality speaks volumes about the nature of Jews and Jewishness. I was first made aware of this issue in an unlikely ethnographic setting. In the spring of 1997, while teaching anthropology at a campus of New York's City University, I illustrated a point from the textbook with an anecdote from Crown Heights. Apropos of nothing, a Black student raised her hand to ask why the Jews in Crown Heights are always "running around." I was taken aback, and mumbled something vague about the danger of stereotypes. But really, I had no idea how to respond. The image was new to me, and I wasn't sure what to make of it. Most of my students were familiar with it, however, and a few jumped right in: "Yeah," they wanted to know, "what's up with that? Why are they always in such a rush?" They saw the Hasidim—or perhaps all Jews—walking distinctively quickly around the streets of New York.

I began asking Crown Heights residents about fast-walking Hasidim, and as soon as I started thinking about them I began to see them myself. But I was still surprised to discover that this distinctive Hasidic gait had been raised in past discussions of Black-Jewish relations. In the documentary film *Blacks and Jews*, David Lazerson—the Hasidic cofounder of the 1990s community organization Project CURE—describes the dialogues he helped organize between Black and Jewish teenagers after the violence of 1991. As soon as these kids got together, Lazerson recalls:

> It was boom, boom, boom—firing all these questions at each other: What's with the beanie on your head? What's with the dreadlocks? What's with the beard? Um . . . what's with these white strings over

here? Just physically—what's with the ankh symbol that you wear? Physically, there were a zillion questions that they had about appearance. How come you Hasidim always seem to be in a rush? You know, walking down the street. And then the Jewish kids saying: Well how come you guys are always hanging out on the corner?[48]

These teenagers' gazes were fixed on many of the signs I have discussed thus far, but they put these signs in motion, observing Black and Jewish bodies "walking down the street" and "hanging out on the corner." Lazerson distinguished these "questions . . . about appearance" from what he described as the "real issues" of culture and politics. But the everyday field of racial and religious visibility cannot be separated so easily from the issues that divide Blacks and Jews in Crown Heights, as the smallest details of bearing and behavior are thought to provide hints of underlying identities.

To many Black observers, a Hasid in a long black coat walking briskly down Eastern Parkway is a picture of Jewish "arrogance," or at least "insularity" and "insensitivity." Blacks in Crown Heights often complain that their Hasidic neighbors aren't so neighborly, that they rush around unconcerned with others, without making eye contact or saying hello. Indeed, Lubavitchers often acknowledge that many in their community are somewhat brusque in public. They claim, however, with some justification, that they're just as rude to each other as they are to their Black neighbors. Once, as I entered a grocery store on Kingston Avenue, I stopped to hold the door open for a Hasidic woman leaving the store with a half-dozen bags and two toddlers in a stroller. She smiled and thanked me, then looked me up and down and asked, "You're not from this neighborhood, are you?" Some Hasidim (like other New Yorkers) take a certain pride in their no-nonsense rudeness, while others bemoan what they describe as a lack of "refinement" in their community. But all tend to argue that these manners and mannerisms have nothing to do with race or religion.

Yet when I asked Lubavitchers about their reputation for rushing, a number of more complex readings emerged. While some insisted their distinctive gait had no significance whatsoever, others saw it as indicative of their efforts to balance both spiritual and material concerns. One woman expressed this view, then went on to explore the deeper implications of this hectic lifestyle. She said she worried sometimes that when Blacks in the neighborhood "see us *rushing* to the mikvah, *rushing* to shopping, *rushing* to make Shabbos, and *rushing* to make Yuntef, there must be a feeling of 'Well, I'm being left out.'" I described my anthropology students' concern with the issue, and she tried to explain:

> Shachris [the morning prayer] has a time-frame, Mincha [the afternoon prayer] has a time-frame, Maariv [the evening prayer] has a time-frame, Shabbos has a time-frame, Yuntef [a general term for all holidays] has a time-frame. And that's why Jews are always rushing. And that's supposed to keep us in line, that's supposed to keep us out of trouble. This whole thing is supposed to keep us spiritual, connected to God. That's the purpose of this, and this is supposed to make us a better people. However, the fallout is that people wonder. They consider us insular, they consider us snotty, they consider us—but that's just ignorance.

Here the distinctive gait of a rushing Hasid indexes his fulfillment of the commandments of the Torah—and it is mostly a matter of "his" fulfillment, as Jewish women are exempt from most of the time-bound commandments described here (though they too must often rush to fit Shabbos and holiday preparations into their busy lives). To some Hasidim, all this rushing shows they are "connected to God." It is a visible sign of divine chosenness—a spiritual phenotype, or an exterior reflection of their godly souls. Their Black neighbors, however, take it as a sign that the Hasidim are insular or arrogant. Either way—or rather, both—the meanings of this Hasidic gait emerge at the intersection of race and religion.

BUT THE NATURE of Jewishness is not perceived solely in the behavior of Jews. Indeed, many Hasidim find compelling evidence of their Jewishness in what they see as the antisemitic behavior of Gentiles. Lubavitchers in Crown Heights often locate antisemitic intent in the smallest details of their Blacks neighbors' actions. For some Lubavitchers, though by no means all, experiences of antisemitism are woven throughout the fabric of everyday life. And in Hasidic eyes, this animosity reveals the true identities of Gentiles and Jews. Their chosenness may best be seen, perhaps, in the hostile gazes of others.

Lubavitchers in Crown Heights clearly do face antisemitism from a small minority of their neighbors. But they also attribute antisemitic intent to a broad range of seemingly ambiguous behaviors. Black animosity appears, in Hasidic eyes, in a number of subtle guises. One Hasid told me: "You get a lot of antisemitism living here. We get a lot of times, people yelling out, y'know, comments. And the spitting, and—." Shocked, I interrupted her to ask: "The spitting?" She had said it in an off-hand way, but I could hardly believe my ears. "Oh yeah," she replied, "They spit when they see Jews, a lot of them. They deliberately spit." Not at you, she clarified, but on the street as you pass. Has she seen it herself, I asked? "Oh yeah," she nodded. She then described an incident she had experienced not long before: "Last year, I was getting on the subway at Nostrand Avenue and I had a guy deliberately ram me with his backpack. . . . It wasn't an accident, it was a deliberate action. I mean, you can tell when people hate you. They come at you, and make comments, and you get the—you can tell." Once one learns how to see them, the everyday behaviors of Black Crown Heights residents can be recast into striking images of antisemitism. Another Lubavitcher recalled glimpsing Hitler's storm-troopers in a pair of Black children walking with their family: "I remember one time I was walking down Eastern Parkway, and there were some parents who were preceded by their two children, and the children were goose-stepping, walking like this, y'know—." He sat up in his chair, his back stiff and his chin jutting out, and started waving his arms aggressively, imitating the march of these young Black Nazis, demonstrating how they were walking, "goose-stepping at me, in mockery."

Such perceptions rest upon a basic understanding of Gentile identity held by many Hasidim and other ultra-orthodox Jews. In essence, according to many Lubavitchers, non-Jews inherently hate the Jews. Although individual Gentiles may struggle successfully against their antisemitic instincts, these instincts are universal and eternal. They stem (as we'll see in chapter 5) from Esau's undying hatred of Jacob, and from Gentile jealousy of Jewish chosenness. As a prominent Lubavitch scholar explained to a class of newly orthodox yeshiva students, "Since we were chosen as the chosen people, a Goy intrinsically and innately hates a Yid." Or as a Lubavitch community activist told me, jabbing his finger at my chest for emphasis, "All of these people—the Schvartzes, the Palestinians, the Syrians, the Italians, the Germans—they all hate you! They all want to kill you! You!"

When Lubavitchers see signs of this hatred in Crown Heights, their neighbors appear to them as Gentiles rather than Blacks. Evidence of antisemitism makes religious difference visible in everyday life. Much like long black coats, hostile Black people show the Lubavitch Hasidim that they are, in fact, Jews. Yet these perceptions of Gentile hostility alternate with other perceptions of identity. Even among Hasidim (with the exception of a few extremists), the enmity of their neighbors isn't always so clear. Gentile antisemitism is at once conceptually axiomatic and perceptually fleeting. Most of the time, thank goodness, signs of antisemitism come and go with the turn of a head. A Hasid may do a double-take, looking back at the Black man she heard muttering a slur, or saw spitting by her feet, and find him looking away, paying her no mind, or smiling instead and nodding hello.

For example, when I told one of my Lubavitch neighbors I was researching a book on Black-Jewish relations, he responded by telling me of the time, just a few days before, when he was walking to his car and a little Black boy, maybe five years old, looked up at him and said, "Heil Hitler!" I'd occasionally heard such comments myself from Black teenagers in and around Crown Heights,[49] but I was nevertheless surprised that this incendiary slogan could have come from such a young child. My neighbor explained that the kid's mother, who was with him at the time, must have put him up to it. I was still skeptical, however, and my neighbor backed away from his claim just a bit: "I was like 98 percent sure," he said. "I was going to say something to him, or to his parents. I was just waiting for him to say it again."

But he never did, so my neighbor was left wondering, with his Jewishness flickering before him, not quite instantiated on the streets of Crown Heights. He could almost make out his chosenness in the words of a five-year-old-boy, but then again he couldn't. Or at least not quite. This sense of suspended perception—waiting nervously for a sign, or confirmation of a hunch—is extremely common in today's Crown Heights, as Black and Jewish experiences of difference are caught in the tensions between race and religion.

Suits and Souls, Identity and Visibility

My neighbor's experience of "waiting for him to say it again" could hardly be more different from a yeshiva student's confident claim that the Jewish soul "just shines out." The diverse perceptions of Jewishness I've explored in this chapter clearly complicate Crown Heights residents' efforts to tell Jews when they see them on the streets of their neighborhood.

But what about the Jewish soul? Or rather, leaving aside Hasidic theology, what about the interior, spiritual dimensions of Jewish identity? There is, of course, far more to *being* a Jew than just *looking* like one. The visual images I have examined in this chapter do not determine the truth of Jewishness in Crown Heights, or anywhere else. Anthony Graziosi, for example, did not become a Jew simply because he looked like one in the eyes of his killers. Black Jews and Hasidic women are no less Jewish than Hasidic men, simply because their identities are less obvious in the eyes of some observers. My goal is certainly not to cast doubt on their Jewishness. Quite the contrary, I hope I have shown that there are Jews in Crown Heights who may not "look Jewish" according to popular images of the "typical" Jew.

Yet the inner core of Jewish identity cannot be sheltered from the historical flux of Jewish visibility. The perceptions and performances I have described shape what it means to be a Jew in today's Crown Heights, not just what it means to look like one. These perceptions were a matter of life and death in the murder of Yankel Rosenbaum, and of insult and injury in the assault I described on an African American orthodox girl. In their own different ways, the Lubavitch Hasidim, Black orthodox Jews, and Black Hebrew Israelites all stress the importance of performing their Jewishness—marking and reinforcing their Jewish identities with black coats, colored kippahs, flowing robes, and other signs. Being a Jew on the "inside" can never be reduced to looking like one on the "outside," but the inside and outside of Jewishness are inextricable in everyday life. According to a young Lubavitcher in Washington Square Park, the Jewish soul "shines out" like a beacon in a complex world. But on the streets of Crown Heights, the dappled rays of a diverse society shine back in. Jewish identities, and others, are defined in this kaleidoscopic play of light.

5

The Voices of Jacob on the Streets of Brooklyn

Israelite Histories and Identities

Throughout this book, I have often distinguished between the racial and religious discourses of Blacks and Jews, respectively. In chapter 1, for example, the underlying contrast between race and religion was reflected in the distinction between a "riot" and a "pogrom." In chapter 3 it took the form of "segregation" and "insularity," as well as "culture" and "kashrus." It was muddied substantially in chapter 4, but reemerged in a contrast between "phenotype" and "fashion"—racialized bodies and religious dress. Given these divergent discourses of difference, it may come as a surprise to learn, in this chapter, that Blacks and Jews in Crown Heights use strikingly similar—or at least parallel—narratives of biblical history and Israelite descent to define what I have described as racial and religious identities. Much as they share and contest a Brooklyn neighborhood, Crown Heights residents share and contest the history and identity of the biblical Israelites, as well as the coveted status of God's chosen people.

These Israelite histories sit, uncomfortably at times, on the conceptual boundaries of "religion" and "race." Although Lubavitchers tend toward a religious understanding of Jewishness, and their neighbors generally tend toward racial understandings of Blackness, they each claim relationships with the biblical Israelites that cannot be defined in terms of race or religion alone. To make sense of these claims, we must treat categories and identities like "race" and "religion," "Blackness" and "Jewishness," much as the historian and social theorist Michel Foucault treated scholarly fields like "biology" and "economics" in *The Archaeology of Knowledge:* "These pre-existing forms of continuity," he wrote, "all these syntheses that are accepted without question, must remain in suspense. They must not be rejected definitively of course, but the tranquility with which they are accepted must be disturbed."[1] This chapter will place Blackness and Jewishness "in suspense" by focusing on claims of Israelite descent. It will "[disturb] the tranquility" of race and religion by focusing on history and genealogy. It will not dispense with these familiar categories—categories that have structured my own analyses—but it will explore their boundaries and limitations.

Crown Heights may seem an unlikely site at which to question, or deconstruct, such categories and identities. Especially since the violence of 1991, the neighborhood has often been divided along racial and religious lines—under the grip, it would seem, of Black-Jewish difference. Yet a brief interaction across these lines of difference points out the limitations of such simplistic binary framings. In an unpublished letter to a local Jewish newspaper, a Lubavitcher who lives just steps from the scene of the accident that killed Gavin Cato, and the epicenter of the violence that followed his death, described a tense conversation soon after this violence in which "One lone rioter from down the block (and his Doberman Pincher) gave a great 45 minute monologue on who the true Jews are (meaning them) and how the fakers (meaning us) would soon be 'dead meat' in more ways than one." Here the difference between Blacks and Jews is articulated in terms of—and thus complicated by—a distinction between "true Jews" and "fakers." Jewishness itself seems to shift back and forth between Blacks and Jews, defined simultaneously by race and/or religion. This vision of Blacks as "true Jews" rests on an unstated assumption that Black Americans are direct descendants of the tribes of ancient Israel. As one Crown Heights Rasta told a journalist in chapter 4: "We are the real Jews. We are the Israelites. . . . It's in the Bible mon."[2]

These Black claims of Jewishness fly in the face of Lubavitchers' basic assumptions about Black-Jewish difference—and, for that matter, those of many other Americans. Yet they capture the ways many Crown Heights residents, both Black and Jewish, define identities in terms of biblical histories. According to the Lubavitch Hasidim, Jewishness ultimately rests on the genealogical ties binding Jews throughout the world to the biblical patriarch Jacob. Like many other Jews, Lubavitchers see themselves (and all others they consider Jews) as descendants of Jacob, who was renamed Israel before fathering the twelve tribes that bear his name. By the same token, as I discussed in chapter 1, they often describe non-Jews as descendants of Jacob's vilified brother Esau, and interpret conflicts between Gentiles and Jews as manifestations of Jacob and Esau's undying hatred. One Crown Heights yeshiva student gave voice to this common Hasidic sentiment when he explained the history of conflict in his neighborhood by telling me simply, "Esau hates Jacob and Jacob hates Esau." He then appealed to the historical logic that supports this view, when he picked up a Bible and asked me, pointedly, "Do you think this is just a storybook? Do you think the Torah is a thing of the past?"

Crown Heights residents generally agree that the Torah is not "a thing of the past." Indeed, as we saw in chapter 4, the Lubavitch Hasidim are hardly the only Crown Heights community to define its identity in terms of biblical history. In and around Crown Heights (and throughout the United States) there are a number of small but thriving communities of Black Hebrew Israelites, who see African American and Afro-Caribbean peoples as the true descendants of the patriarch Jacob, and who sometimes describe White "so-called Jews" as descendants of Esau—and insidious imposters. The Hebrew Israelites practice syncretic forms of Judaism, outside the mainstream of American Jewish life, yet in a complex dialogue with Black orthodox Jews (who are often among their harshest critics). Much like Lubavitchers, they invoke symbolically charged biblical texts to demonstrate their descent from the Israelites of the scriptures. Moreover, their narratives of Israelite history are echoed, at least in part, by many Rastafarians, Black Muslims, Afrocentric Christians, secular Black nationalists, and other Black Brooklynites who may have no real interest in being "Israelites" themselves but are nevertheless certain that the "real Jews" were Black.[3] All told, at least a substantial minority of Black Crown Heights residents feel some sort of tie with the biblical Israelites, and thus doubt or contest their Hasidic neighbors' claims of Israelite descent.

These competing narratives of Israelite history are often tied to criteria of identity one may certainly describe as "racial" and "religious." As I discussed in chapter 4, many Rastas and Hebrew Israelites use phenotypic signs of Blackness—like distinctive skin and hair—to define the boundaries between Israelites and others. Indeed, Black Hebrew Israelites often draw connections between Israelite descent and racial identity, using narratives of Jewish—or rather, Israelite—history to define the spiritual meanings of Blackness. Lubavitchers, by contrast, draw no explicit connection between Israelite descent and racial Whiteness. As I discussed in the introduction and elsewhere, most Lubavitch Hasidim believe that Jews are ultimately distinguished from Gentiles by a unique "godly soul" inherited from their patriarchs, rather than by external or bodily signs. When I asked Lubavitchers how this Jewish soul was transmitted from the patriarchs to present-day Jews, many took pains to distinguish this theory of Jewish descent from racial biology (an understanding of Jewishness they tend to associate with Nazi antisemitism). One Lubavitch community activist defined the Jewish people as "the seed of Abraham" and the "first family of monotheism," and when I asked why this family is only reckoned matrilineally he replied, impatiently, "We're talking about a soul—the inheritance of a soul, or a type of soul. It's metaphysics, not genetics."

Yet despite their divergent ties to popular discourses of race and religion—bodies and souls, genetics and metaphysics—both Lubavitch Hasidim and Black Hebrew Israelites ultimately claim nothing more or less than an inherited relationship with an eternal God. This embodied chosenness transgresses the distinction between "race" and "religion," as these categories are typically understood. We must therefore bracket our easy assumptions about the racial and religious differences between Blacks and Jews, and instead explore the underlying vision of collective identity that is shared—and contested—across the boundaries of these communities. Above all, we must examine the ways Crown Heights residents link race and religion to history and genealogy.

Collective Identity and Inherited Memory

The past is remarkably present in today's Crown Heights. Indeed, one can hardly walk the streets of the neighborhood without coming face to face with "history." The cinder-block walls of a bowling alley on Bedford Avenue are covered with a huge mural depicting the glories of ancient Egypt, as well as a pantheon of pop stars and political figures, from Marcus Garvey and Jean-Jacques Dessalines to Duke Ellington and Mohammad Ali.

The walls of most Hasidic homes are adorned with portraits of the Rebbe and his predecessors. And at Judaica World, on Kingston Avenue, Hasidic children can buy "Torah Cards" depicting biblical prophets, patriarchs, and kings, or a do-it-yourself model of the ancient temple in Jerusalem.

These signs of history reflect a fundamental assumption about collective identity that is widely shared—and rarely questioned—in Crown Heights and elsewhere. We multicultural Americans tend to believe that "peoples" and "cultures" are defined by continuity with their "histories" and "traditions." Collective identities therefore must—or at least should— be grounded, in some way, in these histories. Blackness is thought to require some understanding of African American and/or African history, while Jewishness is imagined as an ongoing dialogue with ancient religious texts and/or cultural traditions. Immigrant ethnicities are founded, in part, on memories of the "Old Country" and the "Old Neighborhood," wherever they may be. Even Christianity—which disrupts these assumptions, to some extent, by encouraging individual conversions to the faith— often calls upon Christians to emulate the early church.[4] In Crown Heights and elsewhere, the consensus is clear: for a "people" to have an authentic "identity," its past must play a part in its present. New York City's popular hip-hop station, Hot 97, may have put it best with its 1998 Black History Month slogan: "If you know your past, you know your self."[5]

But how, exactly, do we know our pasts? The past confronts us all across a gulf of discontinuity—opened by the fact of ceaseless historical change, and the existential reality of death. There is an inescapable disjuncture between today's Crown Heights and its various histories, biblical and otherwise. As the Reverend Clarence Norman, Sr., of the First Baptist Church of Crown Heights, put it when I asked him about his Lubavitch neighbors' biblical interpretations of contemporary politics: "Jacob and Esau have been dead three thousand years, and their hand does not reach from the grave." Perhaps especially in the tangled web of diasporas that makes up today's Crown Heights, it can be difficult for Blacks and Jews alike to sense a connection between their presents and pasts. Despite the central role of "roots" and "origins" in the construction of many diasporic identities, scholars and others have often argued that diasporic communities have particularly fraught relationships with history—that migrants and their children may be cut off from their pasts in distinctive ways.[6] For example, in his essay "Imaginary Homelands," the novelist and critic Salman Rushdie writes:

> It may be argued that the past is a country from which we have all emigrated, that its loss is part of our common humanity. Which seems to me self-evidently true; but I suggest that the writer who is out-of-country and even out-of-language may experience this loss in an intensified form. It is made more concrete for him by the physical fact of discontinuity, of his present being in a different place from his past, of his being "elsewhere."[7]

In a neighborhood populated by chosen peoples in exile—by descendants of immigrants, refugees, and slaves, ostensibly uprooted from their collective pasts following the Nazi Holocaust and the Atlantic slave trade—Crown Heights residents must work to fill a troubling gap between past and present, origins and elsewhere.

In this context, and others, it can be difficult to determine which of the many available histories is actually relevant to one's social life. How, exactly, do we know which past is our own? Are Crown Heights residents inheritors of ancient Israel or Egypt? Of Jacob or Esau? George Washington's revolution or Toussaint L'Ouverture's? Of the Dutch who settled Breukelen or the countless immigrants who followed? Historical threads of various kinds may be traced from these, and countless other, pasts to the present-day lives of Blacks and Jews in Crown Heights. Given this embarrassment of historiographic riches, Blacks and Jews alike turn to another fundamental, and rarely questioned, assumption: the equation, or conflation, of history and genealogy. They tend to assume that they inherit the legacy—the words and deeds, accomplishments and experiences, sorrows and triumphs—of those people to whom they are tied by biogenetic descent. Memory, they believe, is a property of blood. Social experience is a family heirloom. This equation of history and genealogy helps to construct, and is simultaneously constructed by, collective identities like Blackness and Jewishness.[8]

At their core—and in some sense prior to the invocation of categories like race and religion—the collective identities of Lubavitchers and Hebrew Israelites rest on claims to inherit the memory of ancient Israel, through a mysterious combination of genetics and metaphysics. These claims are not entirely different from the claims of many Irish Americans, for example, to inherit the memory of the Irish potato famine, or the claims of many American Jews to inherit the memory of New York's Lower East Side—or for that matter the claims of countless amateur genealogists to inherit the memories of their distinguished ancestors.[9] But claims of Israelite history and genealogy are distinctive in a number of crucial ways. Perhaps above all, the ancient Israelites are widely regarded as God's chosen people, "a kingdom of priests and a holy nation" (Exodus 19:6). This singular status lends cosmological depth and eschatological significance to any claim of Israelite descent. Yet while Israel's importance is relatively clear—at least to people who read the Bible as a divinely authored text—its identity lies shrouded in the mists of time. Even if one accepts the historical reality of biblical figures like Abraham, Isaac, and Jacob (as Lubavitchers, Hebrew Israelites, and many others do), it may be difficult to trace one's family tree to a patriarch who died 3,500 years ago.

This, I think, is where "race" and "religion" come into play. They are, among other things, historiographic tools—techniques for suturing oneself to history.[10] Tenuous claims of descent may be bolstered by evidence of a fundamental similarity between ancestors and descendants, whether a distinctive body, a distinctive soul, or distinctive practices and beliefs. These symbolically charged analogies between past and present are shaped by the available categories of identity formation—race, religion, ethnicity, or what have you—but they ultimately support claims of historical continuity that cannot be reduced to such categories alone.[11] Race and religion offer Crown Heights residents and others ready-made terms with which to articulate their ties to the past—hardly an insignificant task—but these terms are mixed and mingled, fairly indiscriminately, in the service of history and genealogy. The result, in Crown Heights, is a shared and contested field of overlapping categories, narratives, and identities.[12]

The Lubavitch Hasidim and Black Hebrew Israelites use these symbolic resources in dramatically different ways, and tell dramatically different stories of Israelite history. But their collective identities nevertheless take shape within a common set of discourses, and therefore can't be distinguished quite as clearly as Blackness is from Jewishness, or race from religion. We may get a better sense of these commonalities and differences

by examining the ways Lubavitchers and Hebrew Israelites interpret biblical narratives of Israelite history.

"The Voice Is the Voice of Jacob, and
the Hands Are the Hands of Esau"

To trace the ties between race, religion, history, and genealogy in Lubavitch Hasidic understandings of Jewishness, we must turn—as Lubavitchers
themselves often do—to the Hebrew Bible's narrative of the origins of Israel. In Genesis 25, in the Torah portion known as Toldos (which may be
translated, tellingly, as both "Generations" and "Stories," genealogies and
histories), the patriarch Isaac's wife Rebecca gives birth to twin sons,
Jacob and Esau. It was not an easy pregnancy, as the Bible relates:

> The children struggled in her womb, and she said, "If so, why do I
> exist?" She went to enquire of the Lord, and the Lord answered her
> [in verse]: "Two nations are in your womb, / Two separate peoples
> shall issue from your body; / One people shall be mightier than the
> other, / And the older shall serve the younger." When her time to
> give birth was at hand, there were twins in her womb. The first one
> emerged red, like a hairy mantle all over; so they named him Esau
> [a pun on the Hebrew word for "hair"]. Then his brother emerged,
> holding on to the heel of Esau; so they named him Jacob [a pun on
> "heel"]. (Genesis 25:22–26)

According to orthodox Jewish tradition, as I've noted, Jacob went on to father the twelve tribes of Israel and thus the entire Jewish people—passing
God's covenant with Abraham down to his descendants—while Esau fathered Israel's bitter enemy the Edomites and thus (by a complex logic I
will discuss below) the entire Gentile world. Indeed, according to many
Lubavitchers the moral characters of Jacob and Esau determine the social
identities of Jews and Gentiles to this day, and their eternal struggle constitutes the central narrative of world history. We may thus learn a great
deal about Lubavitchers' understandings of Jewish-Gentile difference by
examining how they interpret the relationship between these twins.

The Bible paints ambivalent portraits of both Jacob and Esau, yet according to rabbinic commentaries on the text—which are read as infallible

accounts by contemporary Hasidim—the life of Esau was a sordid tale of idolatry and crime, while the life of Jacob was a heartwarming story of selfless devotion to his parents and their God. Even before birth, there were subtle signs of their divergent characters. Rebecca felt the twins "struggl[ing] in her womb" (25:22), the great sage Rashi explains, because whenever she passed a synagogue or a heathen temple Jacob and Esau were drawn to the Torah and to idol worship, respectively, and fought to get out of the womb. Once they were born, their differences became clearer. The text tells us, for example, that "Esau became a skillful hunter" (25:27), which the rabbinic tradition has long taken to mean a vicious murderer as well. It tells us that "Jacob was a mild man who lived in tents" (25:27), which means he spent his days studying the Torah in a yeshiva.[13]

Esau's love of hunting may have won him his father's favor, thanks to Isaac's taste for game (25:28), but it cost him his birthright as the firstborn son when, famished after a long day outdoors, Jacob convinced him to trade his claim on God's covenant with Abraham for a bowl of lentil stew (25:29–34). Years later, when Isaac was on his deathbed, Jacob made good on this deal by dressing in his brother's clothes, placing goatskins on his arms to mimic his brother's hair, and receiving the blessing Isaac intended for Esau. According to the text, a blind and dying Isaac was at first confused—though ultimately deceived—by the hair on Jacob's arms, and wondered aloud why "The voice is the voice of Jacob, but the hands are the hands of Esau" (27:22). According to rabbinic commentators, however, Isaac's seeming confusion over his sons' identities captured the very essence of their characters, and the enduring difference between their descendants. As I noted in chapter 1, Isaac's reference to "the voice of Jacob" has long been interpreted by orthodox Jews as a prophetic allusion to the intellect and spirituality of the children of Jacob, while his reference to "the hands of Esau" has been interpreted as an allusion to the brutality and materialism of the children of Esau.

Moments after Isaac unwittingly blessed Jacob, Esau came to his father to receive his blessing. Isaac was furious to learn he had been tricked by his younger son, but told Esau it was too late—a blessing is a blessing, and he couldn't take it back. Esau was distraught, and pleaded with Isaac: "'Have you but one blessing Father? Bless me too Father!' And Esau wept aloud" (27:38).[14] Isaac blessed Esau as best he could, but Jacob and his heirs nevertheless inherited the coveted status of God's chosen people. Not surprisingly, the text states that Esau "harbored a grudge against Jacob because of the blessing which his father had given him" (27:41). Indeed, it recounts Esau's oath to kill his brother after their father's death. Yet it also recounts how the brothers eventually reached an uneasy peace. When they meet again, years later, the Bible describes a joyous reunion: "Esau ran to greet [Jacob]. He embraced him and, falling on his neck, he kissed him; and they wept" (33:4).

Most rabbinic commentators, however, have divorced Esau's "grudge against Jacob" from the narrative context of their sibling rivalry, and instead described his jealous rage as a defining feature of all relationships between the brothers' descendants—the ultimate source of what some consider the Gentile world's undying hatred of Jews. As the historian Gerson Cohen writes, in a study of rabbinic views of Esau, "The dominant feeling in all of Hebrew literature is summed up in [the renowned] Rabbi Simeon bar Yohai's comment: 'It is an axiom: Esau hates Jacob.' "[15] This hatred is the interpretive key to the shifting identity of Esau's descendants within the rabbinic imagination. The Bible describes Esau as the father of the Edomites, a neighboring tribe with whom the Israelites had a history of intermittent warfare. But by the first or second century CE, while living under the yoke of Roman imperialism, rabbinic commentators came to identify Esau with the Roman Empire. As Cohen writes: "Scripture named Edom, and history pointed at Rome. By the most elementary syllogism, the two became one."[16] A thousand years later, facing new aggressors, many medieval European Jews identified Esau and Edom with the Catholic Church and European Christendom.[17] And for some contemporary orthodox Jews, Esau has come to signify the entire non-Jewish world—and above all the threat of Gentile antisemitism. According to one recent Torah commentator, Esau symbolizes "the wicked kingdom, which comprises all the forces of evil from time immemorial, which has always clashed with the spiritual world of Israel in different ways and forms."[18]

A symbolically charged picture of the children of Jacob and Esau thus emerges in canonical rabbinic literature and contemporary Hasidic discourse: an image of Jews and Gentiles as opposing peoples and principles, locked in eternal hatred and struggle. These peoples are defined by a number of intersecting criteria, many of which resonate with contemporary understandings of racial and religious identity. They are marked, in large part, by their ancestors' bodies—by birth and kinship, as well as hair and color (although their common descent from Isaac and Rebecca stands at odds with contemporary views of race). Yet these embodied signs are inextricably tied to moral values and ritual practices—a "wicked kingdom" at war with a "spiritual world." And their lineages are distinguished, above all else, by their different relationships with an omnipotent God.

Of course, the Hebrew Bible's genealogical view of collective identity pre-dates contemporary categories like "race" and "religion" by thousands of years. But history and genealogy are tied to racial and religious identity, as Lubavitchers draw on the narrative of Jacob and Esau to make sense of Black-Jewish difference in Crown Heights. We may trace this process by re-examining Shmuel Butman's claim that "the hands of Esau" murdered Yankel Rosenbaum during the violence of August 1991.

AS I DESCRIBED in chapter 1, Rabbi Butman spoke in August of 1996 at a public event held by the Crown Heights Jewish Community Council to mark the fifth anniversary of the violence of 1991, and to support the recently announced federal prosecutions of Charles Price and Lemrick Nelson for the murder of Yankel Rosenbaum. It was, in fact, five years to the day since Rosenbaum's stabbing, so the event was at once a rally, a press conference, and a memorial service. A number of Hasidic community leaders and prominent politicians spoke before a few hundred Hasidim, a handful of Blacks, a few police officers and Guardian Angels, and eight or ten television news cameras. They spoke from a stage set up on the corner of President Street and Brooklyn Avenue—the very site where Rosenbaum had been stabbed to death.

Not surprisingly, most speakers urged the crowd to remember Yankel Rosenbaum's murder and the violence of 1991. These calls to "remember" resonated with the broader Lubavitch concern for historical continuity. Indeed, nearly every Lubavitcher who spoke at the memorial situated Rosenbaum's death within a Hasidic narrative of Jewish history by referring to the violence of August 1991 as a pogrom. The chairman of the Jewish Community Council, for example, spoke gravely of "the first pogrom here on American soil." But this vision of Jewish history and identity did not go uncontested. Even during the memorial, there were conflicting narratives of the violence of 1991. For example, then Senator Alfonse D'Amato—a vociferous supporter of the Lubavitch community—proclaimed that: "Striking

out violently against a person because of his race, his color, his creed, his
sexual orientation, because he or she may be different, is absolutely in-
tolerable." By equating Rosenbaum's murder with hate crimes based on
race and sexuality (in the one sound-bite from the event to make it onto
the evening news), D'Amato undermined Lubavitch efforts to situate the
violence of 1991 within a specifically Jewish history. Yankel Rosenbaum's
death might therefore have marked the Lubavitch community's dislocation from its past, as victims of a "race riot" or a crime equivalent to gay-
bashing.

Even Yankel's brother Norman Rosenbaum seemed to question the
relationship between Yankel's death and the history of anti-Jewish violence. At one point in his brief remarks he denied that his brother's murder had anything to do with his Jewishness, arguing instead that "The
people that murdered my brother are criminals. Firstly and foremostly
and only are they criminals, and criminals do not have the capacity to differentiate between race, creed, or color." At another point he described
his brother as the victim of an antisemitic attack, yet reflected candidly
on his own tenuous relationship with the concrete reality of this attack.
Commenting on the lovely weather we were enjoying, he observed: "The
sun is shining, the skies are blue. The scene here is so far removed from
violence, virtual anarchy, racism and antisemitism, and hatred. But to
think back five years, that this is where—the exact same—where my
brother was not only attacked, but where that attack took place amongst
cries of 'Kill the Jew.' It's beyond belief." A number of previous speakers
had buttressed their pleas to remember Yankel's murder by reminding us
that we stood on the scene of the crime—using our physical presence as a
mnemonic device, or a medium for historical continuity. Norman Rosenbaum, however, took this spatial proximity as an ironic sign of discontinuity. Standing just five years later on "the exact same" site where his
brother was stabbed, the murder was already "beyond belief." Yankel
Rosenbaum's memory was thus threatened by a sense of historical disjuncture. The audience was asked to remember his death—but how?

A number of speakers drew on biblical texts to make Rosenbaum's
death a living memory for Lubavitch Hasidim and other audience members. As interpreted through the lens of biblical narrative, the violence of
August 1991 became a bitter reaffirmation of the ties that bind the

Lubavitch community to Yankel Rosenbaum—and contemporary Jews to their ancient patriarchs. The first major speaker (and the only Lubavitcher to give a lengthy address) was Rabbi Shmuel Butman, director of the Lubavitch Youth Organization. The chairman of the Jewish Community Council introduced him by saying, "We have the pleasure to hear a few words from the Lubavitcher Rebbe, as given over to us by Rabbi Shmuel Menachem Mendel Butman." To the extent that Lubavitchers in the audience imagined Rabbi Butman to be speaking on behalf of their Rebbe, his comments were themselves authoritative words of Torah, so I will discuss them at some length.[19]

After greeting the politicians and community members gathered before him, Rabbi Butman immediately shifted the historical ground on which they stood. He began his speech by observing that: "As we gather here, five years to the day—on the general calendar—from the murder of Yankel Rosenbaum, we are reminded of what we just read this Sabbath in the [Torah] portion of the week." Butman thus marked the fact that the rally commemorated Rosenbaum's murder by the Gregorian rather than the Hebrew calendar—on the nineteenth of August rather than the tenth of Elul (which fell on August 25 in 1996). He then turned, in the same breath, from this secular—or Christian—sense of time and history to a history structured by the text of the Torah, by invoking the previous week's Torah portion and demonstrating its relevance to the matter at hand.[20] He discussed a passage from Deuteronomy 21 that details the sacrificial offering a community is required to make if they cannot identify the murderer of a corpse found near their town, and equated this ancient ritual with the American judicial process in order to place the Torah's authority behind the upcoming prosecutions of Charles Price and Lemrick Nelson. "In our case," Butman argued, "it is the responsibility not only of the Crown Heights Jewish community, and not only of the community of the City of New York, but of the entire community of mankind, to investigate and reinvestigate this case until everyone can say 'We have not spilled this blood' [Deut. 21:7]."

After drawing his audience, through the previous week's Torah portion, into a Hasidic sense of historical time—a history defined by the intimate ties between the biblical text and contemporary social life—Rabbi Butman turned to a pair of biblical narratives that helped him

articulate the meaning of Yankel Rosenbaum's death. He first compared
Rosenbaum's stabbing to Cain's murder of Abel, "the first murder in history." He quoted God's warning to Cain that "The voice of the blood of
your brother cries out to me from the ground" (Genesis 4:10) and told the
crowd: "It is the same thing in our case. The voice of the blood of our
brother Yankel Rosenbaum . . . is screaming to us." He then paused to
welcome Governor George Pataki—shifting yet again between past and
present—and after a round of applause for the governor, he picked up the
thread of his exegesis with the story of Jacob and Esau:

> We further see in the Bible, at the second time where the word
> "voice" is mentioned, and it says: "Hakol kol Yaakov, v'hayadayim
> y'dai Esav." "The voice is the voice of Jacob, and the hands are the
> hands of Esau." After the hands of Esau have committed this atro-
> cious murder, on this very spot, the voice of Jacob—and in our case
> the voice of Jacob Rosenbaum—is calling out and says to all of us: "I
> have waited, day after day, week after week, month after month,
> year after year, for everyone who attacked me to be apprehended,
> and it is the responsibility of everyone, of all public officials, of all
> honest and decent citizens, to work that every one of those attack-
> ers should be apprehended and that justice should finally be done!"

Rabbi Butman then went on to discuss the legal proceedings against Rosenbaum's killers and his hopes for the future of communities like Crown
Heights—as well as his hopes for the messianic redemption of creation.
But the rhetorical crux of Butman's address was the contrast he drew between "the hands of Esau" and "the voice of Jacob." For Lubavitchers in
the audience, this invocation of the biblical text linked the violence of August 1991 to the essence of Jewish and Gentile identity—equating Rosenbaum's killers with the entire Gentile world, and Rosenbaum himself with
the entire Jewish people. But how were these symbolic equations sustained? How was Rabbi Butman able to hear—and ultimately speak—the
voice of Jacob on the streets of Brooklyn?

Butman used a number of rhetorical strategies to establish the historical continuity between Yankel Rosenbaum and the patriarch Jacob.
Rosenbaum, like many Jews, was named after the biblical patriarch
(Yankel is a diminutive form of Yaakov), and this allowed Rabbi Butman
to shift fairly easily between "the voice of Jacob" and "the voice of Jacob

Rosenbaum." Unlike Rosenbaum, however, the biblical patriarch was not a murder victim, so Butman first drew an analogy between Rosenbaum's stabbing and the murder of Abel. He then used the long-established rabbinic principle that passages in the Torah may be linked interpretively through linguistic similarities to read "the voice of the blood of your brother" alongside "the voice of Jacob"—linking Jacob/Yankel to Abel as innocent victims of violence.[21] And finally, he used a disarmingly simple act of rhetorical ventriloquism to merge his own voice with those of Abel, Jacob and Yankel (not to mention that of the Lubavitcher Rebbe, whose words he was said to be "giv[ing] over"). Butman prefaced his thoughts on Rosenbaum's legacy by claiming that "the voice of Jacob—and in our case the voice of Jacob Rosenbaum—is calling out and says to all of us . . ." Speaking in the first-person voice of a murder victim, and the composite voice of Jewish tradition, he called upon New York's political elite to pursue Yankel Rosenbaum's killers. Through this merging of rhetorical voices, Rabbi Butman brought millennia of Jewish history, as most Lubavitchers see it, to bear in today's Crown Heights. Rather than an event on the "general calendar," Yankel Rosenbaum's death became an exemplary moment in a history shaped, since the days of Jacob and Esau, by Gentile violence and hostility.

YET AS PERSUASIVE as these rhetorical strategies may have been, I doubt they conveyed Rabbi Butman's understanding of Yankel Rosenbaum's murder to anyone in the audience aside from his fellow Hasidim. The success of his rhetoric ultimately depended on the fact that Lubavitchers are taught, from a very young age, to imagine the difference between Jews and Gentiles in terms of the story of Jacob and Esau. From preschool on, Hasidic children are taught the contents of each week's Torah portion, or *parsha*, along with highlights from relevant rabbinic commentaries—and are taught to view the events described as incontestable historical facts with infinite layers of symbolic meaning. The story of Jacob and Esau in Parsha Toldos is hardly an exception to this rule.

On a Friday night in November of 1997, during the week that Parsha Toldos is read in synagogue services, I went to the home of a Hasidic friend for Shabbos dinner. Like most Friday nights, my friend's entire family was there, including her eldest daughter, her son-in-law, and their two-year-old son. The young couple told my friend's husband that his grandson had learned the parsha that week, and he wanted his grandfather to give him a parsha quiz. The "parsha quiz" is a fixture of Lubavitch Shabbos meals, in which a parent or grandparent of a school-age child asks a series of questions about the parsha of the week, sometimes using a "parsha stencil" supplied by the child's teacher. Depending on the quizzer, the parsha quiz can be a harrowing exercise of religious authority or a touching moment of intergenerational intimacy. In this case, the quizzer was a gentle, soft-spoken man, and the quizzee—though shy—was eager to show himself a big boy, with a knowledge of Torah. Grandpa smiled broadly as his grandson peered at him from behind the bangs of a boy who had not yet had his first haircut.[22] It was a very tender moment. And it encapsulated, in a few simple questions, the central themes of the biblical narrative sketched above. Grandpa's first question cut to the heart of the matter: "Which was the good boy, and which was the bad boy?" Even a two-year-old knew, with no hesitation, that Yaakov was the good boy, and Esav the bad boy. "Which boy wanted to get out [of the womb] when Rivka passed a yeshiva?" Yaakov. "And who made the soup?" Yaakov. "And who ate the soup?" After a moment of hesitation, my friend's grandson answered enthusiastically: "Esav gobbled it up!" Here, in a nutshell, is an orthodox Jewish vision of Jewish-Gentile difference: There is a good boy and a bad boy. The good boy wants to go to yeshiva, and the bad boy "gobbles" his soup like an animal. Most Lubavitch Hasidim learn to think in such terms at an early age, and to ground these images in the biblical text.

Young Lubavitchers also learn to attribute antisemitism to the children of Esau. For example, on a cassette tape of Bible stories for children, a Lubavitch storyteller narrates Parsha Toldos in simple English, with lavish details drawn from rabbinic commentaries and moral lessons drawn from Hasidic thought. At the crucial moment of Isaac's deathbed blessings, the storyteller quotes directly from the Torah, for the first time on the tape, to stress Isaac's statement that: " 'Hakol kol Yaakov.' The voice is Yaakov's voice. But 'Hayadayim y'dai Esav.' The hands are Esav's hands." He then breaks the frame of the story to tell his listeners:

> Kinderlach [children], our hachamim [sages] tell us that these words were also ruach hakodesh [the spirit of prophecy] talking about the future of the two nations, of Yaakov and Esav. Which

FIGURE 18 Imagining Esau. In this multilayered image (drawn from a flyer for a Torah study class, or *shiur*, in Crown Heights), Esau is pictured as a racialized, if not animalistic, figure. His minions call to mind Nazi stormtroopers, but chant slogans—"We want justice"—that call to mind Black American protest politics. Ironically, however, Esau decides to attend a shiur rather than attack Jacob.

means that, "Hakol kol Yaakov" the voice, the sound of Torah and tefilah [prayer], that is Yaakov's portion. While the hands, "Hayadayim y'dai Esav," the hands which means force, and fighting, and ammunition, those are the hands of Esav.

Later, near the end of the tape, he describes how Esau passed his hatred of Jacob down to his children and his children's children: "Esav gave over his hatred towards Yaakov to his son Eliphaz. Eliphaz passed it on to his family, and like this it went from one family to the next—the hatred against Yaakov and his children. . . . As our hachamim say: 'Halacha hi b'yduah, sh'Esav soneh l'Yaakov.' It is a well known halacha—a Torah rule—that Esav hates Yaakov." Here, in the second such use of Hebrew on the entire tape, Parsha Toldos is made relevant to contemporary Hasidic children. The voice of Jacob speaks to young Lubavitchers, telling them that Gentiles will always hate them.[23]

Needless to say, Hasidic adults often bracket this "Torah rule" in their everyday lives, building respectful—if not intimate—relationships with Gentiles. Like everyone else, most Lubavitch Hasidim draw complex distinctions between communal belief and personal experience. For example, a Hasidic woman who was active in the Black-Jewish women's group Mothers to Mothers acknowledged that Esau's eternal hatred is "the Torah version" of antisemitism, but explained that this story doesn't match her own experience. She was extremely concerned with antisemitism, but attributed it to the Jewish history of diaspora—rather than to the relationship between Jacob and Esau—and said she didn't see it in most of the Gentiles she knew. She seemed somewhat pained, however, by the tension between her personal view and the absolute truth of the Torah. She told me in a quiet, halting voice: "Halachically and Torahdikly and as an observant Jew, I've got to believe in the Esav stuff, but for me it's not as logical as what I know now." Many Hasidim make such difficult distinctions, setting aside Esau's undying hatred to accommodate their experiences of a diverse society.

For others, however, Jacob and Esau bring order to the ambiguity of the social world. And for most Lubavitchers, Esau's jealous rage offers a compelling account of Gentile antisemitism. For example, another Hasidic acquaintance once told me that antisemitism is essentially the same in all times and places, regardless of any superficial historical changes. When I tried to explain why I tended instead to interpret phenomena like antisemitism in terms of their shifting social contexts, she replied: "You're on to something very interesting. Because according to [Hasidic thought], and according to a Torah perspective, there are very deep spiritual reasons for antisemitism, having nothing to do with sociology." "Like what?" I asked. She replied in a definitive tone:

> Esav hates Yaakov. It goes back to that. Now you've gotta talk to a rabbi about this, not me, but Esav hates Yaakov. That was one of the givens in the world, until—until Moshiach [the coming of the messiah], until we ultimately have the redemption in front of our eyes. That's a given: Esav hates Yaakov. . . . It's something that's just inherent. It's like, uh—like you talk about water, y'know. Water condenses, it has certain properties. A non-Jew has certain properties, y'know, and a Jew has certain properties. Like we say a leaf is made up of such-and-such—it's the same thing. It's one of those givens, that Esav hates Yaakov.

"But how," I asked, "does this hatred go from Esav and Yaakov in the Torah—y'know, thousands of years ago—down to today?" She replied:

Again, you have to go to a rabbi, I'm just theorizing. But y'know, Esav hates Yaakov, these are the ruling powers of the world. Like Rome was descended from Esav, that's what they say. . . . And I guess the Roman Empire, y'know, left its mark. Even today, like you have the pope. So there's still that thing: Rome versus Yaakov. . . . Rome set the pace, y'know, Rome sets the pace. Which it did with Christianity. Most of the world is Christian, right?

Unlike the children of Jacob, the children of Esau may or may not be defined by genealogical continuity with their biblical patriarch. But this Hasid nevertheless saw a historical continuity in "the ruling powers of the world" from biblical times to the present. She bridged the gap between today's Crown Heights and her Israelite origins through a seemingly effortless shift from past to present tense: "Rome set the pace, y'know, Rome sets the pace." But still, I pushed, does she see a real relationship between her Black neighbors and ancient Rome? "We're not really dealing with 'Rome' out on the streets here," I said. "Yeah," she replied, gesturing toward her window, where the muffled sound of tape-recorded bells wafted in from the bell-tower of the Episcopal church next door, "but there's a church."

Like most Lubavitch Hasidim, this woman interprets Black-Jewish difference in terms one might loosely describe as religious—in terms of Judaism and Christianity, church bells and the pope, the authority of the Torah and the coming of the messiah. Yet she naturalizes this religious difference in ways that resonate with biological race—describing Gentile antisemitism as "something that's just inherent. . . . Like we say a leaf is made up of such-and-such." These simultaneously "racial" and "religious" differences help support her narrative of Israelite descent. They merge within—and perhaps emerge from—an underlying equation of history, genealogy, and collective identity.

"The Lord Will Send You Back to Egypt in Ships"

However, the identities of Jacob and Esau are not as clear as Lubavitchers imagine. As I've noted, a broad range of Black Crown Heights residents—whom Lubavitchers and most other Jews consider Gentiles—claim varieties of Israelite history and identity. Even Black Christians, who make no consistent claim to Jewishness, often express a sense of continuity with ancient Israel. For example, in addition to the local Episcopal church, my Hasidic acquaintance's living room window looked out over the home of the late James E. Davis—an African American Baptist minister and politician, whose childhood memories of the Lubavitcher Rebbe were quoted above, in chapter 4. When we spoke in the fall of 1997, Davis explained that Christians are linked to Jews through their common devotion to "the God of Abraham" and shared ties to "the father of faith." Then, in the same breath, he shifted from symbolic descent to genealogy, from theology to history, religion to race:

> Now me, as a Black man—and other Blacks—we go a step further. We believe that we're Jewish! Not only from the standpoint of our connection to Judaism from Christianity—Watch this now!— there's many of us who believe that there's something called Ethiopian Jews, who are Jewish but they're Black. . . . And there has been documented proof that slaves, many slaves, came out of those Ethiopian Jewish groups. Now some people say no, Black people came from the Muslim religion. But there were many Blacks—I believe there were many Blacks that came from the Ethiopian Jews, and other Blacks that practiced Judaism. So, because we don't have a history, how can a Jewish person of Crown Heights—how can a Jewish person tell me that I'm not Jewish? He can't, 'cause he doesn't know my history! So therefore, I'm more Jewish—I'm more their brother than they even realize.

And moments later, on a historiographic roll, Davis mused about the "Lost Tribes" of Israel. With tongue only partially in cheek, he said: "I'll tell you where they are! They're right here in Brooklyn. They're in Crown Heights. They're called *Black* people!"

Across the street from a Hasidic home in which Blacks (with the exception of Black orthodox Jews) are distinguished from Jews by their descent from Esau, we thus find an African American home in which Blacks and Jews alike are defined by shared descent from Jacob. Here we see the complex pattern of residential integration and social segregation that characterizes Black-Jewish relations in Crown Heights: two homes, two histories, not twenty yards apart. Yet we may also glimpse an underlying commonality: these divided communities both define their identities through Israelite history and genealogy, at a charged intersection of "race" and "religion."

James Davis's narrative of Black Jewish history is not universally shared by Black Christians in Crown Heights, but it does reflect a central theme of Black Christian discourse and collective identity. As a number of prominent historians have noted, African American Christians have felt an affinity with the biblical Israelites since at least the late eighteenth century, when many began to read and preach the biblical narrative of the exodus from Egypt as a story of their own redemption in the Americas.[24] This Black-Jewish identification was central to the rhetoric of the twentieth-century civil rights movement (as evidenced by Martin Luther King, Jr.'s, self-identification with Moses in his renowned "I've Been to the Mountaintop" sermon) and it remains an element of many African American Christian identities to this day. For a range of reasons, Afro-Caribbean Christians may not have developed such ties with the biblical Israelites as early as did their African American counterparts. But similar forms of Black-Jewish identification were prevalent in the Anglophone Caribbean by the early twentieth century, and helped define such social and religious movements as Ethiopianism, Rastafarianism, and Garveyite Black nationalism.[25]

Throughout my field research—in interviews and casual conversations, as well as sermons, spirituals, and Bible-study courses—I heard both African American and Afro-Caribbean Christians express various forms of affinity with the scriptural Israelites and/or contemporary Jews. Some Black Christians, in Crown Heights and elsewhere, come to identify with Jews through the Jewishness of Jesus. For example, a young Jamaican Pentecostal preacher I knew told me he considered himself a Jew due to his relationship with Jesus: "Don't [the Bible] say He's the king of the Jews? Well . . . He's my king!" Other Black Christians draw specific historical or political parallels between Blacks and Jews or ancient Israelites. For example, the Reverend Al Sharpton told me in an interview: "I see fighting for African Americans [through political activism] in the same light that the ministers in the Old Testament fought for the children of Israel." Sharpton repudiated the image of Black Americans as a "chosen people," but suggested instead, "By saying that we're the people *in these times* that have been oppressed and exploited, and therefore must rally as the Israelites did, I think you get to the same place, though you start from a different premise." The rhetoric of chosenness is, in fact, extremely common in Black Crown Heights politics. In August of 1997, for example (a month before our interview), James Davis appealed to the largely Black audience at his annual "Love Yourself, Stop the Violence" march by paraphrasing 1 Peter 2:9 to tell the crowd: "We are a mighty people! We are a great people! We are a beautiful people! A royal priesthood! A holy nation! Peculiar people! God loves my people! Realize that you are a chosen people. Chosen from Ethiopia—and y'know there was Ethiopian Jews too."

Davis's assertion, above, that "we [Black people] don't have a history" highlights the historiographic stakes in such claims of Israelite descent. Like many Black Crown Heights residents, Davis drew upon narratives of Black Jewish history as he crafted a response to what he saw as the historical discontinuity at the heart of the African diaspora—the painful gap between Black Americans and their African origins, following the dislocation of collective memory wrought by the horrors of the Atlantic slave trade.[26] Davis described slavery as a time when "our history was thrown out the window, and the Devil attacked a whole people," but this traumatic experience opens a space of possibility. He said Black Americans may seem "down and out" now, but he confidently predicted: "How great a Black people we will be when we know our history. Then we can jump on some of them blessings of Abraham!"

THIS IS, in some sense, what a small but substantial number of African American and Afro-Caribbean people have done over the past century. For these Black Hebrew Israelites, the longstanding Black Christian identification with Israel has developed into an enduring Israelite identity. Before examining the biblical and historical narratives at the heart of this identity, I will trace the history of the Hebrew Israelite movement itself, and examine the links Hebrew Israelites establish between racial Blackness and Israelite descent.

There were a number of short-lived Black Jewish sects in the nineteenth-century American South, but today's Hebrew Israelite communities may generally be traced to the Black nationalist milieu of Harlem in the 1910s and 1920s, where Black identification with ancient

Israel was combined with a growing knowledge of Jewish ritual gained, in part, from firsthand experiences of immigrant Jewish life in New York.[27] There were at least eight different synagogues of Black Jews or Hebrew Israelites in Harlem in the 1920s, most of which were founded by Afro-Caribbean immigrants affiliated to varying degrees with Marcus Garvey's Universal Negro Improvement Association. Although the Hebrew Israelite movement initially seems to have provided these immigrants with a means to differentiate themselves from African Americans, it soon grew to include a diverse cross-section of the African diaspora. By the mid-twentieth century, a single synagogue—the Commandment Keepers Congregation of the Living God, founded by Rabbi Wentworth A. Matthews—emerged as the preeminent voice of the movement, and most of the eight or ten Hebrew Israelite synagogues in the New York area today claim ties of some kind to Rabbi Matthews and his congregation. New York City remains the center of gravity of the movement, but there are a broad range of Hebrew Israelite sects and synagogues based throughout North America, and in the state of Israel.[28]

During my field research, in the mid- to late 1990s, there were two Hebrew Israelite synagogues in the area of north Brooklyn surrounding Crown Heights, each of which drew congregants from throughout Brooklyn and the rest of the city.[29] The liturgical contrasts between these synagogues demonstrate the internal diversity of the Hebrew Israelite movement. One is housed in a former private home in Bedford-Stuyvesant that was first used as a synagogue by the modern orthodox Young Israel movement, and although a returning Young Israel member would consider few of its congregants Jewish, he or she would hardly feel out of place in its services. The liturgy is marked as "African" in countless subtle ways—for example by the distinctive cadence and pronunciation of the congregants' spoken Hebrew—but is essentially identical to an orthodox Jewish prayer service. Ten blocks away, however, on the border of Bed-Stuy and Bushwick, another Hebrew Israelite synagogue holds services that consist largely of original songs sung in Hebrew and English, to the accompaniment of exuberant "African" drumming. The traditional Torah reading is complemented here by a sermon in which formal translations of the weekly Torah portion alternate line-by-line with fiery commentaries in vernacular English. As the vice president of this synagogue told

me: "We do our own thing here. Not like [the other synagogue], they're
more conservative there."

These liturgical contrasts are linked to significant differences in the
synagogues' interpretations of their Israelite identity. The first—and far
smaller—of the two congregations leans somewhat closer to a "religious"
Jewishness and is a bit more open to White American Jews, while the second leans closer to a "racial" Blackness and a separatist brand of Black
nationalist thought. But all Hebrew Israelites, from the movement's origin
to the present day, articulate identities on the conceptual margins of religion and race. All share the central defining claim that Black people in the
Americas are the true descendants of ancient Israel, and thus the chosen
people of God. Although their Israelite descent is marked and defined by
religious phenomena like biblical narrative, ritual practice, and supernatural belief, it does not entail a religious identity separable from race.
Rather, it reveals the true meaning of Blackness.

Many Hebrew Israelites stress the significance of race by clearly distinguishing "Israelites" from "Jews"—a distinction not only between Blackness and Whiteness, but between race and religion as such. For example,
the Brooklyn-based author Cohane Michael Ben Levi argues that: "An Israelite is a descendant of the ancient nation of Israel, while a Jew is a
member of a religion called Judaism which attempts to practice the laws
and customs of ancient Israel. . . . One may change his (or her) religion
many times. On the contrary, one may never change who you are at birth,
namely your nationality."[30] Or as one congregant at the second synagogue
described above explained when I told him that my parents' families came
to the United States from Germany and Russia: "Then you're a Germano-
Russian, or a Russo-German, whose fathers converted to the Hebrew God
some time back there. Because there sure weren't no Europeans in Israel."
This concern with "nations" and "nationality" marks the distance between
most Hebrew Israelites and mainstream American views of race. Indeed,
just as they eschew conventional Jewishness, Hebrew Israelites are often
deeply critical of conventional Blackness—describing themselves and other
Black Americans as "so-called Negroes." Yet most nevertheless imagine a
binary opposition between Israelites and "Europeans," and as we saw in
chapter 4, they rely on phenotypic signs of Blackness and Whiteness to define the boundaries of Israelite identity. Hebrew Israelites thus tend to

read contemporary American racial identities into the biblical text. They imagine their continuity with ancient Israel in terms of a shared, and inherited, racial Blackness.

Yet this "racial" identity remains closely tied to a range of "religious" discourses. For example, in a pivotal moment of the Sabbath liturgy at the "more conservative" congregation described above, continuity with ancient Israel is envisioned in terms of the Torah's transmission from generation to generation.[31] Immediately after the reading of the Torah, congregants chant a prayer that is not contained in their modern orthodox prayer book. Speaking in unison, in cadenced, reverential tones, they proclaim: "This is our Torah. This is our Law. Our fathers delivered it. Intact, it was to us transferred. Intact, we will transfer it." With the exception of brief weekly sermons and occasional spontaneous prayers, this is the only time in a four-hour-long service that congregants depart from the Hebrew text of their prayer books—a liturgical innovation that accentuates their expression of Jewish continuity. Much like Lubavitchers, Hebrew Israelites claim ties with the biblical Israelites that cannot be defined in racial or religious terms alone.

Yet unlike those of the Lubavitch Hasidim, Hebrew Israelite claims of continuity with ancient Israel are often complemented—though not contradicted—by an acute sense of historical discontinuity, which Hebrew Israelites often attribute to their displacement from their ancient homeland. Like James Davis, many describe the Atlantic slave trade as a time when "our history was thrown out the window." For example, one congregant at the "more conservative" synagogue described above explained that in the wake of their dispersion, Israelites in the Americas have been forced to rebuild their traditions from "drops of Torah." He gave one example from his childhood in Trinidad:

When we were growing up my mother would always make a cross of salt, somewhere in the room, when we went to sleep at night. To protect from evil spirits—and in Trinidad we had spirits! But it was only a few weeks ago that [my rabbi] showed me where this is from in the Torah, and the importance of salt in Torah—like when you bless the bread, you put it in salt. So we were following the Torah and we didn't even know it!

But these "drops" aren't as "intact" as his synagogue's liturgy claims—indeed, they may even take the form of a cross. A profound uncertainty is introduced if one can "[follow] the Torah and [not] even know it." Hebrew Israelites accommodate this ambivalent sense of continuity and discontinuity through a distinctive narrative of Israelite history.

ACCORDING TO HEBREW ISRAELITES and orthodox Jews alike, the ancient Israelites were conquered and exiled from their promised land in 70 CE because they failed to follow the laws of the Torah. The Roman Empire merely executed God's judgment against his wayward chosen people. According to contemporary Hebrew Israelites, most of the ancient Israelites then fled to Africa, where they settled among other ancient Black peoples and established a diasporic civilization stretching from West Africa to the Fertile Crescent—*From Babylon to Timbuktu*, in the title of Rudolph Windsor's influential 1969 work of Black Israelite history.[32]

According to Windsor, the ancient Israelites maintained their history and identity throughout this early period of dispersion. "The black Jews," he argues, "had an advantage over the African tribes: they carried their culture, history, laws, and written records with them. . . . Because of the stability of black Jewish culture, the Jews were not absorbed into the autochthonous population."[33] But more recent Hebrew Israelite authors are generally less optimistic about the fate of the Israelites' identity in exile. According to the Brooklyn-based author Melchizedek Lewis: "With the final dispersion of Israel after the destruction of the Second Temple in 70 CE, began the complete infusion and submersion of the Israelites within the nations of the world. . . . The Scriptures indicate [in Nahum 1:14] that the nations of the Gentiles are the graves of the Israelite people."[34] And according to nearly all Hebrew Israelites, this "infusion and submersion" was ultimately accomplished in the slave trade—when Israel was brought to the Americas in chains, as an ongoing punishment for its disobedience, and finally lost all knowledge of its true identity.

Instead the White "so-called Jews"—whom some Hebrew Israelites see as Edomite impostors—are nearly universally considered the children of Israel. How did this tragic reversal take place? According to Hebrew Israelites, orthodox Jews, and academic historians alike, Israel conquered Edom in the second century BCE and forcibly converted many Edomites to

Judaism. According to historians, the conflict between Israel and Edom then subsided, and the boundaries of these peoples gradually blurred.[35] According to Hebrew Israelites, however, the ancient Edomites adapted elements of Israelite culture and religion without surrendering their hatred of Israel. This complex period of assimilation and resistance marks the origin of today's "Jews." As Cohane Michael Ben Levi explains: "Through their adoption of Israelite culture and practices the Edomites appeared, at least outwardly, to be Israelites. It was the gradual degradation and cross-culturalizing of Israelite practice and the Hebrew language by the Edomites that led to the coining and eventual use of the term 'Jew.'"[36] Ultimately, according to the Hebrew Israelites, Israel's defeat by Rome allowed Edom—the Jews—to assume Israel's rightful place. Esau, it seems, has reclaimed his birthright. As the true Black Israelites dispersed through Africa, White Edomites slowly filtered into Europe—passing as Israelites and gaining converts to their "Jewish" religion.[37] This history explains why the identity of Israel is, in the words of another New York Israelite, "the world's best-kept secret."[38]

Yet unlike the Hasidic history outlined above, this Hebrew Israelite history seems to introduce a troubling gap between past and present. It supports Black claims of continuity with ancient Israel, yet is built around a tale of discontinuity and loss. While Lubavitchers narrate a seemingly motionless history, frozen in the eternal simultaneity of Israel, Hebrew Israelites narrate a history wracked and distorted by dramatic change. It is a history of reversal and deception, lost and found identity, the death and rebirth of a people—a history, in the words of Melchizedek Lewis, that "[begins] with the three patriarchs and [culminates] in the startling revelation of a people who have become strangers to themselves."[39] Even if one accepts all of its factual claims (which many, of course, do not), it does not seem to establish an intimate bond between today's Black Brooklynites and their Israelite origins.

But we have yet to examine the central text of Hebrew Israelite historiography—the skeleton key that unlocks the hidden continuity of Israel's past. Much like Lubavitch Hasidim, Black Hebrew Israelites use the biblical text as a historiographic tool. Yet while Hasidic historiography rests on the narrative of Israel's origin in Genesis 25, Hebrew Israelite historiography rests on the narrative of Israel's dispersion in Deuteronomy

28. According to the Hebrew Israelites, every twist and turn of their painful history was prophesied by Moses as the Israelites stood on the banks of the Jordan, at the end of their forty-year exodus from Egypt, waiting to enter their promised land.

In the first few verses of Deuteronomy 28, Moses promises Israel that if they obey God's law, God will help them defeat their enemies and bless them with material plenty. But in verse 15, Moses warns Israel that if they disobey the law, God will curse them instead. And then—in a series of passages of unparalleled brutality—Moses threatens Israel with a litany of curses, the prophetic price of their future disobedience. For example:

> Cursed shall you be in the city and cursed shall you be in the country. Cursed shall be your basket and your kneading bowl. Cursed shall be the issue of your womb and the produce of your soil, the calving of your herd and the lambing of your flock. Cursed shall you be in your comings and cursed shall you be in your goings. The Lord will let loose against you calamity, panic, and frustration in all the enterprises you undertake, so that you shall soon be utterly wiped out because of your evildoing in forsaking me. . . . The Lord will strike you with [boils], with hemorrhoids, boil-scars, and itch, from which you shall never recover. The Lord will strike you with madness, blindness, and dismay. You shall grope at noon, as a blind man gropes in the dark; you shall not prosper in your ventures, but shall be constantly abused and robbed, with none to give help. . . . The Lord will scatter you among all peoples, from one end of the earth to the other, and there you shall serve other gods, of wood and stone, whom neither you nor your ancestors have experienced. . . . The Lord will send you back to Egypt in ships, by a route which I told you you should not see again. There you shall offer yourselves for sale to your enemies as male and female slaves, but none will buy. (Deut. 28:16–20, 27–29, 64, 68)

These are "the terms of the covenant" (28:69), the threats—and just a few of the worst—that accompanied God's promises to his chosen people.

Some three thousand years later, in Brooklyn in the late 1980s, a man I later met at a Hebrew Israelite synagogue was searching for his spiritual roots. He had been raised an Anglican, but had never felt comfortable with Christianity. As a teenager he studied African history and Islam. And then, in his early twenties, he decided to take a closer look at the Bible. At the time, he later told me, he was living in Brooklyn and working in the Bronx, so he bought the Bible on tape and listened during his long commutes. He listened to the whole thing—Old and New Testaments, from Genesis to Revelation—sitting in his car with a Bible open on the passenger seat, stopping at red lights to highlight key passages. One can imagine, perhaps, the voice of Charlton Heston or James Earl Jones resonating in the hermetic space of a car crossing the Brooklyn Bridge. In this deep voice, and ancient text, my acquaintance finally found what he'd been looking for: "When the tape got up to Deuteronomy 28, it was just 'Wow!' I had to stop the car, and I played the tape over and over, and I knew it was talking about us." He told me he started to cry, sitting in his car on the side of the road, overwhelmed by the power of his realization: "The dispersal from the land, taken in slave ships, the breakdown of the family, and health problems like Glaucoma, and skin problems. These are all the things that afflict African people in America! I knew it had to be us." And, he said, he knew what he had to do. Although he kept going to church for a little while, he claims he knew from the moment he heard Deuteronomy 28: "All that had to change. I had to change my life to begin keeping Shabbat."

Of course, children raised as Hebrew Israelites need not come to such dramatic realizations, as they are taught from a young age to interpret their history through the lens of Deuteronomy 28. For example, at a Passover seder held at a Hebrew Israelite synagogue, one young girl was reluctant, at first, to taste the bitter herbs the liturgy asks Jews to eat, in memory of slavery in Egypt. As the girl sat pouting, her lips firmly sealed, a woman in her thirties patiently explained that the herbs would help her remember the bitterness of slavery. The girl thought it over for a moment, then turned and pointed to a poster hung prominently in the synagogue's social hall: an image of a slave bound around the neck in irons and chains; a haunting reproduction of an antique photograph from the American South, captioned with a number of biblical texts, including Deuteronomy 28:48: "You shall serve—in hunger and thirst, naked and lacking everything—the enemies whom the Lord will let loose against you. He will place an iron yoke upon your neck until He has wiped you

FIGURE 19 "An iron yoke upon your neck." Israelite slavery in the Americas, as interpreted through Deuteronomy 28:48. Note the striped garment, which a number of Hebrew Israelites identified as a traditional Jewish prayer shawl.

out" (see figure 19). Gesturing toward this chilling image of Israelite slavery in the Americas, the young girl said emphatically: "*That's* slavery." She then turned and ate her bitter herbs.

These moments of identity formation rest on the central premise of nearly all Hebrew Israelite historical narratives: that the curses of

Deuteronomy 28 are a prophetic history of the slavery and racism Israelites have suffered during their exile in the Americas. As Cohane Michael Ben Levi explains:

> In their own unique manner, the prophecies and words of the Holy Scriptures describe the punishment meted out to the so-called Negroes for their disobedience and rejection of God's law.... If Africans and African-Americans understood this important fact, they would see these writings as a mirror of themselves. The particular experience, as it is written, explains and clarifies the peculiar mystery behind the loss of identity of the Black man and his scattering among the nations of the earth. Many nations have been enslaved, yet the nation of Israel alone bears all the signs described in the curse pronounced against them by their Creator. No other nation on earth has a historical experience which comes close to fulfilling the words of Deuteronomy 28.[40]

Like many Hebrew Israelite authors, Ben Levi then catalogs the parallels between Deuteronomy 28 and Black history as he sees it.[41] According to Hebrew Israelites, Moses's threat that Israel will be cursed "in the city" (Deut. 28:16) has been fulfilled in gang violence, while his threat of a cursed "basket" and "kneading bowl" (28:17) speaks of poverty and underdevelopment. The "strange and lasting plagues" (28:59) he warned of are none other than AIDS and the other diseases that disproportionately afflict Black Americans. The "ruthless nation" he said would "swoop down [on Israel] like the eagle" (28:49) is clearly the United States, whose Great Seal contains an eagle.[42] And above all else, Moses's threat that "The Lord will send you back to Egypt in ships" (28:68) undoubtedly foresaw the Middle Passage itself. In all of recorded history, Hebrew Israelites often ask, what other nation has been taken into slavery on ships?

The curses of Deuteronomy 28 thus help Black Hebrew Israelites craft historical continuity from the very stuff of discontinuity, by reading the history of the African diaspora in the text of the Hebrew Bible. The identity of Israel remains secure in spite of the fact—no, *because* of the fact—that God's chosen people have been "scatter[ed] . . . from one end of the earth to the other" (Deut. 28:64). Like Lubavitch narratives of Israel's origin, this narrative of Israel's exile draws on popular images of both "race" and "religion"—on slave ships and sacred texts, American politics and biblical prophecy, urban violence and divine chosenness. Much like Lubavitchers, Hebrew Israelites fuse the racial and religious aspects of their identity through an underlying equation of history and genealogy.

THE POWER OF SUCH NARRATIVES to constitute identities was demonstrated in a conversation I had on the subway with a man whose name I never knew. It was after one in the morning, on a Thursday night turned Friday in November of 1997, and I was headed home to Crown Heights. To pass the time, I started to read and edit an essay I was working on—an embryonic version of this chapter—and after a few minutes, I noticed a middle-aged Black man reading over my shoulder.[43] He soon noticed that I'd noticed him, and after a brief exchange of glances he asked whether it was my own work I was reading. "You been to all these places?" he wanted to know. I said yes, and told him about my research. He said he was an Israelite, born and raised in Bed-Stuy. He wore no visible signs of his Israelite identity—no distinctive jewelry, yarmulke, or dreadlocks—just a frayed but neat jacket over blue jeans and work boots. A short salt-and-pepper Afro and a neatly trimmed beard framed his weathered and gently wrinkled face. He held a leather-bound book, with a pen and Post-it notes, that could have been a Bible or just a day-planner. But even though he didn't quite look the part, I was delighted to meet a Black Hebrew Israelite who took an interest in my research. I introduced myself and offered a handshake. "Naah," he told me, "I don't touch. I'm consecrated."

Oh well, I thought, so much for the ethnographic dream of "rapport." But despite this less than promising introduction, we chatted warmly for a while, both pleasantly surprised by the other's openness. As we sat through a half-hour train delay, he quizzed me on the major themes of Hebrew Israelite historiography and religious thought—some I have touched on here, and others I have not. Did I know that "Jewish" is just an adjective? "Jew-*ish*," meaning "about or related to Jews, not the real thing." The suffix "ish," he explained, actually comes from Russian, and was attached to the word "Jew" by the Khazars. Did I know what the "Torah" is? The five books of Moses, he said, and nothing more: "Talmud, Gemora, and all that—that's not related to Israel. That's only got to do with Jewish, and that's got nothing to do with Israel."[44] The country they call "Israel" these days isn't even the real Holy Land. The true land of Israel is in the highlands of the Nile, between Egypt and Ethiopia. What they're calling "Israel," he told me, is the land of the Edomites. He told me again and again how important it is to learn the original names of things—to look past the web of White deception and get the truth directly from the Torah—and especially to learn the true name of Israel. He said it was prophesied in the Torah that Israel would be called by a series of false names: "You know they're Israel, but the Europeans called them African, Black, Negro, Nigger. They're calling them by all these different names— until the time comes." Yeah, I said, it was prophesied in Deuteronomy 28. He was extremely pleased I knew the reference. Of course, I replied, that's an important text—lots of heavy stuff in there. He nodded gravely and said, "Our whole history is in that thing there."

And this, I think, is the key. After thousands of years of diaspora and deception, the world, it seems, has been turned upside-down. The true identities of peoples have been lost or stolen. Even he couldn't quite keep track of things. He was uncertain, for example, about the origins of the Edomites—telling me at one point they were the children of Ishmael, then correcting himself and calling them the children of Esau. Yet thanks to Deuteronomy 28, he was absolutely certain about the identity of Israel: "Our whole history is in that thing there." And the true identity of Israel is the key to the future in these last days—as "the time comes," he hinted, when God will return his chosen people to their former glory. With this redemption in mind, my new acquaintance tried to impress on me the importance of my research. He told me in an ominous tone, "I don't think you understand how serious all this is." I assured him I take my work very seriously, and promised to seek the truth as best I could. He seemed pleased, and asked me how long it would be before I published my research, and made the truth known. I told him it would take a number of years, and he replied: "You might wanna do it faster than that. There's not much time left." "Before what?" I asked. But he wouldn't say.

History, Identity, and Destiny

In these last elliptical comments, my acquaintance gestured at what many Lubavitch Hasidim and Black Hebrew Israelites consider the most important difference between Israelites and others, in Crown Heights and elsewhere. They may disagree about the relationship between race and religion, not to mention the facts of Israelite history, but Lubavitchers and Hebrew Israelites tend to agree that the descendants of Jacob—whoever they may be—have been chosen by God to play a unique and decisive role in the apocalyptic end of history, while others simply have not.

The implications of this chosenness are far more complex and ambivalent than simple divine favor. God's chosen people have had to endure centuries of exile, as well as the unrelenting hostility of jealous Gentile nations. And in the end, according to all Hasidim and most Hebrew Israelites, the messiah will redeem every one of God's creations, not merely a chosen few. Yet according to many Crown Heights residents, and others, the children of Israel are destined to play a starring role in the drama of redemption—a drama unfolding as we speak, or in the near future. The Israelites stand at the center of this story, as God's chosen agents in human history.[45] For Lubavitchers and Hebrew Israelites, as well as many Christians and others, this is a history, identity, and destiny worth fighting for. A Hebrew Israelite I knew fairly well, for example, was perfectly happy to accept the Jewishness of White Jews—indeed, he often expressed a desire for greater contact and solidarity with his Hasidic neighbors—but he nevertheless insisted that the messiah could not come until the entire world acknowledged the Blackness of ancient Israel. He was well aware of the messianic fervor sweeping the Lubavitch community in the 1990s, but scoffed at the messianic claims surrounding the Lubavitcher Rebbe. The Torah, he reminded me, states quite clearly that the messiah will be a descendant of King David. "And let's face it," he said with a smile, "their Rebbe don't look much like David."

This claim clearly rests on a racialized understanding of what it means to "look like David," but it is not simply a claim about race. As I have argued, discourses of "race" and "religion" shape the contours of the struggle over chosenness in Crown Heights, but they do not determine its ultimate goals. Both Blacks and Jews use these conceptual categories—in different combinations, and with varying emphases—to bolster their claims of Israelite descent. But these claims are at once simpler and more complex than Blackness or Jewishness, race or religion. They are claims to a noble past thought to set Israelites apart from their neighbors (although their neighbors, ironically, claim this past as well), to a present that transcends their long and painful exile, and a future that gives meaning to their everyday lives.

This sense of purpose—of historical agency—is one of the many basic human realities that scholars and others often attempt to gloss with conceptual categories like race and religion. Terms such as these have come to define our perceptions of self and other, identity and community, society and history. These terms may sometimes help us to understand our world—to make sense of our neighbors, not to mention our selves—but they ultimately obscure as much as they reveal. As I have shown in this chapter, they highlight significant differences between Black and Jewish Crown Heights residents, while masking a number of underlying similarities. No identity or community—or discourse for that matter—is simply "racial" or "religious," "ethnic" or "national," "gendered" or "sexual," "cultural" or what-have-you. Even in a polarized neighborhood like Crown Heights, people's lives and beliefs—their histories and destinies—are more complex, and more interesting, than such categories imply.

CONCLUSION

"Stiffnecked Peoples" and American Multiculturalism

While the Hebrew Bible describes the children of Israel as "a kingdom of priests and a holy nation" (Ex. 19:6), it nevertheless paints an ambivalent picture of the relationship between God and his chosen people. Over the course of their forty-year exodus from Egypt, both God and Moses often refer to the Israelites as a "stiffnecked people"—stubbornly attached to their idolatrous ways, and fiercely resistant to divine authority. In the book of Deuteronomy, for example, as the Israelites are about to embark on their divinely ordained conquest of Canaan, Moses is careful to remind them of what he, at least, sees as their failings:

> Know, then, that it is not for any virtue of yours that the Lord your God is giving you this good land to possess; for you are a stiffnecked people. Remember, never forget, how you provoked the Lord your God to anger in the wilderness: from the day that you left the land of Egypt until you reached this place, you have continued defiant toward the Lord. (Deut. 9:6–7)

This tradition of defiance is alive and well in Crown Heights, where today's chosen peoples continue to resist or subvert the expectations of power. But the target of this resistance seems to have shifted, over time, from divine to worldly forms of authority—from the laws of God to the unwritten rules of American multiculturalism.

In the early twenty-first century, following decades of growing transnational migration, many Americans see themselves as members of a "multicultural" society. Of course, the United States has long been seen as a "nation of immigrants," home to people—and peoples—from throughout the world. But while America once demanded assimilation to a false monocultural ideal, more and more of its citizens now celebrate their diversity, working to create space in American society for other cultures and communities. Many New Yorkers, in particular, take a great deal of pride in their city's cosmopolitanism. Indeed, I'm one of those New Yorkers, and I'm often deeply moved by these efforts to embrace our increasing diversity. Our "multiculturalism" clearly does mark progress from the "melting pots" of the past. But the question remains: What *kinds* of space has multiculturalism made available to marginalized communities like the Afro-Caribbean immigrants, African Americans, and Hasidic Jews who make their homes in today's Crown Heights? What *forms* of diversity do we celebrate these days, and what forms do we continue to suppress or deny?

All too often, I think, our understanding of diversity remains limited by reductive conceptual categories like "race," "religion," "ethnicity," and "culture." We are eager to embrace diversity, but only when it comes in easily recognizable forms. In addition to structuring our perceptions of self and other, these conceptual categories have been institutionalized in programs designed—with the best intentions—to promote mutual understanding. Taken together, these perceptions and programs require Crown Heights residents and others to define their identities in terms imposed, more or less subtly, by the state and social elites—as, for example, when the Brooklyn borough president called on Blacks and Jews in Crown Heights to share their "cultural traditions." In order to gain public recognition, and more tangible benefits, all sorts of communities must remake themselves as "racial," "religious," or "ethnic" groups, with "cultures" comparable to those of their neighbors.[1] American society no longer insists upon *substantive* assimilation to a shared national culture, but it continues to insist upon *structural* assimilation to an underlying model of identity and difference. "Its hegemony," as Richard Wilk has argued in a related context, "is not of content but of form."[2] Yet this is, we must remember, a brand of hegemony nonetheless—a taken-for-granted principle of social order that demands compliance if one wishes to participate in public life. The first commandment, so to speak, of American multiculturalism: Thou shalt define thyself in terms we understand.

This is precisely the commandment resisted, to varying degrees, by the stiffnecked chosen peoples of Crown Heights.[3] Crown Heights residents often articulate ambiguous identities that trouble the boundaries of "race" and "religion," as these categories are understood in contemporary American society—as, for example, when Lubavitch Hasidim claim inherited Jewish souls, or their Black neighbors claim descent from ancient Israel. When they do articulate identities that seem "racial" or "religious" in straightforward terms—as in debates over the violence of 1991—they inevitably do so in tension with each other, sparking a heated contest over Black-Jewish difference that casts doubt on the very categories it invokes. This categorical contest is shaped by a number of social forces, as I've shown throughout this book. But above all, I have argued, it may be traced to the efforts of the Lubavitch Hasidim to live by a spiritual vision of Jewishness, in a neighborhood—and nation—where collective identities are generally defined in terms of race. Of course, Black Crown Heights residents have extremely complex collective identities as well, and these Black identities sometimes elude the familiar categories of race and religion. But it's ultimately Lubavitchers—more than their neighbors—who have upset the hegemonic patterns of identity formation in multicultural America.

And, to be blunt, more power to them. I certainly do not share the Lubavitch community's vision of Jewishness—in fact, I am deeply troubled by their essentialist account of Jewish identity and Jewish-Gentile difference—but I respect and admire their determination to define their identities in their own terms. My goal, as I stated in the introduction, is to defend the ability of Lubavitchers and others to conduct their lives in ways that are meaningful to them. It may be tempting to argue that the Lubavitch community's stubborn insistence on foundational beliefs at odds with those of their neighbors—and most other Americans—has exacerbated the conflict between Blacks and Jews in Crown Heights. Indeed, one must admit, it's not always easy to live next door to a chosen people. A "kingdom of priests" devoted to a transcendent god may occasionally be blind to their immediate social context—placing eternal truths, as they see them, above the give and take of civic life. This tendency toward absolutism sometimes tests the limits of multicultural coexistence. A diverse society, many claim, simply cannot accommodate such sectarian communities.

But what sort of "diversity" are we trying to foster if we force people to surrender their deeply held beliefs as the price of entry into the public sphere? What's the point of a "multiculturalism" limited to predictable variations on established themes? Is there no room in our society for radical forms of difference? Is there no way to imagine—and someday create— an America with conceptual and political space for all the chosen peoples of Crown Heights?

These questions do not speak to Crown Heights residents alone—or to immigrants, or members of sectarian religious communities, or to Blacks or Jews, or others imagined as different by the so-called mainstream of American society. In the end, I would argue, we are *all* chosen peoples. We are all somewhat stiffnecked, in one way or another. We may not claim ties to a transcendent god, but we all claim identities that don't quite fit the reductive terms of hegemonic categories. Blacks and Whites are not simply "racial." Jews and Gentiles are not simply "religious." Immigrant communities are not simply "ethnic." No one's life is neatly circumscribed by their "cultural traditions." This is not to say that we're just "individuals," as our lives are shaped in countless ways by such categories of identity and the hierarchies they structure. But these categories ultimately fail to capture the living, breathing, luminous reality of our shared social world. By exploring the limits of categorical thought, I hope I have contributed, in some small way, to a richer understanding of this world.

NOTES

PROLOGUE   "BLACKS" AND "JEWS" AT THE LAUNDROMAT

1. See Bronislaw Malinowski's path-breaking 1922 ethnography *Argonauts of the Western Pacific* (Prospect Heights, IL: Waveland Press, 1984), esp. 18–20. For a more recent reflection on "the matter of factness of the everyday" see Michael Taussig's essay "Tactility and Distraction," in his collection *The Nervous System* (New York: Routledge, 1992), 141–148. Quote on 147.

INTRODUCTION   RACE, RELIGION, AND THE CONTEST
OVER BLACK-JEWISH DIFFERENCE IN CROWN HEIGHTS

1. Like most Crown Heights residents, I usually use "Black" as a catch-all term for people of recognized African descent, including both native-born African Americans and Afro-Caribbean immigrants. I usually capitalize terms denoting racial and religious categories and identities, because standard English usage requires me to capitalize "Jew" and simple fairness requires me to treat Blacks and Jews alike in such textual details.

2. Richard Girgenti, *A Report to the Governor on the Disturbances in Crown Heights, Vol. 1: An Assessment of the City's Preparedness and Response to Civil Disorder* (Albany: New York State Division of Criminal Justice Services, 1993), 132.

3. In addition to extensive media coverage, the violence in Crown Heights has been discussed, above all, by authors concerned with the history of Black-Jewish relations in the United States. Most use the story of "Crown Heights" to mark the decline of the "grand alliance" forged by Black and Jewish leaders in the civil rights movement of the 1960s—a narrative that contains a grain of truth, but pays scant attention to the complex details of the conflict in Crown Heights. A few, however, have developed subtle analyses of Crown Heights itself. See for example: Richard Goldstein, "The New Anti-Semitism: A Geshrei," in *Blacks and Jews: Alliances and Arguments*, ed. Paul Berman (New York: Delta, 1994), 204–216; Jonathan Rieder, "Reflections on Crown Heights: Interpretive Dilemmas and Black-Jewish Conflict" in *Antisemitism in America Today*, ed. Jerome Chanes (New York: Birch Lane Press, 1995), 348–385; Patricia Williams, "On Imagining Foes, Imagining Friendship" in *Struggles in the Promised Land: Toward a History of Black-Jewish Relations in the United States*, ed. Jack Salzman and Cornel West (New York: Oxford University Press, 1997), 371–384. In addition to these essays on the conflict itself, scholars of

Hasidic and Caribbean Brooklyn have sometimes touched on the violence of 1991 in the course of their work on related themes. See for example: Philip Kasinitz, *Caribbean New York: Black Immigrants and the Politics of Race* (Ithaca, NY: Cornell University Press, 1992), xii–xiv; and Jerome Mintz, *Hasidic People: A Place in the New World* (Cambridge, MA: Harvard University Press, 1992), 139–153, 236–247, 328–347. Finally, one remarkable work stands out among these journalistic and scholarly accounts, thanks to its careful attention to the complex details of conflict, identity, and everyday life in Crown Heights. This is Anna Deavere Smith's 1992 play *Fires in the Mirror: Crown Heights, Brooklyn, and Other Identities* (New York: Anchor Books, 1993), a one-woman performance based on extensive interviews conducted by the playwright in the months after the violence of 1991.

4. The summer of 2003 witnessed Lemrick Nelson's third, and most likely final, trial for the stabbing of Yankel Rosenbaum. Nelson was found guilty, but sentenced to little more than "time served"—a verdict that satisfied no one. I will describe the various legal proceedings stemming from the violence of 1991 in detail in chapter 1.

5. As many readers are no doubt aware, over the past couple of decades a growing number of scholars in the social sciences and humanities have reevaluated the process of collective identity formation. At its core, this research has constituted a radical critique of the widely shared assumption that the social world may be divided into stable and clearly bounded units—whether these units are described as "races," "nations," "classes," "religions," "genders," "cultures," "communities," or what-have-you. This is absolutely *not* to say that these painstakingly produced categories and identities don't "really" exist. They are undeniably, and often brutally, real as social and historical facts. But recent research has shown that collective identities are never inherently distinct, and are rarely clearly or stably so. They are products of complex social processes, and thus always work in some sort of fitful progress. The interdisciplinary literatures on collective identity are far too large and diverse to summarize here, but for critical ethnographies of identity formation one might start out with: Jacqueline Nassy Brown, *Dropping Anchor, Setting Sail: Geographies of Race in Black Liverpool* (Princeton, NJ: Princeton University Press, 2005); Virginia Domínguez, *White by Definition: Social Classification in Creole Louisiana* (New Brunswick, NJ: Rutgers University Press, 1986); Allen Feldman, *Formations of Violence: The Narrative of the Body and Political Terror in Northern Ireland* (Chicago: University of Chicago Press, 1991); Steven Gregory, *Black Corona: Race and the Politics of Place in an Urban Community* (Princeton, NJ: Princeton University Press, 1998); Richard Handler, *Nationalism and the Politics of Culture in Quebec* (Madison: University of Wisconsin Press, 1988); Susan Harding, *The Book of Jerry Falwell: Fundamentalist Language and Politics* (Princeton, NJ: Princeton University Press, 2000); John Hartigan, *Racial Situations: Class Predicaments of Whiteness in Detroit* (Princeton, NJ: Princeton University Press, 1999); Liisa Malkki, *Purity and Exile: Violence, Memory, and National Cosmology Among Hutu Refugees in Tanzania* (Chicago: University of Chicago Press, 1995); Michael Taussig, *Shamanism, Colonialism, and the Wild Man* (Chicago: University of Chicago Press, 1987); Mary Weismantel, *Cholas and Pishtacos: Stories of Race and Sex in the Andes* (Chicago: University of Chicago Press, 2001).

6. Patricia Williams, *The Alchemy of Race and Rights* (Cambridge, MA: Harvard University Press, 1991), 10. See also Avery Gordon, *Ghostly Matters: Haunting and the Sociological Imagination* (Minneapolis: University of Minnesota Press, 1997), esp. 3–28. Gordon draws on Williams's insights into life's complexity in an effort to reimagine social theory, and to "treat race, class, and gender dynamics and consciousness as more dense and delicate than these categorical terms often imply" (5).

7. I will often use the term "multiplicity" as a noun—referring, for example, to the "multiplicity of difference" rather than simply "multiple differences." This usage, which may be unfamiliar to nonacademic readers, is intended to highlight the *irreducible* plurality of the differences that divide Blacks and Jews in Crown Heights. The "multiplicity of difference" (like, say, a fish, or any other common noun) is an object in its own right, not easily broken into component parts. But "multiple differences" (with multiplicity demoted to an adjective) offer the false promise of reducing these different differences to expressions of a single underlying phenomenon. For philosophical meditations on the concept of multiplicity, see Gilles Deleuze and Félix Guattari, *A Thousand Plateaus: Capitalism and Schizophrenia*, trans. Brian Massumi (Minneapolis: University of Minnesota Press, 1987).

8. Since the late eighteenth century or so, Americans and others have generally assumed that "racial" identities are based upon immutable biological differences. Over the course of the twentieth century, however, research in a broad range of fields demonstrated quite clearly that these identities are, in fact, the historically contingent products of social and political forces. Although "race" continues to structure hierarchy and inequality in the Americas and elsewhere, it is, quite simply, a biological fiction—the historical product of prejudice, cloaked in the mantle of spurious science. For recent critiques of racial essentialism see, for example, the essays collected in: Henry Louis Gates, Jr., ed., *"Race," Writing and Difference* (Chicago: University of Chicago Press, 1986); David Theo Goldberg, ed., *Anatomy of Racism* (Minneapolis: University of Minnesota Press, 1990); Steven Gregory and Roger Sanjek, eds., *Race* (New Brunswick, NJ: Rutgers University Press, 1994); Wahneema Lubiano, ed., *The House That Race Built* (New York: Vintage Books, 1998). For the social and intellectual history of the concept of race, see: George Fredrickson, *Racism: A Short History* (Princeton, NJ: Princeton University Press, 2002); Winthrop Jordan, *White Over Black: American Attitudes Toward the Negro, 1550–1812* (Chapel Hill: University of North Carolina Press, 1968); George Mosse, *Toward the Final Solution: A History of European Racism* (New York: H. Fertig, 1978); Michael Omi and Howard Winant, *Racial Formation in the United States, From the 1960s to the 1990s* (New York: Routledge, 1994); Audrey Smedley, *Race in North America: Origin and Evolution of a Worldview*, 2nd ed. (Boulder, CO: Westview Press, 1999).

9. Much like "race," the concept of "religion" is a product of social, historical, and political forces. Many, if not all, societies and cultures have developed systems of thought and practice oriented around perceptions of supernatural or nonempirical entities of some kind. But in recent years, an increasing number of scholars have argued that "religion"—the conceptual category thought to embrace *all* of

these diverse systems—is a product of Western, and Christian, thought and society. For recent analyses of the social construction of religious difference see the essays collected in: Henry Goldschmidt and Elizabeth McAlister, eds., *Race, Nation, and Religion in the Americas* (New York: Oxford University Press, 2004); Craig Prentiss, ed., *Religion and the Creation of Race and Ethnicity: An Introduction* (New York: New York University Press, 2003); Peter Van Der Veer and Hartmut Lehmann, eds., *Nation and Religion: Perspectives on Europe and Asia* (Princeton, NJ: Princeton University Press, 1999). On the social and intellectual history of the concept of religion, see: Talal Asad, *Genealogies of Religion* (Baltimore: The Johns Hopkins University Press, 1993); David Chidester, *Savage Systems: Colonialism and Comparative Religion in Southern Africa* (Charlottesville: University of Virginia Press, 1996); Tomoko Masuzawa, *The Invention of World Religions* (Chicago: University of Chicago Press, 2005); Jonathan Z. Smith, "Religion, Religions, Religious" in *Critical Terms for Religious Studies*, ed. Mark C. Taylor (Chicago: University of Chicago Press, 1998), 269–284.

10. This critique of America's culinary multiculturalism is inspired, in part, by Richard Handler's image of a row of equivalently "ethnic" restaurants (Handler, *Nationalism and the Politics of Culture*, 195). My phrasing—"not too spicy please"—is borrowed in part from the Brooklyn Funk Essentials song "Got Cash" (2000, lyrics by Everton Sylvester). I will explore the ties between food and "culture" in chapter 3.

11. The quotes are from Parliament Funkadelic's hit song "Chocolate City" (1975, lyrics by George Clinton, Bootsy Collins, and Bernie Worrell). For a critique of the racial economy of White flight see George Lipsitz, *The Possessive Investment in Whiteness* (Philadelphia: Temple University Press, 1998), 5–8, 25–33. On the history of suburbanization in the United States, see Kenneth Jackson, *Crabgrass Frontier* (New York: Oxford University Press, 1985). On the complex roles of Jews in these nationwide trends, see: Karen Brodkin, *How Jews Became White Folks & What That Says About Race in America* (New Brunswick, NJ: Rutgers University Press, 1998), esp. 25–52; Gerald Gamm, *Urban Exodus: Why the Jews Left Boston and the Catholics Stayed* (Cambridge, MA: Harvard University Press, 1999); Jonathan Rieder, *Canarsie: The Jews and Italians of Brooklyn Against Liberalism* (Cambridge, MA: Harvard University Press, 1985).

12. Statistics drawn from the *Community Planning Handbook: Brooklyn Community District* 8 (New York: City Planning Commission, 1973), table 3.3.

13. On the post-1965 wave of Afro-Caribbean immigration and Caribbean settlement in Crown Heights, see Kasinitz, *Caribbean New York*, 26–32, 59–64.

14. On these early conflicts, see Mintz, *Hasidic People*, 141–143.

15. On the pivotal role of the Ocean Hill–Brownsville teachers' strike in reshaping relations between African Americans and American Jews, see Jonathan Kaufman, *Broken Alliance: The Turbulent Times Between Blacks and Jews in America* (New York: Charles Scribner's Sons, 1994), 127–164; and Jerald Podair, *The Strike That Changed New York: Blacks, Whites, and the Ocean Hill–Brownsville Crisis* (New Haven, CT: Yale University Press, 2002).

16. For a useful summary of Hasidic beliefs about the charismatic leadership of a Rebbe, see Solomon Poll, "The Charismatic Leader of the Hasidic Community:

The Zaddiq, The Rebbe," in *New World Hasidim: Ethnographic Studies of Hasidic Jews in America*, ed. Janet Belcove-Shalin (Albany: State University of New York Press, 1995), 257–275. For a sketch of the Lubavitch dynasty, see Rhonda Berger-Sofer, "Political Kinship Alliances of a Hasidic Dynasty," *Ethnology*, vol. 23, no. 1 (1984):49–62.

17. The Lubavitch community has been well known, and controversial, in recent years for the messianic expectations that surrounded the Rebbe in the last decade of his life. For social analyses of Lubavitch messianism, see: Mintz, *Hasidic People*, 348–364, and a series of three essays by William Shaffir: "Jewish Messianism Lubavitch Style: An Interim Report," *The Jewish Journal of Sociology*, vol. 35, no. 2 (1993):115–128; "Interpreting Adversity: Dynamics of Commitment in a Messianic Redemption Campaign," *The Jewish Journal of Sociology*, vol. 36, no. 1 (1994):43–53; and "When Prophecy is not Validated: Explaining Unexpected in a Messianic Campaign," *The Jewish Journal of Sociology*, vol. 37, no. 2 (1995):119–136. For historical and theological analyses, see: Rachel Elior, "The Lubavitch Messianic Resurgence: The Historical and Mystical Background, 1939–1996" in *Toward the Millennium: Messianic Expectations from the Bible to Waco*, ed. Peter Schäfer and Marc Cohen (Leiden: Brill, 1998), 383–408; Menachem Friedman, "Habad as Messianic Fundamentalism: From Local Particularism to Universal Jewish Mission" in *Accounting for Fundamentalisms*, ed. Martin Marty and R. Scott Appleby (Chicago: University of Chicago Press, 1994), 328–357; and Aviezer Ravitzky, "The Contemporary Lubavitch Hasidic Movement: Between Conservatism and Messianism" in *Accounting for Fundamentalisms*, ed. Martin Marty and R. Scott Appleby (Chicago: University of Chicago Press, 1994), 303–327. And for a non-Hasidic orthodox critique and Lubavitch response, see David Berger, *The Rebbe, The Messiah, and the Scandal of Orthodox Indifference* (London: The Littman Library of Jewish Civilization, 2001) and Chaim Dalfin, *Attack on Lubavitch: A Response* (Brooklyn: Jewish Enrichment Press, 2002).

18. On the central role of nigunim in Lubavitch religious practice, see Ellen Koskoff, *Music in Lubavitcher Life* (Urbana: University of Illinois Press, 2001).

19. I am indebted to my old friend Simon Steiner for this remarkable quote, which I've drawn from his manuscript "Ten Interviews on the Subject of the Farbrengen."

20. The Rebbe nearly always spoke in Yiddish at farbrengens, and his words were later printed and circulated in Hebrew translation. This extended quote, and the one in the next paragraph, are translated from the Hebrew by Edward Hoffman in *Despite All Odds: The Story of Lubavitch* (New York: Simon and Schuster, 1991), 146–147. The shorter quotes in these paragraphs are my own translations from the published text in Menachem Mendel Schneerson, *Likutei Sichot, Vol. 6: Shemot* (Brooklyn: Kehot Publication Society, 1972), 350–356.

21. Kasinitz, *Caribbean New York*, 143.

22. Kasinitz, *Caribbean New York*, 59–66. See also Department of City Planning, *Caribbean Immigrants in New York City: A Demographic Survey* (New York: Department of City Planning, 1988).

23. For analyses of the Labor Day Carnival, see Kasinitz, *Caribbean New York*, 133–159, and Philip Scher, *Carnival and the Formation of a Caribbean Transnation* (Gainesville: University Press of Florida, 2003).

24. For example, Stephen Bloom's deeply flawed yet oddly engrossing account of the tension between Lubavitchers and their neighbors in the Iowa town of Postville (where a Lubavitch family opened a kosher slaughterhouse) documents bitter conflicts framed in terms of religion, class, and culture. But despite the author's own references to "olive-skinned" Hasidim (pgs. xiii, 23), there is no evidence that Jews or Gentiles in Postville ever imagined Jewish difference in racial terms. See Stephen Bloom, *Postville* (New York: Harcourt, 2000).

25. I am not using the term "ideology" in the Marxist sense of a false belief masking an underlying reality. Rather, I am trying to convey the fact that Lubavitch understandings of Jewishness form a more or less systematized program for cultural activism, identity formation, and community organization.

26. I am reluctant to use the term "ultra-orthodox," as the prefix "ultra" carries pejorative connotations of irrational extremism. However, Hasidic and non-Hasidic ultra-orthodox Jews must often be distinguished, as a group, from "modern orthodox" Jews (another deeply problematic term), who interpret the laws of the Torah far less stringently, and participate more fully in secular society.

27. On the Baal Shem Tov, see Moshe Rosman, *Founder of Hasidism: A Quest for the Historical Ba'al Shem Tov* (Berkeley: University of California Press, 1996).

28. For an overview of Hasidic life and thought, see Mintz, *Hasidic People*, 1–8. For an overview of ultra-orthodox Jewry (including Hasidic and non-Hasidic communities) see Samuel Heilman, *Defenders of the Faith* (New York: Schocken Books, 1992), esp. 11–39. For more detailed analyses of American Hasidic life, and an introduction to the ethnographic literature on American Hasidim, see Mintz, *Hasidic People*; Janet Belcove-Shalin, ed., *New World Hasidim: Ethnographic Studies of Hasidic Jews in America* (Albany: State University of New York Press, 1995); and the documentary film by Menachem Daum and Oren Rudavsky, *A Life Apart: Hasidism in America* (New York: First Run/Icarus Films, 1997). And for detailed analyses of Hasidic history and thought, as well as an introduction to the literatures on Hasidism in the field of Jewish studies, see Gershon Hundert, ed., *Essential Papers on Hasidism: Origins to Present* (New York: New York University Press, 1991); Ada Rapoport-Albert, ed., *Hasidism Reappraised* (London: Vallentine Mitchell, 1996).

29. The term "Chabad" is an acronym for the kabbalistic concepts and cosmological principles *Chochma—Bina—Da'as*, or "Wisdom—Understanding—Knowledge," which are central terms in Chabad-Lubavitch theology.

30. The Lubavitch community's "outreach" to secular Jews must be clearly distinguished from Christian evangelism. Most Lubavitchers have no interest whatsoever in converting non-Jews to Judaism. They are, however, profoundly interested in increasing Jewish observance of the commandments of the Torah, as they understand them. For the intellectual roots of this outreach project, see Naftali Loewenthal, *Communicating the Infinite: The Emergence of the Habad School* (Chicago: University of Chicago Press, 1990).

31. For analyses of these outreach campaigns and their complex consequences, see Sue Fishkoff, *The Rebbe's Army: Inside the World of Chabad-Lubavitch* (New York: Schocken Books, 2003); Friedman, "Habad as Messianic Fundamentalism," in *Accounting for Fundamentalisms*, ed. Marty and Appleby; Hoffman, *Against All Odds*.

32. The concept of the "godly soul" draws on a longstanding kabbalistic tradition inspired, in part, by the work of the twelfth-century philosopher and poet Judah Halevi. It was systematized, however, in Rabbi Schneur Zalman's seminal 1796 work *Likutei Amarim—Tanya* (Brooklyn: Kehot Publication Society, 1993). In the 1950s, the Lubavitcher Rebbe decreed that the chapters of *Tanya* devoted to the godly soul (chaps. 18 and 19) are so significant that Lubavitch schoolchildren should learn them by heart. For more on the godly and animal souls, see Koskoff, *Music in Lubavitcher Life*, 32–34; Loewenthal, *Communicating the Infinite*, 54–57.

33. Although the messianic movement surrounding the Lubavitcher Rebbe has been extremely controversial in the orthodox Jewish world (and within the Lubavitch community itself), the fundamental assumption that Torah observance is the key to redemption has been an accepted element of Jewish orthodoxy for centuries. It is a central principle in work of the influential sixteenth-century mystic Isaac Luria. For a sketch of Lurianic messianism, see Gershom Scholem, *The Messianic Idea in Judaism* (New York: Schocken Books, 1971), 43–48.

34. For analyses of the relationships among racial, ethnic, and national identities in Caribbean-American communities, see for example: Nina Glick Schiller and Georges Fouron, *Georges Woke Up Laughing* (Durham, NC: Duke University Press, 2001); Kasinitz, *Caribbean New York*; Elizabeth McAlister, "The Madonna of 115th Street Revisited: Vodou and Haitian Catholicism in the Age of Transnationalism," in *Gatherings in Diaspora: Religious Communities and the New Immigration*, ed. R. Stephen Warner and Judith Wittner (Philadelphia: Temple University Press, 1998), 123–160; Constance Sutton and Elsa Chaney, eds., *Caribbean Life in New York City: Sociocultural Dimensions* (New York: Center for Migration Studies, 1987); Mary Waters, *Black Identities: West Indian Immigrant Dreams and American Realities* (Cambridge and New York: Harvard University Press and the Russell Sage Foundation, 1999).

35. This quick (and somewhat oversimplified) sketch of American Jewish racial history draws on a number of key sources. See for example: Brodkin, *How Jews Became White Folks*; Sander Gilman, *The Jew's Body* (New York: Routledge, 1991); Eric Goldstein, "'Different Blood Flows in Our Veins': Race and Jewish Self-Definition in Late Nineteenth Century America," *American Jewish History*, vol. 85, no. 1 (1997): 29–55; Matthew Jacobson, *Whiteness of a Different Color* (Cambridge: Harvard University Press, 1998), esp. 171–199; Rieder, *Canarsie*; Michael Rogin, *Blackface, White Noise: Jewish Immigrants in the Hollywood Melting Pot* (Berkeley: University of California Press, 1996).

36. Daniel Itzkovitz, "Secret Temples," in *Jews and Other Differences: The New Jewish Cultural Studies*, ed. Jonathan Boyarin and Daniel Boyarin (Minneapolis: University of Minnesota Press, 1997), 180.

37. Itzkovitz, "Secret Temples," 179–180.

38. This is, however, one way to read Will Herberg's argument in his brilliant but infuriating essay on "The 'Chosenness' of Israel and the Jew of Today," in *Arguments and Doctrines*, Arthur Cohen, ed. (New York: Harper & Row, 1970), 270–283.

39. On these and other Israelites, see for example: Michael Barkun, *Religion and the Racist Right: The Origins of the Christian Identity Movement* (Chapel Hill: University

of North Carolina Press, 1994); Sacvan Bercovitch, *The American Jeremiad* (Madison: University of Wisconsin Press, 1978); Barry Chevannes, *Rastafari: Roots and Ideology* (Syracuse, NY: Syracuse University Press, 1994); Yvonne Chireau and Nathaniel Deutsch, eds., *Black Zion: African-American Religious Encounters with Judaism* (New York: Oxford University Press, 2000); Arnold Eisen, *The Chosen People in America: A Study in Jewish Religious Ideology* (Bloomington: Indiana University Press, 1983); Albert Raboteau, "African-Americans, Exodus, and the American Israel" in *A Fire in the Bones* (Boston: Beacon Press, 1995), 17–36; Theophus Smith, *Conjuring Culture: Biblical Formations of Black America* (New York: Oxford University Press, 1994); Werner Sollors, "Typology and Ethnogenesis" in *Beyond Ethnicity* (New York: Oxford University Press, 1986), 40–65; Ernest Tuveson, *Redeemer Nation: The Idea of America's Millennial Role* (1968; reprint, Chicago: University of Chicago Press, 1980).

40. I develop this argument at greater length in the introduction to Goldschmidt and McAlister, eds., *Race, Nation, and Religion in the Americas*, from which some of the text in this section is drawn. See esp. 6–11.

41. Religion has been a major focus of research on African-American and Afro-Caribbean communities since at least the pioneering work of W. E. B. Du Bois, whose writing on the subject has been collected by Phil Zuckerman in *Du Bois on Religion* (Walnut Creek, CA: AltaMira Press, 2000). The scholarly literatures on Black religions in the Americas are far too large and diverse to summarize here, but for useful introductions see the essays collected in: Barry Chevannes, ed., *Rastafari and Other African-Caribbean Worldviews* (New Brunswick: Rutgers University Press, 1998); Timothy Fulop and Albert Raboteau, eds., *African-American Religion: Interpretive Essays in History and Culture* (New York: Routledge, 1997); Patrick Taylor, ed., *Nation Dance: Religion, Identity, and Cultural Difference in the Caribbean* (Bloomington: Indiana University Press, 2001); Gayraud Wilmore, ed., *African American Religious Studies: An Interdisciplinary Anthology* (Durham: Duke University Press, 1989).

42. See for example the essays in: Helen Ebaugh and Janet Chafetz, eds., *Religion and the New Immigrants* (Walnut Creek, CA: AltaMira Press, 2000); R. Stephen Warner and Judith Wittner, eds., *Gatherings in Diaspora: Religious Communities and the New Immigration* (Philadelphia: Temple University Press, 1998). Scholars of religion and migration are deeply indebted to Will Herberg's classic analysis of religion, ethnicity and nationalism, *Protestant-Catholic-Jew* (New York: Doubleday, 1956), but Herberg was largely blind to issues of race.

43. See the works on Jews and race cited above in note # 35.

44. See for example: Diane Austin-Broos, *Jamaica Genesis* (Chicago: Chicago University Press, 1997); John Burdick, *Looking for God in Brazil* (Berkeley: University of California Press, 1993); Stephen Glazier, ed., *Perspectives on Pentecostalism: Case Studies from the Caribbean and Latin America* (Washington, DC: University Press of America, 1980); Nicole Rodriguez Toulis, *Believing Identity: Pentecostalism and the Mediation of Jamaican Ethnicity and Gender in England* (Oxford: Berg, 1997).

45. See for example: James Aho, *The Politics of Righteousness: Idaho Christian Patriotism* (Seattle: University of Washington Press, 1990); Barkun, *Religion and the Racist*

Right; Ann Burlein, *Lift High the Cross: Where White Supremacy and the Christian Right Converge* (Durham: Duke University Press, 2002).

46. See for example: Jean and John Comaroff, *Of Revelation and Revolution: Christianity, Colonialism and Consciousness in South Africa, Volume One* (Chicago: University of Chicago Press, 1991); Robert Hefner, ed., *Conversion to Christianity: Historical and Anthropological Perspectives on a Great Transformation* (Berkeley: University of California Press, 1993); Vincente Rafael, *Contracting Colonialism: Translation and Christian Conversion in Tagalog Society under Early Spanish Rule* (Ithaca: Cornell University Press, 1988); Peter Van Der Veer, ed., *Conversion to Modernities: The Globalization of Christianity* (New York: Routledge, 1996).

47. See for example: Paul Brass, ed., *Riots and Pogroms* (New York: New York University Press, 1996); Fred Halliday, *Nation and Religion in the Middle East* (Boulder, CO: Lynne Rienner Publishers, 2000); Malkki, *Purity and Exile*; Martin Marty and R. Scott Appleby, eds., *Religion, Ethnicity, and Self-Identity: Nations in Turmoil* (Hanover, NH: University Press of New England, 1997); Peter Van Der Veer, *Religious Nationalism: Hindus and Muslims in India* (Berkeley: University of California Press, 1994).

48. The literatures on religious fundamentalism rarely engage with questions of race, but often reflect on ethnicity and nationalism, and explore the role of religion in identity formation. For an introduction see the essays collected by Martin Marty and R. Scott Appleby in the five volumes of *The Fundamentalism Project* (Chicago: Chicago University Press, 1991–1995).

49. There are, of course, important exceptions to this critique as well—but unfortunately not so many of them. For examples, see the essays collected in Goldschmidt and McAlister, eds., *Race, Nation, and Religion in the Americas*, as well as some of the essays collected in Prentiss, ed., *Religion and the Creation of Race and Ethnicity*. For a similar analysis of race and religion as "articulated identities," see Aisha Khan's important new work *Callaloo Nation: Metaphors of Race and Religious Identity among South Asians in Trinidad* (Durham, NC: Duke University Press, 2004).

50. Evelyn Brooks Higginbotham, "African-American Women's History and the Metalanguage of Race," *Signs*, vol. 17, no. 2 (1992):251–274. Higginbotham adapts the term "metalanguage" from Roland Barthes, *Mythologies*, trans. Annette Lavers (New York: Hill & Wang, 1972), esp. 111–117.

51. Higginbotham, "Metalanguage," 255.

52. Judith Butler, *Bodies that Matter: On the Discursive Limits of "Sex"* (New York: Routledge, 1993), 168.

53. I develop this argument at greater length in the introduction to Goldschmidt and McAlister, eds., *Race, Nation, and Religion in the Americas*, from which some of the text in this section is drawn. See esp. 11–15.

54. For analyses of the links between race and modernity, see Zygmunt Bauman, *Modernity and the Holocaust* (Ithaca, NY: Cornell University Press, 1989); Paul Gilroy, *The Black Atlantic: Modernity and Double Consciousness* (Cambridge, MA: Harvard University Press, 1993); and Robyn Wiegman, *American Anatomies: Theorizing Race and Gender* (Durham, NC: Duke University Press, 1995).

55. For a range of perspectives on the contested relationship between modernity and secularization, see the essays collected in: Steve Bruce, ed., *Religion and Modernization: Sociologists and Historians Debate the Secularization Thesis* (New York: Oxford University Press, 1992); William Swatos and Daniel Olson, eds., *The Secularization Debate* (Lanham, MD: Rowman and Littlefield Publishers, 2000). The argument that secularization is a necessary aspect of modernization generally draws on Max Weber's classic analysis of the "disenchantment" of the modern world. See Weber's 1918 lecture on "Science as a Vocation," in *From Max Weber: Essays in Sociology*, ed. H. H. Gerth and C. Wright Mills (New York: Oxford University Press, 1946), 129–156. For a particularly subtle, and conditional, rearticulation of the secularization thesis, see Jose Casanova, *Public Religions in the Modern World* (Chicago: University of Chicago Press, 1994). For an innovative analysis of culturally specific ideologies of secularism, see Talal Asad, *Formations of the Secular: Christianity, Islam, Modernity* (Stanford, CA: Stanford University Press, 2003).

56. Lis Harris, *Holy Days: The World of a Hasidic Family* (New York: Summit, 1985), 57.

57. Harris, *Holy Days*, "ordinary world" on page 13, "dream" on page 14.

58. Audrey Smedley, " 'Race' and the Construction of Human Identity," *American Anthropologist*, vol. 100, no. 3 (1998):695.

59. Fredrickson, *Racism: A Short History*, 3.

60. Ann Stoler, *Race and the Education of Desire* (Durham, NC: Duke University Press, 1995), 72. In the passage quoted, Stoler is outlining Foucault's genealogy of the concept of race, as developed in his unpublished 1976 Collège de France lectures.

61. Asad, *Formations of the Secular*, 15. Asad is, I should note, somewhat less insistent on this point than I have been. He poses this image of a nonbinary world as an open question, placing it in tension with analyses of the ways various social actors have divided the world into "modern" and "nonmodern." For a comparable critique of binary thinking about modernity, see also Bruno Latour, *We Have Never Been Modern*, trans. Catherine Porter (Cambridge, MA: Harvard University Press, 1993).

CHAPTER 1   COLLISIONS

1. I obtained weather data for August 19, 1991, and the rest of the summer, from the North East Regional Climate Center. The relatively cool, dry weather of August 19 belies the popular assumption linking outbreaks of urban violence to excessive heat and humidity.

2. Smith, *Fires in the Mirror*, 79. I have disregarded the frequent line-breaks used by Smith to accentuate the rhythms of her interviewees' speech. Though I share Smith's concern with the idiosyncratic and culturally patterned contours of speech, I will quote her text in prose.

3. Rieder, "Reflections," in *Antisemitism in America Today*, ed. Chanes, 377.

4. Joan Scott, "The Evidence of Experience," in *Critical Inquiry*, vol. 17, no. 4 (summer 1991): 797.

5. Susan Harding, "Imagining the Last Days: The Politics of Apocalyptic Language," in *Accounting for Fundamentalisms*, ed. Martin Marty and R. Scott Appleby (Chicago: University of Chicago Press, 1994), 61. For further analyses of the links between narrative and collective identity, see for example: Homi Bhabha, ed., *Nation and Narration* (New York: Routledge, 1990); Gates, ed., *"Race," Writing and Difference*; Harding, *The Book of Jerry Falwell*; Malkki, *Purity and Exile*; Werner Sollors, *Beyond Ethnicity* (New York: Oxford University Press, 1986); Mary Steedly, *Hanging Without a Rope: Narrative Experience in Colonial and Postcolonial Karoland* (Princeton, NJ: Princeton University Press, 1993); Kathleen Stewart, *A Space on the Side of the Road: Cultural Poetics in an "Other" America* (Princeton, NJ: Princeton University Press, 1996); Weismantel, *Cholas and Pishtacos*; Yael Zerubavel, *Recovered Roots: Collective Memory and the Making of Israeli National Tradition* (Chicago: University of Chicago Press, 1995). And for classic anthropological analyses of myth, see for example: Bronislaw Malinowski, "Myth in Primitive Psychology," in *Magic, Science and Religion and Other Essays* (Boston: Beacon Press, 1948); and Claude Levi-Strauss, "The Structural Study of Myth" in *Structural Anthropology* (New York: Basic Books, 1963).

6. Of course, I am not the first scholar to examine the relationships between narrative and conflict. See for example: Paul Brass, *Theft of an Idol: Text and Context in the Representation of Collective Violence* (Princeton, NJ: Princeton University Press, 1997); Beth Roy, *Some Trouble with Cows: Making Sense of Social Conflict* (Berkeley: University of California Press, 1994); Ted Swedenburg, *Memories of Revolt: The 1936–1939 Rebellion and the Palestinian National Past* (Minneapolis: University of Minnesota Press, 1995).

7. Smith, *Fires in the Mirror*, 135–136.

8. Smith, *Fires in the Mirror*, "numerous numbers" on page 136, "my children" on page 135.

9. The next two paragraphs, describing the first few hours of violence following the death of Gavin Cato, are largely based on Girgenti, *Report to the Governor*, vol. 1, 55–58, 61–65, 232.

10. This extended quote, along with the shorter one in the previous paragraph, is drawn from a document submitted into evidence at the 1997 trial of Lemrick Nelson and Charles Price. The document is a transcript of a September 1995 conversation recorded by the FBI. All other quotes attributed to Price in this and the following paragraph are drawn from witness testimony at the 1997 trial, and my account of Price's role in the violence is largely based on evidence presented in court.

11. The lyric is from Naughty By Nature's hit song "O.P.P." (1991, lyrics by Treach).

12. In addition to the stabbing of Yankel Rosenbaum, there were two nonfatal assaults on Hasidic Jews on the night of August 19. For details, see Girgenti, *Report to the Governor*, vol. 1, 62.

13. For details on Lemrick Nelson's role in the death of Yankel Rosenbaum, see Richard Girgenti, *A Report to the Governor on the Disturbances in Crown Heights, Vol. 2: A Review of the Circumstances Surrounding the Death of Yankel Rosenbaum and the*

Resulting Prosecution (Albany: New York State Division of Criminal Justice Services, 1993).

14. These analyses of the relationships between categories of difference and acts of violence have been developed, above all, by scholars of "communal" conflict in South Asia. See for example: Brass, *Theft of an Idol*; Gyanendra Pandey, *The Construction of Communalism in Colonial North India* (New Delhi: Oxford University Press, 1990); and Roy, *Some Trouble With Cows*. For a comparative analysis of collective violence, see Brass, ed., *Riots and Pogroms*, and for a similar analysis of the violence in Crown Heights, see Rieder, "Reflections" in *Antisemitism in America Today*, ed. Chanes.

15. This footage was shown at the 1997 trial of Lemrick Nelson and Charles Price.

16. Smith, *Fires in the Mirror*, 80.

17. Girgenti, *Report to the Governor*, vol. 1, 55–56.

18. Arthur Hertzberg, "The Ghosts of Crown Heights," in the *New York Times*, December 23, 1992, pg. A19.

19. Smith, *Fires in the Mirror*, 82–83.

20. Smith, *Fires in the Mirror*, 77. Here, and at a number of other points in the book, I have altered Smith's published text slightly, adding text drawn from the 1993 adaptation of her play for the PBS series "American Playhouse." There is, I would argue, no single definitive version of a piece conceived for the theater, and the published text often differs from the videotaped performance in crucial details. I will, of course, note these additions in the future as well.

21. Sharpton's eulogy was reprinted as "Gavin's Death Must Spark a Beginning," in *The City Sun*, August 29–September 3, 1991, pg 3.

22. Girgenti, *Report to the Governor*, vol. 1, 56.

23. Girgenti, *Report to the Governor*, vol. 1, 55.

24. Smith, *Fires in the Mirror*, 126.

25. Smith, *Fires in the Mirror*, 68–69, with added text from "American Playhouse."

26. Smith, *Fires in the Mirror*, 73.

27. For discussions of these accusations, see Alan Dundes, ed., *The Blood Libel Legend: A Casebook in Anti-Semitic Folklore* (Madison: University of Wisconsin Press, 1991); Joshua Trachtenberg, *The Devil and the Jews* (2nd ed., Philadelphia: Jewish Publication Society, 1983 [1943]), 124–155. For an analysis of the violence of 1991 in these terms (by a progressive secular Jew), see Goldstein, "The New Anti-Semitism," in *Blacks and Jews*, ed. Berman.

28. This flyer was posted to advertise a rally held on September 13, 1991. It was signed by a range of Black nationalist organizations and leaders, including Sonny Carson, Reverend Herbert Daughtry, Jitu Weusi, the December 12th Movement, and the rap group X-Clan.

29. Smith, *Fires in the Mirror*, 94.

30. Vinette Pryce, "Many Blacks, No Jews, Arrested in Crown Heights," in the *New York Amsterdam News*, August 24, 1991, pg. 8.

31. This settlement was awarded by the Giuliani administration, and spearheaded by Richard Green of the Crown Heights Youth Collective—who was, by 2001, a fairly close ally of Mayor Giuliani.

32. See Girgenti, *Report to the Governor*, vol. 2, for analyses of this widely criticized trial.

33. Nelson's second prosecution was not (as some Black activists charged) a case of "double jeopardy." His 1997 trial on civil rights violations proceeded under the same legal provision that allowed federal courts in the 1960s to retry the murders of prominent Black leaders, like Medgar Evers, following acquittals in state courts suspected of racial bias.

34. There was, in fact, substantial evidence of negligence in Yankel Rosenbaum's care at Kings County Hospital. In June of 2005, the Rosenbaum family received $1.25 million from the City of New York to settle their malpractice suit against the public hospital. But evidence of medical malpractice has no bearing on Lemrick Nelson's responsibility for Rosenbaum's murder, and therefore was not presented at any of Nelson's trials.

35. Girgenti, *Report to the Governor*, vol. 1, 132.

36. Smith, *Fires in the Mirror*, 77, with added text from "American Playhouse."

37. Smith, *Fires in the Mirror*, 117–119.

38. National Advisory Commission on Civil Disorders, *Report of the National Advisory Commission on Civil Disorders* (New York: Bantam Books, 1968), 1.

39. National Advisory Commission, *Report*, "eruption of disorder" on page 112, "White racism" on page 203.

40. For descriptions of these demonstrations, see Girgenti, *Report to the Governor*, vol. 1, 68–72, 91–94.

41. See Pryce, "Many Blacks," and Peter Noel, "Crown Heights Burning: Rage, Race, and Politics of Resistance" in *The Village Voice*, September 3, 1991, pp. 37–40.

42. Noel, "Crown Heights Burning," 40.

43. Smith, *Fires in the Mirror*, 120–121, with added text from "American Playhouse."

44. For details on this attack, see Girgenti, *Report to the Governor*, vol. 1, 79–81.

45. On the complex history of European pogroms see John Klier and Shlomo Lambroza, eds., *Pogroms: Anti-Jewish Violence in Modern Russian History* (Cambridge: Cambridge University Press, 1992). Ironically, one of the most striking continuities between the violence in Crown Heights and the pogroms of late-nineteenth and early-twentieth-century Eastern Europe seems to lie in the ambiguous and contested nature of collective violence in each context.

46. Smith, *Fires in the Mirror*, 86–87, with added text from "American Playhouse."

47. Rabbi Butman's speech was videotaped by a Hasidic marcher, and copies of the tape circulated widely in the Lubavitch community. I copied it, in turn, from a Lubavitch friend and informant.

48. On police deployment and strategy for August 20–21, see Girgenti, *Report to the Governor*, vol. 1, 209–211.

49. Smith, *Fires in the Mirror*, 125.

50. On police deployment and strategy for August 22, see Girgenti, *Report to the Governor*, 213–215.

51. Quoted in T. J. Collins and George Jordan, " 'Suicide Try' Blamed on Local Tensions," *New York Newsday*, August 27, 1991, pg. 29.

52. Smith, *Fires in the Mirror*, 129–131, with added text from "American Playhouse."

CHAPTER 2   GEOGRAPHIES OF DIFFERENCE

1. For critical analyses of the role of "neighborhoods" in defining the identities of
    New York communities, see for example: Hasia Diner, *Lower East Side Memories: A
    Jewish Place in America* (Princeton, NJ: Princeton University Press, 2000); Gregory,
    Black Corona; John Jackson, *HarlemWorld: Doing Race and Class in Contemporary
    Black America* (Chicago: University of Chicago Press, 2001); and Robert Orsi, *The
    Madonna of 115th Street: Faith and Community in Italian Harlem*, 1880–1950 (New
    Haven, CT: Yale University Press, 1985). For similar analyses in other contexts see
    for example: Brown, *Dropping Anchor*; Hartigan, *Racial Situations*; and Doreen
    Massey, "Double Articulation: A Place in the World," in *Displacements*, ed. Ange-
    lika Bammer (Bloomington: Indiana University Press, 1994), 110–121.

2. Akhil Gupta and James Ferguson, "Culture, Power, Place: Ethnography at the End
    of an Era," in their edited volume *Culture, Power, Place* (Durham, NC: Duke Uni-
    versity Press, 1997), 4. For an introduction to anthropological discussions of place
    and identity, see the essays in Gupta and Ferguson's collection, and those in
    Steven Feld and Keith Basso, eds., *Senses of Place* (Santa Fe, NM: School of Ameri-
    can Research, 1996). For an introduction to comparable discussions in the fields
    of geography and cultural studies, see the essays in Michael Keith and Steve Pile,
    eds., *Place and the Politics of Identity* (London: Routledge, 1993).

3. Jacqueline Nassy Brown, "Enslaving History: Narratives on Local Whiteness in a
    Black Atlantic Port," *American Ethnologist*, vol. 27, no. 2 (2000): 340–370. Quotes
    on 350.

4. Smith, *Fires in the Mirror*, 123–127

5. Reverend Sharpton clearly did bring bus-loads of demonstrators affiliated with
    his National Action Network to Crown Heights. In his autobiography Sharpton de-
    scribes a similar march in January of 1991 in which "five hundred of us got on
    buses and headed out" to the Brooklyn neighborhood of Bensonhurst. See Al
    Sharpton and Anthony Walton, *Go and Tell Pharaoh: The Autobiography of the Rev-
    erend Al Sharpton* (New York: Doubleday, 1996), 174. Sharpton was joined in
    Crown Heights by members of the United African Movement, the Jewish Defense
    League, Jewish Defense Organization, and Guardian Angels, as well as the press,
    the police, the mayor, and quite a few other "outsiders."

6. Sharpton and Walton, *Go and Tell Pharaoh*, 167. Also see 193–207 for Sharpton's
    discussion of his role in Crown Heights.

7. Sharpton and Walton, *Go and Tell Pharaoh*, 168.

8. My discussion of the nineteenth-century prehistory of Crown Heights in the fol-
    lowing paragraphs draws on a number of published sources, including: John
    Manbeck, ed., *The Neighborhoods of Brooklyn* (New Haven, CT: Yale University
    Press, 1998); David Ment and Mary Donovan, *The People of Brooklyn: A History of
    Two Neighborhoods* (Brooklyn: Brooklyn Educational and Cultural Alliance, 1980);
    Robert Swan, "The Origin of Black Bedford-Stuyvesant," in *An Introduction to the
    Black Contribution to the Development of Brooklyn*, ed. Charlene Clay Van Derzee
    (Brooklyn: New Muse Community Museum of Brooklyn, 1977), 72–84; and an
    anonymously written profile of the area in the *Brooklyn Daily Eagle*, August 14,

1873, pg. 3. I have also drawn on the resources of the Brooklyn Collection at the Grand Army Plaza branch of the Brooklyn Public Library, and am deeply indebted to the assistance of the collection's librarians.

9. The outline of the hill is still visible in Crown Heights, though it was leveled slightly to make way for urban development. This hill is a small part of the terminal moraine that extends across much of Long Island, marking the southernmost reach of the glaciers of the last ice age.

10. A few Weeksville houses remain, and have been restored since 1971 by the Society for the Preservation of Weeksville and Bedford-Stuyvesant History. A number of churches and other institutions founded in Weeksville and Carrville still thrive in new locations in Crown Heights and Bed-Stuy.

11. Anonymous, *Brooklyn Daily Eagle*, September 15, 1922, pg. 32.

12. Anonymous, *Brooklyn Daily Eagle*, September 13, 1891, pg. 17.

13. This statistic is drawn from Deborah Dash Moore, *At Home in America: Second Generation New York Jews* (New York: Columbia University Press, 1981), 66. See also 41–51 for the role of Jewish real-estate developers in popularizing new Jewish neighborhoods.

14. Moore, *At Home in America*, 66.

15. Alfred Kazin, *A Walker in the City* (New York: Harcourt Brace, 1951), 9, original emphasis.

16. On Black settlement in Crown Heights and Bed-Stuy in this period, see Harold X. Connolly, *A Ghetto Grows in Brooklyn* (New York: New York University Press, 1977), 54–56. See 56 for a map of Black settlement patterns in 1930.

17. Community Council of Greater New York, *Brooklyn Communities, Volume* 1 (New York: Community Council of Greater New York, 1959), 137.

18. All statistics in this paragraph are drawn from Community Council of Greater New York, *Brooklyn Communities*, 139–144.

19. On the Lubavitch presence in Crown Heights prior to the 1940s, and the Previous Rebbe's arrival in 1940, see Mintz, *Hasidic People*, 139.

20. Linda Nochlin, "Forward: The Couturier and the Hasid," in *Too Jewish?: Challenging Traditional Identities*, ed. Norman Kleeblatt (New York and New Brunswick, NJ: The Jewish Museum and Rutgers University Press, 1996), xvii. I will discuss this image of Hasidic men in detail in chapter 4. I should note here, however, that Nochlin uses this dehumanizing image to critique her own discomfort at Jews who look "too Jewish."

21. The Crown Heights History Project was sponsored by a consortium of local museums, as background research for a series of exhibits conceived in the wake of the violence of 1991. The project's files are available at the Brooklyn Historical Society.

22. In the mid-1960s the anthropologist Jerome Mintz estimated that the Lubavitch and Bobov communities—the two largest Hasidic communities in the neighborhood— each consisted of between one and five hundred families. It is therefore reasonable to suppose that in the 1950s there were about five or six hundred Hasidic families in Crown Heights, or a few thousand Hasidim. See Jerome Mintz, *Legends of the Hasidim* (Chicago: University of Chicago Press, 1968), 42.

23. Community Council of Greater New York, *Brooklyn Communities*, 139–140.

24. For a map of Black settlement patterns in 1950, see Connolly, *Ghetto Grows in Brooklyn*, 131.

25. Paule Marshall, *Brown Girl, Brownstones* (New York: The Feminist Press, 1981 [1959]), 173–174. See also page 70 for "scrub[bing] the Jew floor," and page 74 for "up with the white people," quoted above.

26. Kasinitz, *Caribbean New York*, 143. See also 62–63 for maps of Afro-Caribbean settlement patterns in 1970 and 1980. And for a map of Black settlement patterns in 1970, see Connolly, *Ghetto Grows in Brooklyn*, 133.

27. All statistics in this paragraph are drawn from New York Department of City Planning, *Demographic Profiles* (New York: Department of City Planning, 1992), 118 and 122.

28. For the acrimonious debate surrounding the creation of today's Community Districts Eight and Nine, see Francis Clines, "About New York: A Christmas Sermon, Brooklyn Redistricting" in the *New York Times*, December 28, 1976; and Glenn Fowler, "Hasidim and Blacks Are Disputing New Community Lines in Brooklyn" in the *New York Times*, December 23, 1976.

29. For more on the links between neighborhood and nation, see Henry Goldschmidt, " 'Crown Heights is the Center of the World': Reterritorializing a Jewish Diaspora," *Diaspora: A Journal of Transnational Studies*, vol. 9, no. 1 (2000):83–106.

30. For ethnographic analyses of the links between race, class, and urban space in the United States, see Gregory, *Black Corona*; Hartigan, *Racial Situations*; and Jackson, *HarlemWorld*. For a broader analysis of the links between racial segregation and class formation, see Douglas Massey and Nancy Denton, *American Apartheid: Segregation and the Making of the Underclass* (Cambridge, MA: Harvard University Press, 1993).

31. My account of this incident is drawn from Francis Clines's column, "About New York: When the Wall Fell Down in Crown Heights" in the *New York Times*, April 2, 1977. All quotes are from Clines.

32. These statistics are based on New York Department of City Planning, *Socioeconomic Profiles* (New York: Department of City Planning, 1993), 21, 169, 175. But the figures, like many I rely upon in this section, are plagued by the very question of neighborhood boundaries I am trying to address. There is no single statistical unit that corresponds to "Crown Heights" or its "Jewish neighborhood," so I am forced to approximate as best I can. My figures may not be statistically precise—a colleague once called them "numerical anecdotes"—but they are carefully thought out and fundamentally accurate.

33. Statistics based on New York Department of City Planning, *Socioeconomic Profiles*. See 139 for Bed-Stuy, 205 for Flatbush, 217 for Brownsville, and 223 for East Flatbush.

34. On the history of housing development in Brownsville, see Deborah Dash Moore, "On the Fringes of the City: Jewish Neighborhoods in Three Boroughs," in *The Landscape of Modernity: New York City 1900–1940*, ed. David Ware and Oliver Zunz (Baltimore: The Johns Hopkins University Press, 1992), 256–259.

35. On the history of housing development in Bed-Stuy, see Connolly, *A Ghetto Grows in Brooklyn*, 117–123, 196–200. On New York City's tenements, see Roy Lubove, *The Progressives and the Slums* (Pittsburgh: University of Pittsburgh Press, 1962).

36. My account of housing development in Crown Heights draws largely on a New York Department of City Planning document titled *Strategy: Crown Heights Area Maintenance Program* (New York: Department of City Planning, 1972).

37. Moore, *At Home in America*, 42. Also see 52–58 for a broader analysis of New York's real-estate business at this time.

38. New York Department of City Planning, *Strategy*, 31.

39. For 1970 median incomes, see New York City Planning Commission, *Portfolio: Brooklyn Community District 8* (New York: City Planning Commission, 1979), table 4.2a. For 1990 median incomes and poverty statistics, see New York Department of City Planning, *Socioeconomic Profiles*, 22, 170, 175, 176. Again, I should note that no statistical unit corresponds directly to "north Crown Heights" or "south Crown Heights." I've used figures for Community Districts Eight and Nine, but these may paint too rosy a picture of economic development in north Crown Heights, as District Eight also includes the largely gentrified neighborhood of Prospect Heights.

40. Figures based on my own analysis of data from the 1990 census.

41. Smith, *Fires in the Mirror*, 122.

42. The maps of Afro-Caribbean settlement patterns found in Philip Kasinitz's *Caribbean New York*, 62–63, show a community centered in the relatively well-off area of south Crown Heights that was—and remains—the geographic heart of the Lubavitch community. The horizontal census tract in the middle of Kasinitz's 1970 map, indicating 25 to 50 percent Caribbean population, includes the residential blocks around Kingston Avenue just south of Eastern Parkway.

43. Figures based on my own analysis of data from the 1990 census.

44. Figures based on my own analysis of data from the 1990 census. I should note, again, that these are careful estimates, not precise statistics. I have used a number of different statistical units to approximate "Crown Heights," "south Crown Heights," and "the nicest blocks." And I have interpreted the census data on "White" per capita incomes as "Jewish." The vast majority of Whites in the area are Lubavitch Hasidim, but my figure for Jewish incomes undoubtedly include a handful of non-Jewish Whites.

45. Family income is generally considered a better index of class position than per capita income, but one cannot compare family incomes by race, as the census does not ascribe "race" to families. Moreover, I'm not sure a comparison of family incomes would be an effective gauge of class differences between Blacks and Hasidim, given the expense of raising a large family and such complex variables as the costs of yeshiva education and kosher food.

46. In 1990, as I have noted, Blacks in Crown Heights had per capita incomes 15 percent higher than their Jewish neighbors. At the same time, however, Whites in Brooklyn as a whole had per capita incomes 40 percent higher than Blacks.

47. See note 21, above, on the Crown Heights History Project.

48. The Lubavitch Hasidim were hardly alone in this effort. In the 1960s and 1970s, Crown Heights was a focal point of community organizing and state intervention designed to prevent the "decline" of the neighborhood. The Hasidic community development initiatives I will describe were complemented by a number of state-sponsored programs and interracial grass-roots efforts. As the headline of an article in the *New York Daily News* noted at the time: "Crown Heights [was] Fighting Not to Become a Slum" (April 27, 1970).

49. Carol Bellamy, "A Report on Chevra Machazikei Hashchuna, Inc." (New York City Council Report, 1978). Manuscript available at the New York City Municipal Library.

50. HUD documents cited in Tom Robbins, "Tales of Crown Heights: The Fruits of Harassment," *City Limits*, vol. 2, no. 10 (1981):17.

51. "Collapsed" is actually far too passive a verb. Chevra and its chairman were charged with racketeering in a RICO lawsuit brought by a number of Hasidic investors.

52. On the flap over the double sinks, see Alexis Jetter, "Ethnic Makeup of Building's Tenants Sparks Controversy," *New York Newsday*, May 11, 1989, B23.

53. Such fears of crime are often linked to White American fears of Blackness. On race and crime in the United States, see, for example, Katheryn Russell, *The Color of Crime* (New York: New York University Press, 1998). For a comparable analysis of "muggings" in England, see Paul Gilroy, *"There Ain't No Black in the Union Jack"* (Chicago: University of Chicago Press, 1991), 72–113.

54. On the conflicts surrounding the Maccabees, see Mintz, *Hasidic People*, 141–143.

55. Ironically, although the Rebbe's police escort became an important point of contention in Black-Jewish relations, he was first granted this service when his life was threatened by Satmar Hasidim from Williamsburg in the early 1980s. On the longstanding conflicts between Satmar and Lubavitch, see Mintz, *Hasidic People*, 154–165.

56. Herbert Daughtry, *No Monopoly on Suffering: Blacks and Jews in Crown Heights and Elsewhere* (Trenton, NJ: Africa World Press, 1997), 194. See 194–207 for Daughtry's specific critiques of government policy toward Lubavitch Hasidim. These critiques are called into question, to some extent, by a journalistic investigation conducted after the violence of 1991, which was critical of city policy in the 1970s but found little or no evidence of ongoing "preferential treatment." See Michael Powell and Jennifer Preston, "Little Proof Inequity Persists," *New York Newsday*, September 3, 1991.

57. On federal government support for suburbanization, see Brodkin, *How Jews Became White Folks*, 44–50; Jackson, *Crabgrass Frontier*, 190–219. For the broader contours of this "possessive investment in whiteness," see Lipsitz, *Possessive Investment in Whiteness*, 1–23.

58. For more on this narrative, and its implications for an understanding of the global and local Lubavitch community, see Goldschmidt, "Crown Heights is the Center of the World," in *Diaspora*, vol. 9, no. 1.

59. This pattern of settlement around a spiritual center stands in contrast to the de-centered geography of most Black (and White) Christian communities. Many

Black Crown Heights residents attend churches located throughout the New York metropolitan area, while many churches located in Crown Heights have equally far-flung congregations.

60. The survey was conducted by New York City's Human Rights Commission, and cited in Powell and Preston, "Little Proof Inequity Persists," *New York Newsday*, September 3, 1991.

61. This letter is cited in Dorothy Rabinowitz, "Blacks, Jews, and New York Politics," *Commentary*, vol. 66, no. 5 (1978):45. I was unable to locate the original text, but I may have missed it in a long roll of microfilm.

62. On the global dispersion of the Rebbe's emissaries, and the global network of Lubavitch institutions, see Fishkoff, *The Rebbe's Army*, esp. 9–32.

63. Other estimates have put the worldwide Lubavitch population as high as 250,000. But this figure most likely includes non-Hasidic Jews affiliated with Lubavitch institutions, and may also be inflated by Lubavitchers for public-relations purposes.

64. On transnational and diasporic communities, see for example: Arjun Appadurai, "Patriotism and its Futures," *Public Culture*, vol. 5, no. 3 (1993):411–429; Linda Basch, Nina Glick Schiller, and Cristina Szanton-Blanc, *Nations Unbound* (Langhorne, PA: Gordon and Breach, 1994); James Clifford, "Diasporas," *Cultural Anthropology*, vol. 9, no. 3 (1994):302–338; Robin Cohen, *Global Diasporas* (London: UCL Press, 1997); Peggy Levitt, *The Transnational Villagers* (Berkeley: University of California Press, 2001).

CHAPTER 3   KOSHER HOMES, RACIAL BOUNDARIES

1. Smith, *Fires in the Mirror*, 123.

2. As Hasia Diner insightfully reminded me, the gendered patterns of Hasidic domesticity differ from those of many other Americans, in that Hasidic fathers—and male rabbis—bear ultimate responsibility for managing the home according to religious law. But in the course of everyday life, most Lubavitchers see the home as a woman's space and responsibility. For more on the domestic practice and ideology of Lubavitch women, see Harris, *Holy Days*, and Bonnie Morris, *Lubavitcher Women in America: Identity and Activism in the Postwar Era* (Albany: State University of New York Press, 1998). For other Jewish homes see Susan Braunstein and Jenna Weissman Joselit, eds., *Getting Comfortable in New York: The American Jewish Home*, 1880–1950 (New York: The Jewish Museum, 1990).

3. Menachem Mendel Schneerson, *Letters by the Lubavitcher Rebbe, Vol. 1: Tishrei—Adar* (Brooklyn: Kehot Publication Society, 1979), 199, original emphasis.

4. Smith, *Fires in the Mirror*, 5.

5. Smith, *Fires in the Mirror*, 8, with added text from "American Playhouse."

6. Many Hasidim, and other American Jews, use the Yiddish word "schvartze" to refer to African American and Afro-Caribbean people. "Schvartze" translates literally as "black," but its range of meanings extends from "black" to "nigger"— from a value-neutral description to an extremely derogatory slur—depending, in part, on the speaker's tone. I honestly can't remember how, exactly, the man I'm quoting here used it.

7. For a moving celebration of such fleeting social ties, see Vivian Gornick, "On the Street: Nobody Watches, Everyone Performs," in *Approaching Eye Level* (Boston: Beacon Press, 1996): 1–29.

8. Tamara Hareven, "The Home and the Family in Historical Perspective," in *Social Research*, vol. 28, no. 1 (1991), 259, 262.

9. Hareven, "Home and the Family," 263.

10. Robert Park, "The City: Suggestions for the Investigation of Human Behavior in the Urban Environment," in *Classic Essays in the Culture of Cities*, ed. Richard Sennett (Englewood Cliffs, NJ: Prentice Hall, 1969), 111, 113.

11. Sally Engle Merry, "Urban Danger: Life in a Neighborhood of Strangers," in *Urban Life*, ed. George Gmelch and Walter Zenner (2nd ed., Prospect Heights, IL: Waveland Press, 1980), 65.

12. Golden's comments were excerpted in the Crown Heights Coalition's 1992 report, *Crown Heights: A Strategy for the Future* (Brooklyn: Office of the Brooklyn Borough President, 1992), 22.

13. The anthropologist Terence Turner sketches an even broader context for American multiculturalism, situating this loosely defined movement within "the contemporary conjuncture of the global organization of capital and the concomitant surpassing of the nation state, the rise of ethnic and identity politics, the explosive growth of new informational technologies and media, and the fluorescence of late-capitalist consumerism." See Turner's essay, "Anthropology and Multiculturalism: What is Anthropology That Multiculturalists Should be Mindful of It?" *Cultural Anthropology*, vol. 8, no. 4 (1993):411–429. Quote on 424.

14. Verena Stolke, "Talking Culture: New Boundaries, New Rhetorics of Exclusion in Europe," *Current Anthropology*, vol. 36, no. 1 (1995): 1. Stolke argues that "Western geopolitical conflicts and realignments" are increasingly articulated in terms of "culture," but her analysis of European cultural nationalism speaks, in many ways, to the relationships among American minority communities.

15. I discuss the differences between anthropological and multicultural definitions of culture in more detail in my essay "Food Fights: Contesting 'Cultural Diversity' in Crown Heights," in *Local Actions: Cultural Activism, Power and Public Life in America*, ed. Melissa Checker and Maggie Fishman (New York: Columbia University Press, 2004), 159–183. See also Turner, "Anthropology and Multiculturalism," in *Cultural Anthropology*, vol. 8, no. 4.

16. Richard Wilk, "Learning to Be Local in Belize: Global Systems of Common Difference," in *Worlds Apart*, ed. Daniel Miller (London: Routledge, 1995), 130.

17. For examples of communities that have taken up the concept of culture in their own understandings of collective identity, see: Gerd Baumann, *Contesting Culture: Discourses of Identity in Multi-Ethnic London* (Cambridge: Cambridge University Press, 1996); Jonathan Friedman, *Cultural Identity and Global Process* (London: Sage, 1994); Gilroy, *Ain't No Black in the Union Jack*; Handler, *Nationalism and the Politics of Culture*; Stolke, "Talking Culture"; Richard Wilk, " 'Real Belizean Food': Building Local Identity in the Transnational Caribbean," *American Anthropologist*, vol. 101, no. 2 (1999):244–255; and Wilk, "Learning to be Local." These are just a few examples from a fast-growing literature.

18. This view of Black Americans as a people without a "culture" has its roots in the racist discourse that Melville Herskovitz famously dubbed "the myth of the Negro past." Similar arguments have been voiced, however, by some Black Americans—as indictments of America's racist past. See Melville Herskovitz, *The Myth of the Negro Past* (Boston: Beacon Press, 1941).

19. On the relationships between race, nation, and culture, see, for example: Martin Barker, *The New Racism* (London: Junction Books, 1981); Baumann, *Contesting Culture*; Gilroy, *Ain't No Black in the Union Jack*; Handler, *Nationalism and the Politics of Culture*; Stolke, "Talking Culture"; and Turner, "Anthropology and Multiculturalism." Although the racialization of "culture" stands against the antiracist intellectual legacy of Franz Boas and his students, a number of recent scholars have argued that the anthropological concept itself contains the seeds of racial essentialism. For recent debates over the concept of culture, see for example: Lila Abu-Lughod, "Writing Against Culture," in *Recapturing Anthropology*, ed. Richard Fox (Santa Fe, NM: School of American Research Press, 1991), 137–162; Robert Brightman, "Forget Culture: Replacement, Transcendence, Relexification," *Cultural Anthropology*, vol. 10, no. 4 (1995):509–546; Christoph Brumann, "Writing for Culture: Why a Successful Concept Should Not Be Discarded," *Current Anthropology*, vol. 40, Supplement (1999):S1–S13; James Clifford, *The Predicament of Culture* (Cambridge, MA: Harvard University Press, 1988); Walter Benn Michaels, "Race into Culture: A Critical Genealogy of Cultural Identity," *Critical Inquiry*, vol. 18, no. 4 (1992):655–685.

20. I am, I should note, glossing over the distinction often drawn in Jewish orthodoxy between *halacha* and *minhag*—religious law and local custom. The orthodox Jewish concept of "custom" is actually quite similar to the multicultural concept of "culture," but Lubavitchers and other ultra-orthodox Jews tend to gloss over the distinction between halacha and minhag themselves, imbuing customary practices with the sanctity and authority of religious law. On the decline of minhag in contemporary orthodoxy, see Menachem Friedman, "Life Tradition and Book Tradition in the Development of Ultraorthodox Judaism," in *Judaism Viewed From Within and From Without: Anthropological Studies*, ed. Harvey Goldberg (Albany: State University of New York Press, 1987), 235–255.

21. Wilk, "'Real Belizean Food,'" *American Anthropologist*, vol. 101, no. 2, 244. There are vast scholarly literatures on the social significance of food. Unfortunately, however, most authors on the subject simply restate the commonsense equation of food and identity in authoritative scholarly garb. A few, however, offer subtle analyses of the diverse ways this equation is produced. For a broad overview of these literatures, see Carole Counihan and Penny Van Esterik, eds., *Food and Culture: A Reader* (New York: Routledge, 1997). In addition to Wilk's essays, a few texts that have been particularly helpful to me include: Hasia Diner, *Hungering for America: Italian, Irish, and Jewish Foodways in the Age of Migration* (Cambridge, MA: Harvard University Press, 2002); Donna Gabaccia, *We Are What We Eat: Ethnic Food and the Making of Americans* (Cambridge, MA: Harvard University Press, 1998); and Sidney Mintz, *Tasting Food, Tasting Freedom: Excursions into Eating, Culture and the Past* (Boston: Beacon Press, 1996).

22. William Robertson Smith, *The Religion of the Semites: The Fundamental Institutions* (New York: Schocken Books, 1972 [1889]), 265, 269.

23. Wilk, "Learning to be Local in Belize," in *Worlds Apart*, ed. Miller, 113.

24. Wilk, "'Real Belizean Food,'" *American Anthropologist*, vol. 101, no. 2, 251.

25. Donna Gabbacia also highlights the role of state-sponsored "folk-life" festivals and commercial cookbooks in popularizing regional and ethnic foods as central components of the "new ethnicity" of the 1960s and 1970s. See Gabbacia, *We Are What We Eat*, 175–201.

26. Patricia Williams, "Ethnic Hash," *Transition*, vol. 7, no. 1 (1998): 34, original emphasis.

27. In the context of Crown Heights, it is important to note the prevalence of pork in this woman's list of her "cultural food." On the significance of pork in African American social life, and the gender politics of the Nation of Islam's pork prohibition, see Doris Witt, *Black Hunger: Food and the Politics of U.S. Identity* (New York: Oxford University Press, 1999), 102–125.

28. I have adapted the phrase "cultural objectification" from Handler, *Nationalism and the Politics of Culture.*

29. Gabaccia, *We Are What We Eat*, 5.

30. Despite my best efforts, I was never invited to attend meetings of the Crown Heights Coalition, and was not privy to the inner workings of the organization. My account of its top-down style of program development rests on the comments of a number of coalition members, but would no doubt be disputed by others.

31. Crown Heights Coalition, *Who Are My Neighbors? Answers to Some Questions About the Many Cultures of Crown Heights* (Brooklyn: Office of the Brooklyn Borough President, no date), 26.

32. Crown Heights Coalition, *Who Are My Neighbors?* All discussions of Caribbean and Jewish foods cited in this paragraph are on page 29.

33. Crown Heights Coalition, *Crown Heights: A Strategy for the Future*, 20.

34. Crown Heights Coalition, *Crown Heights: A Strategy for the Future*, 22.

35. Crown Heights Coalition, *Who Are My Neighbors?*, 3.

36. For an analysis of the role of rabbinic law in maintaining social boundaries between Jews and Gentiles in Christian Europe—as well as the striking parallels between rabbinic and canon law on such issues—see Magda Teter's forthcoming essay, "'There Should Be No Love Between Us and Them': Social Life and the Bounds of Jewish and Canon Law in Early Modern Poland," in *Polin: Borders And Boundaries in Early Modern Polish-Lithuanian Jewish History*, ed. Antony Polonsky, Adam Teller, and Magda Teter (Oxford, UK: Littman Library of Jewish Civilization, 2008).

37. Tractate Avodah Zarah, 29b.

38. Smith, *Fires in the Mirror*, 109.

39. Smith, *Fires in the Mirror*, 110–111.

40. These lists of forbidden beasts are the subjects of Mary Douglas's justly famous analysis of the laws of kashrus, "The Abominations of Leviticus," in *Purity and Danger* (London: Routledge, 1966), 42–58. See also Douglas's further reflections on Leviticus, in which she argues that the laws of kashrus form part of a "larger

pattern of social behavior which used very clear, tight defining lines to distinguish two classes of human beings, the Israelites and the rest." Mary Douglas, "Deciphering a Meal" and "Self-Evidence," in *Implicit Meanings* (London: Routledge & Kegan Paul, 1975), 249–318. Quote on 283.

41. Elements of this narrative that may seem remarkable at first glance are, in fact, quite commonplace in Hasidic life. Lubavitchers and other Hasidim often write to their Rebbes, asking for advice on interpersonal relations, spiritual concerns, business decisions, and other aspects of daily life. Rebbes often respond by urging vigilance in an area of ritual observance tied to their petitioner's concerns. And Hasidic folk-tales often focus on a Rebbe's miraculous power to understand and resolve the concerns of his Hasidim. For more on these issues, see Simon Dein, "Letters to the Rebbe: Millennium, Messianism and Medicine Among the Lubavitch of Stamford Hill, London," in *International Journal of Social Psychiatry*, vol. 38, no. 2 (1992): 262–272; Mintz, *Tales of the Hasidim*.

42. Tzivia Emmer, "The Kashrut Connection: Does G-d Really Care What I Eat?" in *Body and Soul: A Handbook for Kosher Living*, ed. Kashruth Division of the Lubavitch Women's Organization (Brooklyn: Lubavitch Women's Cookbook Publications, 1989), 5–6.

43. Emmer, "The Kashrut Connection," 7.

44. For a sketch of the creation myth at the heart of Lurianic cosmology, see Scholem, *The Messianic Idea in Judaism*, 43–48.

45. Anonymous "Preface" to *Body and Soul: A Handbook for Kosher Living*, ed. Kashruth Division of the Lubavitch Women's Organization (Brooklyn: Lubavitch Women's Cookbook Publications, 1989), xi.

46. For profiles of Mothers to Mothers, see Letty Cottin Pogrebin, "The Twain Shall Meet," in the *New York Times*, March 16, 1997, pg. 17 of "The City" section; and Sarah Safer, "Mothers Reshuffle the Race Card in Crown Heights," in *Lilith*, vol. 22, no. 1 (1997): 8.

47. Thanks to Hasia Diner for suggesting this useful parallel.

48. Cited by Mordecai Wilensky in "Hasidism and its Opponents: The Hostile Phase," in *Tolerance and Movements of Religious Dissent in Eastern Europe*, ed. Béla Király (New York: Columbia University Press, 1975), 98.

49. Higginbotham, "African-American Women's History and the Metalanguage of Race," in *Signs*, vol. 17, no. 2. See my discussion of Higginbotham's work in the introduction.

50. There are, I should note, a few organizations working to build relationships between Blacks and Jews in Crown Heights that have pursued nonreductive, conceptually flexible organizing strategies like those I am calling for here. We may, for example, see such an approach at work in the open-ended discussions and personal relationships fostered by the members of Mothers to Mothers. Although I have (gently) criticized their barbecue for creating a "one-way street when it comes to food," I was consistently impressed by the subtlety and sensitivity with which the Mothers negotiated issues of race and religion. A similar openness and sensitivity has characterized the work of the Crown Heights Community Mediation Center, a center for alternative dispute resolution and violence

reduction (among other things) founded in 1998 as a project of the Manhattan-based Center for Court Innovation. The Mediation Center (with which I have been closely associated, as both a long-time volunteer and the husband of a former director) has created a space in which Black and Jewish Crown Heights residents can work together to address their shared concerns, without dwelling upon their collective identities.

CHAPTER 4   WHITE SKIN, BLACK HATS, AND OTHER SIGNS OF JEWS

1. For a similar analysis of racial visibility and urban space, see Cecilia McCallum's fascinating recent essay "Racialized Bodies, Naturalized Classes: Moving Through the City of Salvador da Bahia," in *American Ethnologist*, vol. 32, no. 1 (2005): 100–117.

2. Quoted in Nancy Beiles, "The Crown Heights Laboratory," in *The Brooklyn Jewish Week*, April 17, 1998, 22.

3. This reciprocal view of dress and the body stands in contrast with most research on "ethnic dress," which tends to focus on items of clothing to the exclusion of the (often racialized) bodies that wear them. See for example: Joanne Eicher, ed., *Dress and Ethnicity* (Oxford: Berg, 1995). For a unified analysis of dress and embodiment, see Deborah Durham, "The Predicament of Dress: Polyvalency and the Ironies of Cultural Identity," in *American Ethnologist*, vol. 26, no. 2 (1999): 389–411. My own perspective draws, in large part, on the work of scholars who have examined the role of dress in the racialization of Black Americans. For elements of this history, see: Stuart Cosgrove, "The Zoot-Suit and Style Warfare," in *History Workshop Journal*, no. 18 (1984): 77–91; Robin D. G. Kelley, "Nap Time: Historicizing the Afro," in *Fashion Theory*, vol. 1, no. 4 (1997): 339–352; Kobena Mercer, "Black Hair/Style Politics," in *Out There: Marginalization and Contemporary Cultures*, ed. Russell Ferguson, Martha Gever, Trinh T. Minh-ha, and Cornel West (New York and Cambridge, MA: The New Museum of Contemporary Art and MIT Press, 1990), 247–264; Shane White and Graham White, *Stylin': African American Expressive Culture from Its Beginnings to the Zoot Suit* (Ithaca, NY: Cornell University Press, 1998). For a comparable analysis of yarmulkes and circumcision as marks of Jewish masculinity see Jonathan and Daniel Boyarin's essay "Self-Exposure as Theory: The Double Mark of the Male Jew," in Jonathan Boyarin, *Thinking in Jewish* (Chicago: University of Chicago Press, 1996), 34–62. And finally, on the relationship between medieval European perceptions of dress and contemporary perceptions of racial phenotype, see Colette Guillaumin, "Race and Nature: The System of Marks," in *Feminist Issues*, vol. 8, no. 2 (1988): 25–43.

4. Omi and Winant, *Racial Formation in the United States*, 59, original emphasis.

5. Wiegman, *American Anatomies*, 21.

6. Of course there are many forms of racial hierarchy, like segregation in housing or education, that have little to do with individuals or their appearances. But a number of significant social issues and policies, like employment discrimination and affirmative action, rest on our socially conditioned ability to perceive an

individual's race. New Yorkers and other Americans have been reminded of the political significance of racialized perception by the ongoing debates over racial profiling sparked by the police killing of Amadou Diallo in February of 1999, by the criminalization of "driving while Black," and above all by "homeland security" measures targeted at people of Middle Eastern descent after the terrorist attacks of September 11, 2001. In each case, perceptions of "race" drive social policy.

7. For these discussions of Jewish racial visibility, see Gilman, *The Jew's Body*, esp. 169–193; Jacobson, *Whiteness of a Different Color*, 171–199.

8. Johann Blumenbach, *On the Natural Varieties of Mankind*, trans. Thomas Bendyshe (New York: Bergman Publishers, 1969), 234. This passage is cited and discussed in Jacobson, *Whiteness of a Different Color*, 171.

9. Cited in Jacobson, *Whiteness of a Different Color*, 178.

10. Gilman, *The Jew's Body*, 181.

11. See Zamgba Browne, "Are Police Afraid to Arrest Hasidic Jews in Brooklyn?" in *New York Amsterdam News*, June 11, 1988, 3.

12. Although my goal here is not to offer an ethical judgment or critique, it is important to note that the victim's sister recounted these words with utter contempt—horrified by the Hasid's implication that it would somehow have been acceptable for him to attack her sister if she hadn't been Jewish. It is also important to note that this sort of brazen disregard for non-Jews is not shared by most Hasidim in Crown Heights.

13. The *Too Jewish?* exhibit was held at New York's Jewish Museum in 1996. The exhibit catalog, of the same title, was edited by Norman Kleeblatt (New York and New Brunswick, NJ: The Jewish Museum and Rutgers University Press, 1996).

14. Daniel Segal, "Can You Tell a Jew When You See One? or Thoughts on Meeting Barbra/Barbie at the Museum," in *Judaism*, vol. 48, no. 2 (1999): 236.

15. Segal, "Can You Tell a Jew," 236.

16. Harris, *Holy Days*, 9.

17. Harris, *Holy Days*, 10.

18. See for example Alfred Rubens, *A History of Jewish Costume* (London: Vallentine, Mitchell and Company, 1967), 125–132.

19. I once heard a Hasid from Boro Park, speaking at a Lubavitch community event, tell a long joke that ended with the punch-line: "So I thought, when I walked in here with my streimel, 'Am I the only Jew in here?'" The crowd responded with good-natured but edgy laughter.

20. See his comments on shorts in Chaim Dalfin, ed., *The Rebbe's Advice, Book 2* (New York: Mendelsohn Press, 1998), 9.

21. For examples see Rubens, *A History of Jewish Costume*, 91–124. For a discussion of both rabbinic and canon law concerning distinctive Jewish dress, see Magda Teter's forthcoming essay "'There Should Be No Love Between Us and Them,'" in *Polin: Borders And Boundaries in Early Modern Polish-Lithuanian Jewish History*, ed. Polonsky, Teller, and Teter.

22. The pattern for such decrees was set in 1215, when the Vatican's Fourth Lateran Council bemoaned the fact that in certain parts of Europe, "there has arisen such confusion that no differences [between Christians and others] are noticeable,"

and demanded that "[Jews and Muslims] of either sex, and in all Christian lands, and at all times, shall be easily distinguishable from the rest of the population by the quality of their clothes." Cited in Solomon Grayzel, *The Church and the Jews in the XIIIth Century* (New York: Hermon Press, 1966), 309.

23. For examples see Barbara Schreier, *Becoming American Women: Clothing and the Jewish Immigrant Experience, 1880–1920* (Chicago: Chicago Historical Society, 1994).

24. Jenna Weissman Joselit, *New York's Jewish Jews: The Orthodox Community in the Interwar Years* (Bloomington: Indiana University Press, 1990), 21.

25. Nochlin, "The Couturier and the Hasid," in *Too Jewish?*, ed. Kleeblatt, xvii. I should note that Nochlin presents this disturbing image in a spirit of self-criticism, to explore the discomfort many secular Jews feel at orthodox Jews who look "too Jewish." She then goes on to discuss the 1993 Hasidic-themed runway collection by the controversial fashion designer Jean Paul Gaultier.

26. See Herbert Weiner, "The Lubovitcher Movement," in *Commentary*, vol. 23, no. 3 (1957): 238.

27. This observation is cited in Dalfin, *The Rebbe's Advice*, 4.

28. James Davis was murdered on July 23, 2003. His shooting, in New York's City Council chamber, stunned the city. His sometimes controversial political career was exemplified, ironically, by his tireless work against gun violence.

29. For a more or less balanced discussion of this incident, see Mintz, *Hasidic People*, 146–147.

30. See Daughtry's detailed discussion of this infamous quote in his book *No Monopoly on Suffering*, 37–45.

31. For discussions of their trial see Mintz, *Hasidic People*, 152; Rabinowitz, "Blacks, Jews, and New York Politics," in *Commentary*, vol. 66, no. 5, 45.

32. Technically, the concept of tznius applies to men as well. Indeed, many of the Hasidic men's styles described above are also considered elements of tznius. But on a day-to-day basis, Hasidim associate tznius almost solely with women's dress.

33. On the details of tzniusdik style that Bobov Hasidim in Boro Park use to make visual distinctions among various Hasidic communities, see: Barbara Carrel, "Hasidic Women's Head Coverings: A Feminized System of Hasidic Distinction," in *Religion, Dress and the Body*, ed: Linda Arthur (Oxford: Berg, 1999), 163–179; and Ayala Fader, *The Morality of Difference: Self, Language and Community Among Hasidim in Boro Park* (Doctoral Dissertation in Anthropology: New York University, 2000), 217–247. For a broader analysis of tznius and social identity, see also Ayala Fader's essay "'Ticket to Eden': Modesty Among Hasidic Women and Girls in Brooklyn," forthcoming in *Cultural Anthropology*.

34. Jewish women have often been singled out for styles of dress that seem far less distinctive than the tzniusdik fashions of Hasidic women. In Renaissance Italy, for example, Jewish women were sometimes distinguished from Christians by their hoop earrings. And in today's United States, misogynist myths of the "Jewish American Princess" point to the ostensibly extravagant or tacky clothes of secular Jewish women as ambivalent signs of Jewish identity. For more on these comparative cases, see: Diane Owen Hughes, "Distinguishing Signs: Ear-Rings, Jews and Franciscan Rhetoric in the Italian Renaissance City," in *Past & Present*,

no. 112 (1986): 3–59; and Riv-Ellen Prell, "Why Jewish Princesses Don't Sweat: Desire and Consumption in Postwar American Jewish Culture," in *Too Jewish?*, ed. Kleeblatt, 74–92.

35. On the limited but complex roles of Lubavitch women in public political life, see Morris, *Lubavitcher Women in America*.

36. Ralph Ellison, *Invisible Man* (New York: Random House, 1947), 7.

37. The magazine was initially called *The Black Jew*, and later renamed *Ha Olam* ("The World"). Copies may be found in the library of the American Jewish Committee in Manhattan. For more on Rabbi Coleman's work, see Andy Edelstein, "Black Rabbi Leads Integrated Synagogue, Strictly Halachic," in *The Jewish Week-American Examiner*, December 25, 1977, 16; and Marc Silver and David Szonyi, "Black Jews: Struggling for Acceptance," in *The Baltimore Jewish Times*, August 18, 1978, 36–37.

38. Ironically, no more than a thin wall and a single door separated this eclectic, multiracial Jewish milieu from the yeshiva's own synagogue, where overwhelmingly White secular Jewish men were refashioned into Lubavitch Hasidim. The door between the synagogues was usually kept locked on Shabbos—"to cut down on traffic," as one Hasid explained.

39. Curtis Simmons, "Man of Faith and Color," in the *New York Daily News*, November 29, 1992, 18.

40. For a photo, see Silver and Szonyi, "Black Jews."

41. Wiegman, *American Anatomies*, 21.

42. Fleming Aytes, *The Teaching Black Jew*, 252–253. Publisher unknown, but the text (dated 1927) is available at the New York Public Library's Schomburg Center for Research in Black Culture.

43. Most contemporary translations render this verse: "I am black, but comely," while some read: "I am dark, but comely." The Hebrew Israelites (and many others) dismiss these translations as deliberate attempts to disguise the Blackness of ancient Israel.

44. On the American Protestant penchant for literalist interpretations of the Bible— and much else—see Vincent Crapanzano, *Serving the Word: Literalism in America from the Pulpit to the Bench* (New York: New Press, 2000). On the subtle interpretive strategies required to produce this "biblical realism," see also Harding, *The Book of Jerry Falwell*.

45. Indeed, not all Rastas wear dreadlocks, and many who wear dreadlocks these days are not Rastas. For the complex history and symbolism of dreadlocks, see Barry Chevannes, "The Origin of the Dreadlocks" and "The Phallus and the Outcast: The Symbolism of the Dreadlocks in Jamaica," both in *Rastafari and Other African-Caribbean Worldviews*, ed. Barry Chevannes (New Brunswick, NJ: Rutgers University Press, 1998), 77–96, 97–126.

46. Andy Logan, "Ya Me? Ya You!" in *The New Yorker*, vol. 67, no. 37 (November 4, 1991): 110.

47. For more on the influential yet controversial Twelve Tribes of Israel, see Leonard Barrett, *The Rastafarians* (Boston: Beacon Press, 1977), 225–234.

48. Interview in Alan Snitow and Deborah Kaufman, *Blacks and Jews* (San Francisco: California Newsreel, 1997).

49. Once, while I was walking by a junior high school in Crown Heights (wearing a yarmulke and casual clothes), two or three boys leaned out of a window and chanted at me, in the sing-song voice of a schoolyard taunt: "Hitler, Hitler, Hitler." One then added: "Hitler's my daddy, Hitler's my daddy." Shorn of any recognizable ideology, these taunts demonstrate the talismanic power of "Hitler" in Crown Heights. Lubavitchers would argue that they also demonstrate the deep-seated nature of Gentile antisemitism, but I'm not so sure. Though they clearly draw on the brutal legacy of the Nazi Holocaust, their relationship to this history of genocide and atrocity is tenuous at best.

CHAPTER 5   THE VOICES OF JACOB ON THE STREETS OF BROOKLYN

1. Michel Foucault, *The Archaeology of Knowledge*, trans. A. M. Sheridan Smith (New York: Pantheon Books, 1972), 25.
2. Logan, "Ya Me? Ya You!," in *The New Yorker*, vol. 67, no. 37, 110.
3. This broad discourse on the Blackness of ancient Israel can be traced in the widely read works of the Reverend Walter McCray, *The Black Presence in the Bible* (Chicago: Black Light Fellowship, 1990) and *The Black Presence in the Bible and the Table of Nations, Genesis 10:1–32* (Chicago: Black Light Fellowship, 1990), as well as in the popular 1989 hip-hop song "Why Is That?" by KRS-One / Boogie Down Productions, in which Kris Parker cites the Bible to rap about the Blackness of Abraham, Isaac, Jacob, Moses, and others. Of course, Black Americans and orthodox Jews are hardly alone in such claims to Israelite descent. On a broader historical scale, as I discussed in the introduction, the cast of "Israelites" is almost endless.
4. Of course Judaism also welcomes new converts, although it has rarely encouraged them in quite the same ways Christianity does. Conversions to Judaism may actually reinforce the links between history and identity I'm examining here, as converts are thought to take on the history and genealogy of Israel. Jewish law generally requires converts to mark their new identities by adding the phrase "son/daughter of Abraham and Sarah" to their Hebrew names. Indeed, Hasidim often describe converts as non-Jews who somehow—by inscrutable cosmic design—inherited a Jewish soul. Conversion is thus understood as a belated recognition of one's true history and genealogy.
5. My goal here is not to dispute or debunk these widespread claims about the role of history in collective identity—or at least not exactly. Historical narratives, collective memories, and cultural traditions clearly do help define most communities and identities, but the unquestioned link between history and identity offers an inadequate account of both. The scholarly literatures on history and identity are far too large to summarize here, but for a few recent ethnographic examples, see: Jonathan Boyarin, ed., *Remapping Memory: The Politics of TimeSpace* (Minneapolis: University of Minnesota Press, 1994); Jonathan Friedman, "The Past in the Future: History and the Politics of Identity," in *American Anthropologist*, vol. 94, no. 4 (1992): 837–859; Richard Handler and Eric Gable, *The New History in an Old Museum: Creating the Past at Colonial Williamsburg* (Durham, NC: Duke University

Press, 1997); Michael Lambek, *The Weight of the Past: Living With History in Maha-janga, Madagascar* (New York: Palgrave Macmillan, 2002); Andrew Shryock, *Nationalism and the Genealogical Imagination: Oral History and Textual Authority in Tribal Jordan* (Berkeley: University of California Press, 1997). Also see the works on diasporic history cited below in note 6, as well as the works on Black and Jewish histories cited below in note 10.

6. While many scholars have explored the links between migration and historical discontinuity, others—and often enough the same ones—have documented the uncanny presence of the past in many diasporic communities. For discussions of diaspora and history, see for example: Pamela Ballinger, *History in Exile: Memory and Identity at the Borders of the Balkans* (Princeton, NJ: Princeton University Press, 2003); Matthew Jacobson, *Special Sorrows: The Diasporic Imagination of Irish, Polish, and Jewish Immigrants in the United States* (Cambridge, MA: Harvard University Press, 1995); Malkki, *Purity and Exile*; Salman Rushdie, "Imaginary Homelands," in *Imaginary Homelands* (London: Granta, 1991), 9–21; Andrea Smith, "Place Replaced: Colonial Nostalgia and Pied-Noir Pilgrimages to Malta," in *Cultural Anthropology*, vol. 18, no. 3 (2003): 329–364. Also see the works on Black and Jewish histories cited below in note 10.

7. Rushdie, "Imaginary Homelands," 12.

8. There are, of course, a number of significant exceptions to this broad generalization about genealogy and identity. But these exceptions generally complicate—rather than contradict—the rule. See, for example, my brief discussion of conversion to Judaism in note 4, above. These assumptions about genealogy place identities like Blackness and Jewishness on the familiar, yet shifting, terrain of anthropological kinship analysis. For discussions of Black and Jewish concerns with kinship and identity, see for example: Daniel Boyarin and Jonathan Boyarin, "Diaspora: Generation and the Ground of Jewish Identity," in *Critical Inquiry*, vol. 19, no. 4 (1993): 693–725; Brown, *Dropping Anchor, Setting Sail*, esp. 70–96; Shaye Cohen, *The Beginnings of Jewishness: Boundaries, Varieties, Uncertainties* (Berkeley: University of California Press, 1999), 241–340; Domínguez, *White By Definition*; Susan Khan, *Reproducing Jews: A Cultural Account of Assisted Conception in Israel* (Durham, NC: Duke University Press, 2000); David Schneider, "Kinship, Nationality and Religion in American Culture," in *Symbolic Anthropology*, ed. Janet Dolgin, David Kemnitzer, and David Schneider (New York: Columbia University Press, 1977), 63–71; Regina Schwartz, *The Curse of Cain: The Violent Legacy of Monotheism* (Chicago: University of Chicago Press, 1997), 77–119; Brackette Williams, "Classification Systems Revisited: Kinship, Caste, Race, and Nationality as the Flow of Blood and the Spread of Rights," in *Naturalizing Power*, ed. Sylvia Yanagisako and Carol Delaney (New York: Routledge, 1995), 201–236.

9. This parallel is inspired by the journalist Jack Hitt's insightful and irreverent account of the debate over the "race" of Kennewick Man. Hitt compares White and Native American claims on this 9,200-year-old skeleton to his own childhood claim of descent from Charlemagne. See his "Mighty White of You: Racial Preferences Color America's Oldest Skulls and Bones," in *Harper's Magazine*, vol. 311, no. 1862 (July, 2005): 39–55.

10.   It is hardly news to scholars of identity formation that "race" and "religion" are
      linked to history and memory. However, most scholars have taken racial or reli-
      gious identities as the primary objects of their analyses, then shown how such
      identities are defined through historical narratives. My argument reverses this
      claim by showing how historical narratives themselves are structured by assump-
      tions about race and religion. For discussions of Black and Jewish concerns with
      history and memory, see for example: Nadia Abu El-Haj, *Facts on the Ground:
      Archaeological Practice and Territorial Self-Fashioning in Israeli Society* (Chicago:
      University of Chicago Press, 2001); Jonathan Boyarin, *Polish Jews in Paris: The
      Ethnography of Memory* (Bloomington: Indiana University Press, 1991); Brown,
      Dropping Anchor, Setting Sail, esp. 161–186; Genevieve Fabre and Robert O'Meally,
      eds., *History and Memory in African-American Culture* (New York: Oxford Univer-
      sity Press, 1994); Amos Funkenstein, *Perceptions of Jewish History* (Berkeley: Uni-
      versity of California Press, 1993); Gilroy, *The Black Atlantic*; Stuart Hall, "Cultural
      Identity and Diaspora," in *Identity: Community, Culture, Difference*, ed. Jonathan
      Rutherford (London: Lawrence and Wishart, 1990), 222–237; Schwartz, *The Curse
      of Cain*, 143–176; David Scott, "That Event, This Memory: Notes on the Anthropol-
      ogy of African Diasporas in the New World," in *Diaspora*, vol. 1, no. 3 (1991):
      261–284; Yosef Haim Yerushalmi, *Zakhor: Jewish History and Jewish Memory* (Seat-
      tle: University of Washington Press, 1982); Zerubavel, *Recovered Roots*.

11.   My argument here is informed by the literary critic Steven Knapp's essay "Collec-
      tive Memory and the Actual Past," in *Representations*, no. 26 (1989): 123–149.
      Knapp traces the ways historians construct relationships between the past and
      present through combinations of continuity and analogy. For similarly skeptical
      accounts of historical continuity, see also: Anthony Appiah, "The Uncompleted
      Argument: Du Bois and the Illusion of Race," in *"Race," Writing and Difference*, ed.
      Henry Louis Gates, Jr., 21–37; Michaels, "Race into Culture," in *Critical Inquiry*,
      vol. 18, no. 4.

12.   Taken as a whole, this field forms what Michel Foucault described, in *The Archae-
      ology of Knowledge*, as a "discursive formation."

13.   One of the most remarkable images of historical continuity in orthodox Jewish
      historiography is the common claim that the biblical patriarchs had access to the
      Torah centuries before it was given at Sinai—and spent their days studying its
      text, like the Talmudic sages and some contemporary Jewish men.

14.   See Schwartz, *The Curse of Cain*, for a profound critique of the ideology of scarcity
      that stands behind Esau's poignant question, "Have you but one blessing Father?"

15.   Gerson Cohen, "Esau as Symbol in Early Medieval Thought," in *Jewish Medieval
      and Renaissance Studies*, ed. Alexander Altmann (Cambridge, MA: Harvard Uni-
      versity Press, 1967), 26–27.

16.   Cohen, "Esau as Symbol," 25. The equation of Edom with Rome was, in fact, ex-
      tremely complex. Rome had traditionally been identified with the "Kittim"—a
      people described in Genesis 10:4 as descendants of Noah's son Japheth. Yet Edom,
      like Israel, was a descendant of Noah's son Shem. The rabbis of late antiquity re-
      solved this tension through creative narratives in which Esau's grandson, or

sometimes Esau himself, settles among the Kittim and fathers the ruling elite of the Roman Empire. See Cohen, "Esau as Symbol," 39–44.

17. At the same time, however, medieval Christians often linked themselves to Jacob, and the Jews to Esau, through typological readings of the biblical text. According to Christians, the Jews fulfilled the type of Esau—the spurned elder brother—while the Church fulfilled the type of Jacob—the younger brother who ultimately claims the birthright. See Cohen, "Esau as Symbol," 31–38. On typology as a historiographic method, see: Erich Auerbach, "Figura," in *Scenes From the Drama of European Literature* (New York: Meridian Books, 1959), 11–76; and Sollors, "Typology and Ethnogensis." For a contemporary typological reading of Jacob and Esau, see Harding, *The Book of Jerry Falwell*, 85–104.

18. Yehudah Nachshoni, *Studies in the Weekly Parashah: The Classical Interpretations of Major Topics and Themes in the Torah* (Brooklyn: Mesorah Publications, 1988), 136.

19. Not surprisingly, the JCC chairman's claim that Rabbi Butman spoke on behalf of the Rebbe would be contested by many Lubavitchers. Both men are significant players in a series of heated power struggles within the Lubavitch community leadership.

20. This is an extremely common Hasidic rhetorical strategy. Nearly all Lubavitch community events and festive occasions begin with at least a brief commentary on the weekly Torah portion, and Lubavitchers often interpret current events in terms of the Torah portion with which they coincide.

21. This principle has been known for nearly two thousand years as *gezera sheva*, or "derivation from an equal." For a summary, see Susan Handelman, *The Slayers of Moses: The Emergence of Rabbinic Interpretation in Modern Literary Theory* (Albany: State University of New York Press, 1982), 57–58.

22. Hasidic boys generally don't have their hair cut until their third birthday. The first haircut is celebrated with a ritual, and party, known as an *upshernish*.

23. In fairness I should note that this interpretation is interwoven, throughout the tape, with another that links Jacob and Esau to the good and evil impulses within every Jew, thus locating their eternal struggle in a moral and psychological realm.

24. For the history of African American identification with ancient Israel, see for example: Chireau and Deutsch, eds., *Black Zion*; Lawrence Levine, *Black Culture and Black Consciousness* (New York: Oxford University Press, 1977), 30–55; Raboteau, "African-Americans, Exodus, and the American Israel," in *A Fire in the Bones*; Smith, *Conjuring Culture*; Sollors, "Typology and Ethnogenesis," in *Beyond Ethnicity*. And for the longer history of American national identification with Israel, see: Bercovitch, *American Jeremiad*; Conrad Cherry, ed., *God's New Israel: Religious Interpretations of American Destiny* (Englewood Cliffs, NJ: Prentice Hall, 1971); Sollors, "Typology and Ethnogenesis," in *Beyond Ethnicity*; Tuveson, *Redeemer Nation*.

25. For Afro-Caribbean identification with Israel, see for example: Barrett, *The Rastafarians*, esp. 68–102, 111–133; Chevannes, *Rastafari*, esp. 33–42, 116–188; Elizabeth McAlister, "The Jew in the Haitian Imagination," in *Race, Nation, and Religion in the Americas*, ed. Henry Goldschmidt and Elizabeth McAlister (New York: Oxford University Press, 2004), 61–82.

26. I am not arguing that there actually is—or isn't—such a discontinuity at the heart of Black history. My point here is simply that Black Crown Heights residents often narrate their history in such terms. There has been a great deal of debate among anthropologists, historians, Black activists, and others about the cultural conti- nuities and discontinuities between Black Americans and their West African roots. For the classic anthropological analysis, see Herskovitz, *The Myth of the Negro Past*. For more recent reconceptualizations of these issues, see: Gilroy, *The Black Atlantic*; Hall, "Cultural Identity and Diaspora," in *Identity*, ed. Rutherford; and Scott, "That Event, This Memory," in *Diaspora*, vol. 1, no. 3.

27. Some scholars have speculated that Blacks working in Jewish homes and institu- tions may have disseminated knowledge of Jewish ritual practice. And indeed, I witnessed similar processes of cultural exchange in today's Crown Heights. I knew a number of Haitian men who had worked, for years, as janitors and cooks in a Lubavitch yeshiva, and I often saw them mimicking the distinctive motions of Ha- sidic prayer, and heard them humming Hasidic songs. They were quite familiar with the Jewish dietary laws, and acquainted with aspects of Hasidic thought. One man, who was not committed to any particular religious community, told me he lit a single red candle for Shabbos—or perhaps Ogou?—every Friday night.

28. On the early Hebrew Israelite movement, see: Howard Brotz, "Negro 'Jews' in the United States," in *Phylon*, vol. 8, no. 4 (1952): 324–337, and *The Black Jews of Harlem: Negro Nationalism and the Dilemmas of Negro Leadership* (New York: Schocken Books, 1964); Yvonne Chireau, "Black Culture and Black Zion: African American Religious Encounters with Judaism, 1790–1930, an Overview," in *Black Zion*, ed. Yvonne Chireau and Nathaniel Deutsch (New York: Oxford University Press, 2000), 15–32; Roberta Gold, "The Black Jews of Harlem: Representation, Identity, and Race, 1920–1939," in *American Quarterly*, vol. 55, no. 2 (2003): 179–225; Ruth Landes, "Negro Jews in Harlem," in *Jewish Journal of Sociology*, vol. 9, no. 2 (1967, based on fieldwork done in 1933): 175–189. On today's Hebrew Is- raelite communities see: Graenum Berger, *Black Jews in America* (New York: Fed- eration of Jewish Philanthropies of New York, Commission on Synagogue Relations, 1978); Chester Higgins, "In the Spirit of Abraham," in *CommonQuest: The Magazine of Black-Jewish Relations*, vol. 3, no. 1 (1998): 20–31; Fran Markowitz, "Israel as Africa, Africa as Israel: 'Divine Geography' in the Personal Narratives and Community Identity of the Black Hebrew Israelites," in *Anthropological Quar- terly*, vol. 69, no. 4 (1996): 193–205; Fran Markowitz, Sara Helman and Dafna Shir- Vertesh, "Soul Citizenship: The Black Hebrews and the State of Israel," in *American Anthropologist*, vol. 105, no. 2 (2003): 302–312; Ethan Michaeli, "Another Exodus: The Hebrew Israelites from Chicago to Dimona," in *Black Zion*, ed. Chireau and Deutsch, 73–87; Merrill Singer, "Life in a Defensive Society: The Black Hebrew Israelites," in *Sex Roles in Contemporary American Communes*, ed. Jon Wagner (Bloomington: Indiana University Press, 1982), 45–81, and "Symbolic Identity Formation in an African-American Religious Sect: The Black Hebrew Is- raelites," in *Black Zion*, ed. Chireau and Deutsch, 55–72.

29. There were congregants at each of these synagogues who lived in south Crown Heights, alongside the Lubavitch Hasidim, but they did not form a majority.

Unlike my discussions of the Lubavitch community, my discussions of the Hebrew Israelites will not be focused specifically on Crown Heights. Yet they will nevertheless speak to the collective identities of Crown Heights residents.

30. Cohane Michael Ben Levi, *Israelites and Jews: The Significant Difference* (Temple Hills, MD: Levitical Communications, 1997), 78.

31. This is a central trope of continuity in orthodox Judaism as well. For example, the opening lines of the Mishnaic text *Pirkei Avot* assures Jews that, "Moses received the Torah at Sinai and handed it down to Joshua, and Joshua to the elders" and so on.

32. Rudolph Windsor, *From Babylon to Timbuktu: A History of Ancient Black Races, Including the Black Hebrews* (Atlanta: Windsor's Golden Series, 1969). Windsor's pioneering work has had a huge impact on subsequent Hebrew Israelite authors—most of whom draw extensively on his research and arguments. Windsor often draws, in turn, on Joseph Williams's earlier work, *Hebrewisms of West Africa* (New York: The Dial Press, 1930). Williams was a White American missionary who worked in Jamaica, and seems to have admired Jamaicans far more than Black Americans. His book attempts to explain their supposed superiority by showing that the Jamaicans descended from the Ashanti, who descended in turn from the Israelites, who according to Williams were decidedly not Black (see *Hebrewisms*, 15, 93). Williams's late Victorian racism and diffusionist social thought have thus been put to entirely new uses by contemporary Hebrew Israelites.

33. Windsor, *Babylon to Timbuktu*, 90.

34. Melchizedek Lewis, *History of Edom and Khazaria: The Other Israel* (Brooklyn: M.Y.L. Publishers, 1997), 34–35.

35. See for example Cohen, *The Beginnings of Jewishness*, 110–129.

36. Ben Levi, *Israelites and Jews*, 84.

37. According to some Hebrew Israelites, the Edomites found a uniquely receptive group of converts among the Khazars, a semi-nomadic tribe of the Eurasian steppes who converted to Judaism in the eighth century, and eventually fathered the Ashkenazic Jews of Eastern Europe. Hebrew Israelites generally base their history of the Khazars on Arthur Koestler's vaguely antisemitic text, *The Thirteenth Tribe: The Khazar Empire and its Heritage* (New York: Random House, 1976). Historians agree that the ruling elite of the Khazars did in fact convert to Judaism, but Koestler weaves a web of speculation around this grain of truth to support his claim that contemporary Jews are, "more closely related to the Hun, Uigur and Magyar tribes than to the seed of Abraham, Isaac and Jacob" (17).

38. Ella Hughley, *The Truth about Black Biblical Hebrew-Israelites (Jews): The World's Best-Kept Secret!* (Springfield Gardens, NY: Hughley Publications, 1982).

39. Lewis, *History of Edom*, 34,

40. Ben Levi, *Israelites and Jews*, 3–4.

41. For the parallels mentioned here, and many others, see: Ben Levi, *Israelites and Jews*, 3–16; Hughley, *The Truth*, 18–23; Lewis, *History of Edom*, 132–145; Rudolph Windsor, *The Valley of the Dry Bones: The Conditions that Face Black People in America* (Atlanta: Windsor's Golden Series, 1986), 67–87.

42. The Hebrew Israelites are hardly alone in their biblical interpretation of the American eagle. The eagle has often been glossed by God's claim, in Exodus 19:4, to have borne the Israelites out of Egypt "on eagles' wings," and/or by the eagle in Revelation 12:14, who rescues a woman taken to represent Christ's true church. In each case, it serves as sign of America's chosenness. See Bercovitch, *American Jeremiad*, 124–125; Tuveson, *Redeemer Nation*, 118–119.

43. This moment struck me—and cracked me up—as an ironic reversal of Clifford Geertz's argument that "The culture of a people is an ensemble of texts . . . which the anthropologist strains to read over the shoulders of those to whom they properly belong." See Geertz's classic essay "Deep Play: Notes on the Balinese Cockfight," in *The Interpretation of Cultures* (New York: Basic Books, 1973), 452.

44. In dismissing the significance of "Talmud, Gemora, and all that," my acquaintance was referring to the textual tradition of rabbinic law and biblical interpretation. His use of the term "Gemora" (which designates one of the many components of the Talmud) indicates at least a passing familiarity with this tradition, as does his awareness of the fact that orthodox Jews view these texts as "Torah" in a broad sense of the term.

45. This analysis of chosenness as a form of historical agency is inspired, in part, by Susan Harding's analyses of evangelical Christian end-times narratives. See Harding, "Imagining the Last Days," in *Accounting for Fundamentalisms*, ed. Marty and Appleby.

CONCLUSION "STIFFNECKED PEOPLES" AND AMERICAN MULTICULTURALISM

1. For analyses of this process among other New York communities, see Philip Scher, "West Indian American Day: Becoming a Tile in the Gorgeous Mosaic," in *Religion, Diaspora and Cultural Identity: A Reader in the Anglophone Caribbean*, ed. John Pulis (Langhorne, PA: Gordon and Breach, 1999), 45–66; Madhulika Khandelwal, *Becoming American, Being Indian: An Immigrant Community in New York City* (Ithaca, NY: Cornell University Press, 2002).

2. Wilk, "Learning to be Local," in *Worlds Apart*, ed. Miller, 118. Wilk's essay explores the hegemonic assumptions that structure difference in Belize. For a similar critique of British multiculturalism, see Homi Bhabha, "The Third Space," in Jonathan Rutherford, ed., *Identity: Community, Culture, Difference* (London: Lawrence and Wishart, 1990), 207–221.

3. "Resistance" may not be the best word for the social dynamics I am describing here, as I do not mean to imply that Crown Heights residents are consciously opposed to the explicit demands of external authorities. "Stiffneckedness" may be better, because I am simply arguing that Crown Heights residents often construct identities in terms at odds with those embraced by state institutions and social elites. For a critique of the anthropological tendency to locate "resistance" pretty much everywhere, see Lila Abu-Lughod, "The Romance of Resistance: Tracing Transformations of Power Through Bedouin Women," in *American Ethnologist*, vol. 17, no. 1 (1990): 41–55.

INDEX

Page numbers in *italics* indicate illustrations

Washington Temple, 83
Weeksville, 86, 87, 89
West Indian–American Day Parade, 18, 123
West Indians. *See* Afro-Caribbean community
White, Henna, 153, 154, 155
White flight, 5, 14–15, 17–18, 91, 93–94, 242n11
Whiteness, Jewish, 19, 27, 29
Who Are My Neighbors? (booklet), 139, 140
Wiegman, Robyn, 166, 186
Wilk, Richard, 132, 134–135, 235
Williams, Joseph, 271n32
Williams, Patricia, 9, 135

Williamsburg, 21, 185
Winant, Howard, 166
Windsor, Rudolph, 224, 271n32
Wingate, 83. *See also* Pig Town
women, Lubavitch: in Black-Jewish dialogue, 136, 153–157, 215; distinctive dress of, 179–182, *180*; limited role in public life, 181, 265n35; privileged role in domestic life, 120–121, 257n2

yarmulkes, 162–163, 168, 173, 184–185
Yohai, Simeon bar, 208

Zalman, Shneur ("the Alter Rebbe"), 22, 245n32

ABOUT THE AUTHOR

HENRY GOLDSCHMIDT is currently an assistant professor of religion and society at Wesleyan University. He has also taught cultural anthropology, Jewish studies, and diaspora studies at Rutgers University, Dickinson College, and elsewhere. He received his B.A. in anthropology from Wesleyan University in 1991, and his Ph.D. in anthropology from the University of California at Santa Cruz in 2000. He is the coeditor of the collection *Race, Nation, and Religion in the Americas* (Oxford University Press, 2004) and his essays on Crown Heights have previously been published in a number of journals and edited collections. He grew up in Brooklyn, where he lives with his wife, Jillian Shagan.

www.ingramcontent.com/pod-product-compliance
Lightning Source LLC
Chambersburg PA
CBHW060153280326
41932CB00012B/1742